Software Testing using Visual Studio 2010

A step-by-step guide to understanding the features and concepts of testing applications using Visual Studio

Subashni S

Satheesh Kumar N

BIRMINGHAM - MUMBAI

Software Testing using Visual Studio 2010

First published: November 2010

Production Reference: 1241110

Published by Packt Publishing Ltd.
32 Lincoln Road
Olton
Birmingham, B27 6PA, UK.

ISBN 978-1-849681-40-7

www.packtpub.com

Cover Image by David Guettirrez (bilbaorocker@yahoo.co.uk)

Credits

About the Authors

Subashni S, has a Bachelor's Degree in Computer Science Engineering and around twelve years of experience in software development and testing life cycle, project, and program management. She is a certified **Project Management Professional (PMP)** and **Certified Software Test Manager (CSTM)**. She started her career as DBA in Oracle technology and later developed many software applications using Borland software products for a multinational company based in Chennai, India, and then moved to Bangalore. She is presently working for a multinational company in the area of managing development and testing projects. She is also the co-author of the book, *Software Testing using Microsoft Visual Studio 2008*, by Packt Publishing.

I would like to thank my husband for helping me in co-authoring and supporting me in completing this book. I would also like to thank my other family members and friends for their continuous support in my career and success.

Satheesh Kumar N, has a Bachelor's Degree in Computer Science Engineering and has around fourteen years of experience in software development life cycle, project, and program management. He started his career developing software applications using Borland software products in a company based in India and then moved to the United Arab Emirates and continued developing applications using Borland Delphi and customizing Great Plain Dynamics (now known as Microsoft Dynamics). He moved back to India and spent three years designing and developing application software using Microsoft products for a top multinational company in India and then spent couple of years in Project Management and Program Management activities.

Now he works as a Technical Architect in Bangalore for a top retail company, based in the United States. He works with the latest Microsoft technologies and has published many articles on LINQ and other features of .NET. He is also the author of the books, *LINQ Quickly* and *Software Testing using Microsoft Visual Studio 2008,* by Packt Publishing.

I would like to thank my wife for helping me in co-authoring and supporting me in completing this book. I would also like to thank my other family members and friends for their continuous support in my career and success.

About the Reviewers

YiChun Chen is one of the, five star contributors at MSDN VSTS, TFS forums, as well as Visual Studio forums, and is an enthusiastic TFS expert.

He is familiar with VB.NET, C# development, and is interested in new techniques of VSTS and TFS from Microsoft. He is well versed in the use of databases, including SQL Server and Oracle.

He has worked for Microsoft for about two years as a Senior Support Engineer on MSDN forums to help customers worldwide to solve technical issues on Visual Studio, Team Foundation Sever, and .NET Framework.

Adam Gallant is a Developer Tools Technology specialist with Microsoft Canada, focusing on Visual Studio 2010 Application Lifecycle Management. In his role, Adam works with Microsoft's partners and customers across Canada, helping them understand how to implement the Microsoft ALM platform, in order to deliver high-quality solutions more effectively. Adam has been with Microsoft in various roles focusing on software development for the past 16 years.

Adam can be reached through e-mail at adamga@microsoft.com.

Table of Contents

Preface

The Microsoft Visual Studio 2010 suite contains several features that support the needs of developers, testers, managers, and architects to simplify the development process. Visual Studio provides different editions of the products such as Professional, Premium, and Ultimate with different sets of tools. Visual Studio 2010 is tightly integrated with Team Foundation Server 2010, which is the central repository system that provides version control, process guidance and templates, automated build, automated test, bug tracking, work item tracking, reporting, and supporting of the Lab Center and Test Center.

This book helps developers to get familiarized with the Visual Studio tools and techniques to create automated unit tests, using automated user interface testing, code analysis, and profiling to find out the performance and quality of the code. Testers benefit from learning more about the usage of Test Center and Lab Center, which are very new tools in Visual Studio 2010. This books also covers different types of testing such as Web Performance Test, Load Test, Executing the Manual Test cases, and recording the user actions, rerunning the tests using the recording, Test case execution, and capturing the defects and integrating the requirements, test cases, test results, and defects together is also covered in detail. Testers also get a high level overview on using Lab Center for creating virtual environments for testing multiple users and multiple location scenarios.

Visual Studio provides user interface tools such as Test List Editor, Test View, Test Results, Test Configuration user interfaces, Test Center, and Lab Center to easily manage and maintain multiple test cases, and Test Results in integration with Team Foundation Server. This book provides detailed information on all of the tools used for testing the application during the development and testing phase of the project life cycle.

What this book covers

Chapter 1, Visual Studio 2010 Test Types, provides an overview of different types of testing which help with testing software applications throughout different phases of software development. This chapter also introduces the tools and techniques in Visual Studio 2010 for different testing types.

Chapter 2, Test Plan, Test Suite, and Manual Testing, explains the steps involved in creating the Test Plan, Test cases, and Test Suite used for manual testing. Creating the manual test by recording the user action and running the test with data inputs is also covered as part of this chapter.

Chapter 3, Automated Tests, provides the step-by-step approach to create a Coded UI test from the user action recording. It also explains the steps to provide data to the coded UI test and custom rules for the test.

Chapter 4, Unit Testing, explains the detailed steps involved in creating the unit test classes and methods for the code. It also explains different types of assert methods and parameters for testing the code. Passing a data source with a set of data and testing the code is also explained in detail.

Chapter 5, Web Performance Testing, explains the basic method of web testing using VSTS and features such as adding rules and parameterization of dynamic variables. Microsoft Visual Studio 2010 ultimately provides many new features for the Web Performance Testing such as adding new APIs to the test results, web performance test results in a separate file, looping and branching, new validation and extraction rules, and many more.

Chapter 6, Advanced Web Testing, generates the code for the testing scenario explained in *Chapter 5* using the Generate Code option. This is very useful for customizing tests using the code.

Chapter 7, Load Testing, can simulate the number of users, network bandwidth, a combination of different web browsers, and different configurations. In the case of web applications it is always necessary to test the application with different sets of users and browsers to simulate multiple requests to the server. This chapter explains the steps involved in simulating the real world scenario and testing the application.

Chapter 8, Ordered and Generic Tests, explains both test types, the ones used for testing the existing third party tool or programs which can also be run using the command line, in detail. Visual Studio 2010 provides a feature called ordered test to group all or some of these tests and then execute the tests in the same order. The main advantage of creating the ordered test is to execute multiple tests in an order based on the dependencies. Generic tests are just like any other tests except that they are used for testing the existing third-party tool or program which can also be run using the command line.

Chapter 9, Managing and Configuring a Test, provides different tools that support easy ways of managing and grouping the tests. Using these tools, we can enable and disable the tests or select them to run, filter the tests from the list of all the tests created for the project, and set the properties for the individual test. The Test List Editor is the main interface provided by Visual Studio for managing all tests under the solution. This chapter explains the details of the test settings file and the tools used for managing the tests.

Chapter 10, Command Line, explains the command line tool, *MSTest,* used for running the test with different options and then collecting the output and publishing it to the Team Project.

Chapter 11, Working with Test Results, helps us to verify whether the test methods return the expected results but also to analyze the application quality and to verify the build. We can add the test as part of the Team Foundation Server automated build so that we can verify the build and make sure the latest code is checked in to the source control, and is working as expected. This chapter explains the process of running the tests and publishing the test results to the Team project.

Chapter 12, Reporting, explains the details of accessing the publishing and reporting test results in a specific format. Accessing different types of testing reports and creating new test reports are also explained in this chapter

Chapter 13, Test and Lab Center, is useful for creating the Test Plans and adding Test Cases to the plans. We can also associate the requirements to the test plans. The Lab Center helps us to create and configure different virtual/physical environments for the test runs, test settings such as defining the roles and configuring the data and diagnostics information for the selected roles, configuring the Test Controllers required for the test, and configure the test library to store the environment information.

What you need for this book

This book requires a basic knowledge of any of the versions of Visual Studio and Team Foundation Server. The reader must be familiar with Visual Studio IDE and integration with Team Foundation Server and have a basic knowledge of C#. To generate coded tests and customize the code, the testers should have a basic knowledge of C#. The following tools are required in order to try the samples in all of the chapters of this book:

- Visual Studio 2010 Ultimate
- SQL Server 2008
- Team Foundation Server 2010
- Microsoft Office (Microsoft Word and Microsoft Excel)
- SQL Server Analysis and Reporting Services (for customizing reports)

Who this book is for

If you are a developer, a software tester, or an architect who wishes to master the amazing range of features offered by Visual Studio 2010 for testing your software applications before going live—then this book is for you.

This book assumes that you have a basic knowledge of testing software applications and have good work experience of using Visual Studio IDE.

Conventions

In this book, you will find a number of styles of text that distinguish between different kinds of information. Here are some examples of these styles, and an explanation of their meaning.

Code words in text are shown as follows: "Now assign a name for the new test project. Let us name it as AddNumbersTestProject."

A block of code is set as follows:

```
public double CalculateTotalPrice(double quantity)
{
  double totalPrice;
  double unitPrice;
  // Todo get unit price. For test let us hardcode it
  unitPrice = 16.0;
  totalPrice = unitPrice * quantity;
```

```
    return totalPrice;
}
```

When we wish to draw your attention to a particular part of a code block, the relevant lines or items are set in bold:

```
get
{
    return testContextInstance;
}
```

Any command-line input or output is written as follows:

```
cd c:\Program Files\Microsoft Visual Studio 10.0\Common7\IDE
```

New terms and **important words** are shown in bold. Words that you see on the screen, in menus or dialog boxes for example, appear in the text like this:"After selecting the required counters, click on **Finish** to complete the wizard and start the generation of the actual report".

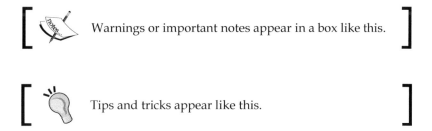

Warnings or important notes appear in a box like this.

Tips and tricks appear like this.

Reader feedback

Feedback from our readers is always welcome. Let us know what you think about this book—what you liked or may have disliked. Reader feedback is important for us to develop titles that you really get the most out of.

To send us general feedback, simply send an e-mail to feedback@packtpub.com, and mention the book title via the subject of your message.

If there is a book that you need and would like to see us publish, please send us a note in the **SUGGEST A TITLE** form on www.packtpub.com or e-mail suggest@packtpub.com.

If there is a topic that you have expertise in and you are interested in either writing or contributing to a book, see our author guide on www.packtpub.com/authors.

Customer support

Now that you are the proud owner of a Packt book, we have a number of things to help you to get the most from your purchase.

> **Downloading the example code for this book**
>
> You can download the example code files for all Packt books you have purchased from your account at http://www.PacktPub.com. If you purchased this book elsewhere, you can visit http://www.PacktPub.com/support and register to have the files e-mailed directly to you.

Errata

Although we have taken every care to ensure the accuracy of our content, mistakes do happen. If you find a mistake in one of our books—maybe a mistake in the text or the code—we would be grateful if you would report this to us. By doing so, you can save other readers from frustration and help us improve subsequent versions of this book. If you find any errata, please report them by visiting http://www.packtpub.com/support, selecting your book, clicking on the **errata submission form** link, and entering the details of your errata. Once your errata are verified, your submission will be accepted and the errata will be uploaded on our website, or added to any list of existing errata, under the Errata section of that title. Any existing errata can be viewed by selecting your title from http://www.packtpub.com/support.

Piracy

Piracy of copyright material on the Internet is an ongoing problem across all media. At Packt, we take the protection of our copyright and licenses very seriously. If you come across any illegal copies of our works, in any form, on the Internet, please provide us with the location address or website name immediately so that we can pursue a remedy.

Please contact us at copyright@packtpub.com with a link to the suspected pirated material.

We appreciate your help in protecting our authors, and our ability to bring you valuable content.

Questions

You can contact us at questions@packtpub.com if you are having a problem with any aspect of the book, and we will do our best to address it.

1
Visual Studio 2010 Test Types

Software testing is one of the most important phases of the **Software Development Life Cycle (SDLC)**. The delivery of the end product is based on better design, better coding, better testing, and meeting the requirements. The quality of the product is measured by testing the product based on functional and non-functional requirements with the help of testing tools and techniques. The tools are useful in simulating a real life situation and the user load. For example, testing a web application with more than 1000 user load is a very time consuming and tedious task if we do it manually. But the performance testing tool that comes along with Visual Studio 2010 can simulate this scenario and test it in a very short period of time. Visual Studio 2010 provides additional tools for testing all type of applications and scenarios such as Unit testing, Load Testing, Web testing, Ordered testing, and generic testing.

This chapter provides a high level overview on all the testing tools and techniques supported by Visual Studio 2010. This chapter covers the following topics:

- Testing as part of the software development life cycle
- Types of Testing
- Test Management in Visual Studio 2010
- Testing Tools in Visual Studio 2010

Software testing in Visual Studio 2010

Before getting into the details of the actual testing using Visual Studio 2010 let us find out the different tools provided by **Visual Studio 2010** and their usage and then we can execute the actual tests. Visual Studio 2010 provides different tools for testing and management such as the Test List Editor and the Test View. The test projects and the actual test files are maintained in **Team Foundation Server (TFS)** for managing the version control of the source and the history of changes. Using Test List Editor we can group similar tests, create any number of Test Lists, and add or delete tests from a Test List.

The other aspect of this chapter is to see the different file types generated in Visual Studio during testing. Most of these files are in XML format, which are created automatically whenever a new test is created.

For the new learners of Visual Studio, there is a brief overview on each one of those windows as we are going to deal with these windows throughout all or most of the chapters in this book. While we go through the windows and their purposes, we can check the **Integrated Development Environment (IDE)** and the tools integration into Visual Studio 2010.

Testing as part of the Software Development Life Cycle

The main objective of testing is to find the defects early in the SDLC. If the defect is found early, then the cost will be lower than when the defect is found during the production or implementation stage. Moreover, testing is carried out to assure the quality and reliability of the software. In order to find the defect as soon as possible, the testing activities should start early, that is in the **Requirement** phase of SDLC and continue till the end of the SDLC.

In the **Coding** phase various testing activities take place. Based on the design, the developers start coding the modules. Static and dynamic testing is carried out by the developers. Code reviews and code walkthroughs are conducted by the team.

Once the coding is complete, then comes the **Validation** phase, where different phases or forms of testing are performed:

- **Unit Testing**: This is the first stage of testing in the SDLC. This is performed by the developer to check whether the developed code meets the stated functionality. If there are any defects found during this testing then the defect is logged against the code and the developer fixes it.

The code is retested and then moved to the testers after confirming the code without any defects for the purpose of functionality. This phase may identify a lot of code defects which reduces the cost and time involved in testing the application by testers, fixing the code, and retesting the fixed code.

- **Integration Testing**: This type of testing is carried out between two or more modules or functions together with the intention of finding interface defects between them. This testing is completed as a part of unit or functional testing and, sometimes, becomes its own standalone test phase. On a larger scale, integration testing can involve putting together groups of modules and functions with the goal of completing and verifying that the system meets the system requirements. Defects found are logged and later fixed by the developers. There are different ways of integration testing such as top-down and bottom-up.

  ○ The **Top-Down** approach is intended to test the highest level of components and integrate first to test the high level logic and the flow. The low level components are tested later.

  ○ The **Bottom-Up** approach is exactly opposite to the top-down approach. In this case the low level functionalities are tested and integrated first and then the high level functionalities are tested. The disadvantage of this approach is that the high level or the most complex functionalities are tested later.

  ○ The **Umbrella** approach uses both the top-down and bottom-up patterns. The inputs for functions are integrated in the bottom-up approach and then the outputs for functions are integrated in the top-down approach.

- **System Testing**: This type of testing compares the system specifications against the actual system. The system test design is derived from the system design documents and is used in this phase. Sometimes system testing is automated using testing tools. Once all the modules are integrated, several errors may arise. Testing done at this stage is called system testing. Defects found in this type of testing are logged by the testers and fixed by the developers.

- **Regression Testing**: This type of testing is carried out in all the phases of the testing life cycle, once the defects logged by the testers are fixed by the developers or if any new functionality changes due to the defects logged. The main objective of this type of testing is testing with the intention of determining if bug fixes have been successful and have not created any new defects. Also, this type of testing is done to ensure that no degradation of baseline functionality has occurred and to check if any new functionality that was introduced in the software caused prior bugs to resurface.

Types of testing

Visual Studio provides a range of testing types and tools for testing software applications. The following are some of those types:

- Unit test
- Manual test
- Web Performance Test
- Coded UI Test
- Load Test
- Generic test
- Ordered test

In addition to these types there are additional tools provided to manage, order the listing, and execution of tests created in Visual Studio. Some of these are the Test View, Test List Editor, and Test Results window. We will look at the details of these testing tools and the supporting tools for managing testing in Visual Studio 2010.

Unit test

Unit testing is one of the earliest phases of testing the application. In this phase the developers have to make sure the code is producing the expected result as per the stated functionality. It is extremely important to run unit tests to catch defects in the early stage of the software development cycle. The main goal of unit testing is to isolate each piece of the code or individual functionality and test if the method is returning the expected result for different sets of parameter values.

A unit test is a functional class method test which calls a method with the appropriate parameters, exercises it, and compares the results with the expected outcome to ensure the correctness of the implemented code. Visual Studio 2010 has great support for unit testing through the integrated automated unit test framework, which enables the team to write and run unit tests.

Visual Studio has the functionality to automatically generate unit test classes and methods during the implementation of the class. Visual Studio generates the test methods or the base code for the test methods but it remains the responsibility of the developer or the team to modify the generated test methods and to include the code for actual testing. The generated unit testing code will contain several attributes to identify the Test Class, Test Method, and Test Project. These attributes are assigned when the unit test code is generated from the original source code. Here is a sample of the generated unit test code.

```
[TestClass()]
public class Form1Test
{
    private TestContext testContextInstance;

    /// <summary> ...
    public TestContext TestContext...

    Additional test attributes


    /// <summary> ...
    [TestMethod()]
    [DeploymentItem("AddNumbers.exe")]
    public void AddNumbersTest()
    {
        Form1_Accessor target = new Form1_Accessor(); // TODO: Initialize to an appropriate value
        double iOne = 0F; // TODO: Initialize to an appropriate value
        double iTwo = 0F; // TODO: Initialize to an appropriate value
        double expected = 0F; // TODO: Initialize to an appropriate value
        double actual;
        actual = target.AddNumbers(iOne, iTwo);
        Assert.AreEqual(expected, actual);
        Assert.Inconclusive("Verify the correctness of this test method.");
    }
}
}
```

A Unit test is used by developers to identify functionality change and code defects. We can run the unit test any number of times and make sure the code delivers the expected functionality and is not affected by new code change or defect fix.

All the methods and classes generated for the automated unit testing are inherited from the namespace Microsoft.VisualStudio.TestTools.UnitTesting.

Manual test

Manual testing is the oldest and the simplest type of testing but yet very crucial for software testing. The tester would be writing the test cases based on the functional and non-functional requirements and then testing the application based on each test case written. It helps us to validate whether the application meets various standards defined for effective and efficient accessibility and usage.

Manual testing comes to play in the following scenarios:

- There is not enough budget for automation
- The tests are more complicated or too difficult to convert into automated tests
- Not enough time to automate the tests
- Automated tests would be time consuming to create and run

The tested code hasn't stabilized sufficiently for cost effective automation.

We can create manual tests by using Visual Studio 2010 very easily. The most important step in a Manual test is to document all the required test steps for the scenario with supporting information, which could be in a separate file. Once all the test cases are created, we should add the test cases to the Test Plan to be able to run the test and gather the test result every time we run the test. The new Microsoft Test Manager tool helps us when adding or editing the test cases to the Test Plan. The following are additional Manual testing features that are supported by Visual Studio 2010:

- Running the Manual test multiple times with different data by adding parameters
- Create multiple test cases using an existing test case to get the base test case first and then customize or modify the test
- Sharing test steps between multiple test cases
- Remove test cases from the test if not required
- Adding or copying test steps from Microsoft Excel or Microsoft Word or any other supported tool

There are a lot of other manual testing features that are supported in Visual Studio 2010. We will see those features explained in *Chapter 2, Test Plan, Test Suite, and Manual Testing.*

Web Performance Tests

Web Performance Tests are used for testing the functionality and performance of the web page, web application, web site, web services, and combination of all of these. Web Performance Tests can be created by recording the HTTP requests and events during user interaction with the web application. The recording also captures the web page redirects, validations, view state information, authentication, and all the other activities. All these are possible by manually building the web tests using the Web Performance Test editor but this takes more time and is more complex. Visual Studio 2010 provides the automated Web test feature which takes care of capturing all HTTP request and response events while recording the user interaction and generating the test.

There are different validation rules and extraction rules used in Web Performance Testing. Validation rules are used for validating the form field names, texts, and tags in the requested web page. We can validate the results or values against the expected result as per the business needs. These validation rules are also used for checking the processing time taken for the HTTP request.

Extraction rules in Web Performance Tests are used for collecting the data from the web pages during requests and responses. Collecting this data helps us in testing the functionality and expected result from the response.

Providing enough data for the test methods is very important for the success of automated testing. Similarly, for Web Performance Tests we need to have a data source from which the data would be populated to the test methods and the web pages would be tested. The data source could be a database, a spreadsheet, or an XML data source. There is a data binding mechanism in Web Performance Tests which takes care of fetching the data from the source and provides the data to the test methods. For example, a reporting page in a web application definitely needs more data to test it successfully. This is also called the **data driven web test**.

Web Performance Tests can be classified into Simple Web Performance Tests and Coded Web Performance Tests. Both of these are supported by VS:

- **Simple Web Performance Tests** generate and execute the test as per the recording with a series of valid flows of events. Once the test is started there won't be any intervention and it is not conditional.

- **Coded Web Performance Tests** are more complex but provide a lot of flexibility. These types of tests are used for conditional execution based on values. Coded web tests can be created manually or generated from the Web Performance Test recording. We can choose the language for generating the code for the Web Performance Test such as C# or VB.NET. Using the generated code, we can control the flow of test events by customizing the code. A coded Web Performance Test is a powerful and highly customizable test for web requests.

Coded UI test

The previous versions of Visual Studio provided all facilities to test application functionality and performance but there is no test type to test the UI part of the application, whether it is Web or Windows. Visual Studio 2010 has a very good new feature for the UI test to access the controls in a web page and verify the values.

The Coded UI test Test can be generated from action recordings coming from MTM or can be recorded and generated directly in Visual Studio. A Coded UI test generates a *UIMap* object that represents the controls, windows, and assertions. Using these objects and methods we can perform actions to automate the test. The coded UI test also creates other supporting files such as:

- `CodedUITest.cs`: A File which contains the test class, test methods, and assertions
- `UIMap.uitest`: The XML model for the UIMap class which contains the windows, controls, properties, methods, and assertions
- `UIMap.Designer.cs`: Contains the code for the `UIMap.uitest` XML file
- `UIMap.cs`: All customization code for the UI Map would go into this file

The following screenshot shows the coded UI test with the default files created for the test:

Load Test

Load Testing is a method of testing used to identify the performance of critical situations and the maximum workload the application can handle. In the case of a desktop or a standalone application the user load is predictable and it is easy to tune the performance, but in the case of a multi-user application or a web application it is necessary to determine the application behavior under normal and peak load conditions.

Visual Studio 2010 provides a Load Test wizard which helps in creating the Load Test for different scenarios. These are the parameters set using the Load Test wizard:

- Load Test pattern defines how the user will run the app at any point

- Test mixes define which tests will be used for testing

- Browser Mix and Network Mix define the possible browser and the network configuration related to the actual

- Counter Sets define which performance counters are collected from the load test agents and the system

- Run settings define the test run such as how long the test should be run

So before we release this web site to the customers or the end users, we should check the performance of the application so that it can support the mass end user group. This is where Load Testing is very useful to test the application along with the Web test or Unit test.

The Load Test is always driven by the collection of Web and Unit tests. The Web Performance Test is added to a Load Test to simulate multiple users opening simultaneous connections to the same web application and making multiple HTTP requests. The Load Test starts with a minimum number of virtual users and then gradually increases the user count to check the performance at the peak user load.

The Load Test can be used to test the performance of the service components to find out the servicing capacity of the component for the client requests. One good example would be to test the data access service component that calls stored procedure in the backend database and returns the results to the client application. Unit tests would be used as part of a Load Test in these cases.

With VS 2010 we have the option of capturing individual tests and saving the entire test result of individual test runs within the Load Test such as a failed Web Performance Test or a failed unit test. This is very helpful when debugging the Load Tests. Results of different tests can be saved in a repository to compare the set of results and improve performance.

VS also provides the Load Test Analyzer, which provides the summary and details of test runs from the Load Test result.

We will see more about setting the Load Test properties, working with tests, and analyzing the Load Test results later in this book in *Chapter 7, Load Testing*.

Ordered test

There are situations where the execution of a test is dependent on another test. In order to execute the dependent test successfully, the parent test should be executed first. Ordered tests merely consist of setting the order for all the tests in an ordered Test List. Sometimes there would be a test B, which depends on the result produced by test A in the list of tests executed. If we don't set the order that test A should be run before running test B then the entire test would fail.VS 2010 provides the feature to set the execution or running order for the tests through the Test View window. We can list all available tests in the Test View and choose the tests in an order using different options provided by Visual Studio and then run the tests. Visual studio will take care of running the tests in the order we have chosen in the list.

Once we are able to run the tests successfully in an order, we also expect the same ordering in getting the results. Visual Studio provides the results of all the tests in a single row in the Test Results window. Actually, this single row result will contain the results of all the tests run in the order. We can just double-click the single row result to get the details of each of the tests run in the ordered test.

An ordered test is the best way to control tests and run tests in an order.

Generic test

We have seen different types and ways of testing applications but there are situations where we might end up having other third party applications for testing, which were not developed using Visual Studio. We might have only the executable or binaries for the application and may not have the supported testing tool for those applications. This is where we need the generic testing method, which is just a way of testing third party applications using Visual Studio.

Generic tests are used to wrap existing tests. Once the wrapping is done then it is just another test in VS.

Using Visual Studio we can collect the test results and gather the code coverage data too. We can manage and run the generic tests in Visual Studio just like others tests. In fact, the test result output can be published to the Team Foundation server to link it with the code build used for testing.

Test management in VS 2010

Visual Studio 2010 has great testing features and management tools for testing. These features are greatly improved from previous versions of VS. The Test Impact View is the new test management tool added to the existing tools such as Test View, Test List Editor, Test Results, Code coverage Results, and Test Runs from the main IDE.

Team Explorer

Team Explorer is the application tier that is integrated into Visual Studio to connect the source control tool, Team Foundation Server. Using this explorer, the developer can browse through the Team Projects in the TFS. TFS is the central source control repository for managing and controlling Team Projects. From Team Explorer IDE, we can connect to the Team Foundation Server, and the Team Project collection, and Team Project. After connecting to the server, we can use Team Explorer to browse through the details of the Team Project.

Team Explorer provides features to work with Team Project details such as:

- Accessing project process guidance documents that explain the process to be followed for the Team Project such as work items, reports, queries, and work products.
- Managing work items such as tasks, defects, issues, and requirements.
- Importing and exporting work items.
- Accessing the project files and source code.
- Adding, removing, configuring, and managing Team Projects.
- Creating, managing, and automating project builds.
- Managing favorites which are the shortcuts to the favorite node of the Team Project.
- Managing reports. It could be defect reporting or any type of work items reporting.

Testing tools introduction

Visual Studio 2010 provides many tools to create, run, debug, and view results of tests. The following is an overview of the tools and windows provided by Visual Studio to view test details and test output details. We will look into more details of the actual usage of these tools later, in *Chapter 9, Managing and Configuring a Test*.

Let us see how we can create a new test project using Visual Studio 2010 and then we will test a sample project to get to know the tools and features.

Open Visual Studio 2010 and open the solution. We will not go into the details of the sample application **AddNumbers** now but we will just create a test project for the sample application and see the features of the tools and windows. The application referred to throughout this chapter is a very simple application for adding two numbers and showing the result.

In the same way as adding the projects and code files to the solution, we have to create the test project and test files, and add the test project to the solution. There are different ways of creating test projects under the solution:

1. Select the solution and add a project using the **Add | New Project...**. Then select the project type as **Test** from the list of project types under the language which we are going to use. Then select the template as **Test Project**.

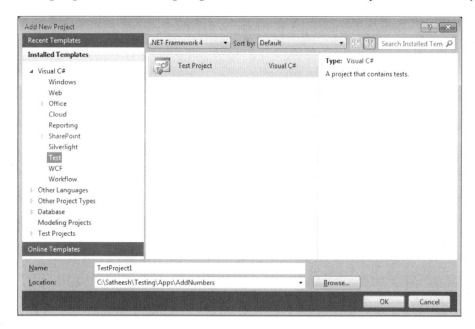

2. Select the solution and then from the top toolbar menu option select the option **Test | New Test...**. This will list all the test type templates to offer the type of template we need for the testing. You can see the option which is a dropdown saying **Add to Test Project** with the options as list of <projectnames>, **Create a new Visual C# test project...**, **Create a new Visual Basic test project...**, and three more options.

For our sample testing application, we will select the second option mentioned previously and choose the simple **Unit Test** type.

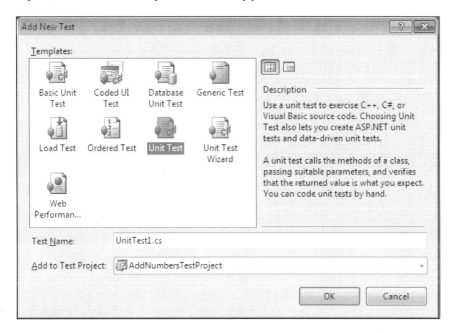

The **Add New Test** dialog contains nine different template options for creating tests. Unit testing templates consist of four types, one is a basic unit test, the second one is Database unit test, the third for the general unit test, and the fourth is for using Unit Test Wizard. The following are the file extensions for each of the VS test types shown in the preceding image:

- .vb or .cs is for all types of unit tests and coded UI tests
- .generictest is for the Generic test type
- .loadtest is for a test which is of type Load Test
- .webtest is for Web Performance Testing

After selecting the test type, give a name for the test in the **Test Name** field. Select the **Create new Visual C# test Project...** in the **Add to Test Project** option. Now assign a name for the new test project. Let us name it AddNumbersTestProject.

Now we can see that there are two files created, <ProjectName>**.vsmdi**, which is the metadata file, and the **Local.testsettings** file created under the solution items for the test projects. The metadata file is an XML file which contains all the information about the tests list. Let us add a couple more tests to this test project to run different tests using the tools available.

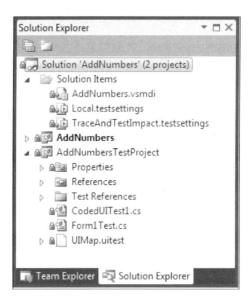

Now let us see the different windows and tools that support all the tests that we can execute using Visual Studio. We will walk through the tools by using the sample unit test.

Test View

Visual Studio 2010 provides the **Test View** window to view the list of all tests available in the current solution. **Test View** provides the option to change the column display, grouping of tests based on test properties, search for specific tests from the list, and select and run the test from the list as well. The test view window is available under the **Test | Windows** menu option in Visual Studio IDE. The following screenshot shows a sample of the **Test View** window which displays the list of all tests created in the current solution:

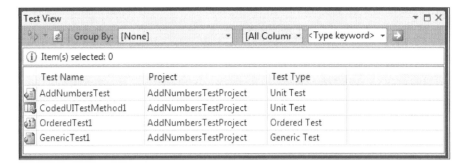

The **Test View** window has its own toolbar for the multiple operations that can be performed on the list. The leftmost option in the toolbar is the **run and debug option** with which we can start and debug the selected tests in the list.

The second and third options in the toolbar are for Filtering the list by choosing the column from the dropdown and entering matching text in the keyword area. When you submit filter conditions using the button to the right, the list gets filtered and only the test matching the condition is shown. For example, the following screenshot shows the list of tests filtered with **Test Type** as **Unit Test**:

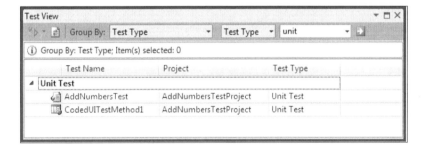

The third option in the toolbar is to group the lists based on some common property of the tests. Clear the above selected filters to list all available tests.

Now select any of the values available from the **Group By** dropdown.

On selecting a value from the dropdown we can see the list regrouped based on the type selected.

The following screenshot shows the tests grouped by **Test Type**. There are two unit tests, one Generic test, and one Ordered test.

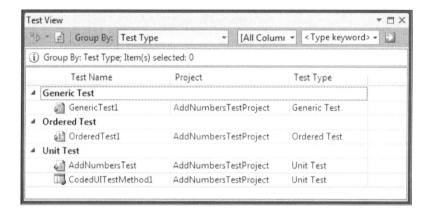

The following screenshot shows the tests grouped by **Class Name**. The Ordered test and Generic test do not have class names as they are not derived from any class and do not have a class.

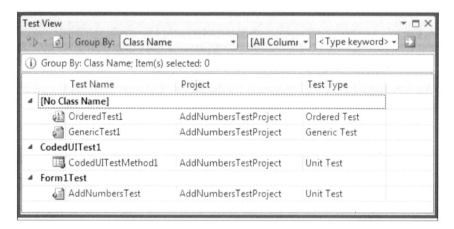

In **Test View,** we can customize the display of columns and the sorting of these columns:

1. Right-click on the columns that are available in the **Test View** window, and select the **Add/Remove Columns** option and the **Add/Remove Columns** dialog box gets displayed.

2. Check and uncheck the columns based on the columns that are needed on the display.

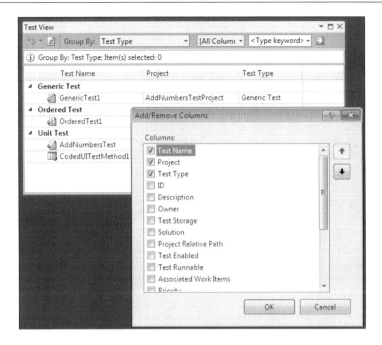

To change the sorting order of the list, just click on the column header. If the same column is already sorted then the sorting order will be changed.

Test List Editor

All features available in Test View are also available in the Test List Editor with some additional features such as creating new Test Lists by selecting multiple tests from the available list of tests.

The following screenshot is the **Test List Editor** opened using the menu option, **Test | Windows | Test List Editor**. The editor shows all available tests under **All Loaded Tests**:

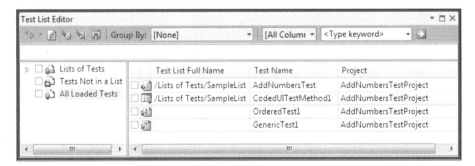

The toolbar in the **Test List Editor** window has the same features as we saw in the **Test View** window. But you can see the detail section of the list window is split into two panes. The left pane of the window has three nodes and the right pane displays all the tests in the lists based on the selection in the left pane. The Test List editor displays the following three options as nodes:

- *List of Tests* displays the available Test Lists and acts as an interface to create a new Test List

- *Tests Not in a List* is the second option, which provides all the tests which are not part of any of the Test Lists

- *All Loaded Tests* is the third option, which provides the list of all the tests in the solution whether the test is part of any list or not

The following screenshot contains a Test List which contains a couple of tests selected from the available list of all tests in the solution. You can right-click on the node and select the **Create New Test List** option and provide the required details to create the new Test List.

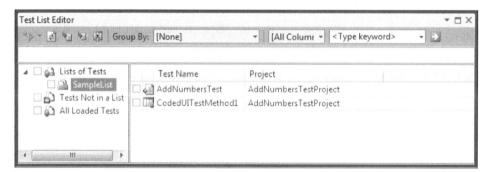

After creating the Test List and adding the required tests to the corresponding list, you may want to check the tests that are not part of any of the list. The screenshot here shows the second option of displaying the tests not part of any of the list:

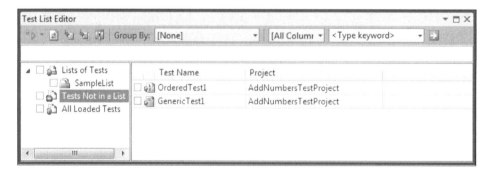

Now we know that there are tests which are part of a Test List and some are not part of any List but how can we see all of the available tests under the solution? To get this, you have to choose the third option, **All Loaded Tests**, from the Editor window.

By listing all tests from the solution we can also move the tests around from one list to another, or remove the test from any list, or add tests to a new list.

Test Results

This window provides the status of all test runs including the error messages and an option to rerun the test irrespective of whether it passed or failed. Using this window, we can export the test results or import the exported results. We can also get detailed information about the test run by double-clicking on the test result. Select the unit test and Coded UI test from **Test View** or **Test List Editor** and run the tests.

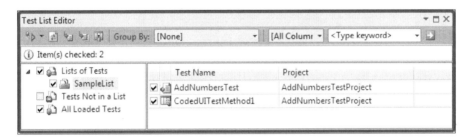

The following screenshot shows the different stages of test runs in the result window. From the following image we see that the first test is still in the process of test execution and the second test is pending execution.

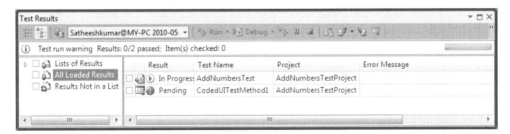

The following image shows the final execution status of the selected tests. One test executed successfully and the other test failed. The error message for the failed test is also displayed. We can also select a test from the result window and rerun a test. This would be very useful in executing a failed test.

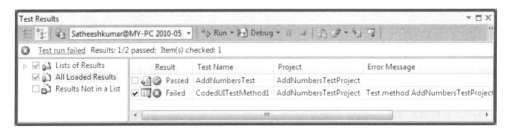

To get more information such as the detailed error message, the stack trace of the error, the time duration of the test run, and other details, just double-click on the test result which will open a new window with more details.

On execution of any test in VS, a test result file is created with all the test result information. The file is automatically created with the username and the machine name with date and the extension `.trx`. In the preceding image the name for the test result file is generated as **Satheeshkumar@MY-PC 2010-05-25 23_24_32**. The test result file is an XML file with all the result information. The following screenshot shows the default folder structure and the files created for the test results:

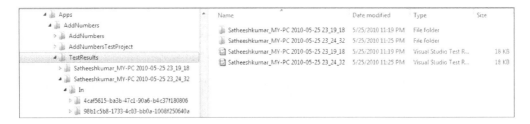

In the case of multiple test runs and multiple tests, we sometimes need the test to be stored somewhere or to keep the copy of the test run trace for future analysis of the test, or we may prefer sharing the result with another team member. In that case we can use **Export Test Run Results** or **Export Selected Test Results** from the toolbar which exports the entire trace file for the tests selected.

Code coverage results

Visual Studio provides this code coverage feature to find out the percentage of code that is covered by the test execution. Through this window, we can find out the number of lines covered in each method by the test. To activate the code coverage for the test project, the test settings have to be changed. This is a little bit different from VS 2008. To configure the test project, open the **local.testsettings** file and select the **Data and Diagnostics** option from the list of settings options.

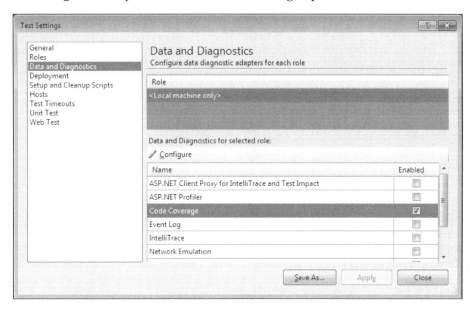

Choose **Code Coverage** from the list of diagnostics and enable it. You can see that the **Configure** option on top of the list is enabled now. Click on **Configure** to open the **Code Coverage Detail** page which would lists all the projects and artifacts available under the solution. Choose the required artifacts from the list for which the code coverage has to be captured during the test run. Apply the settings and close the window.

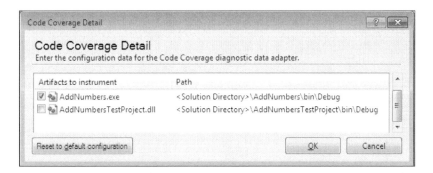

After completing the configuration, select the test from the Test View/List Editor and run the test. The test run will capture the code coverage and store the coverage result in a separate file with the default name of `data.coverage`.

Select the tests run result from the results window and then right-click and choose the code coverage results or open this using **Test | Windows | Code Coverage Results** from the menu option. The following screenshot shows the code coverage results from the test run. The result window provides information such as number of code blocks not covered by the test, percentage of code blocks not covered, covered code blocks, and percentage of covered code blocks from the selected assembly.

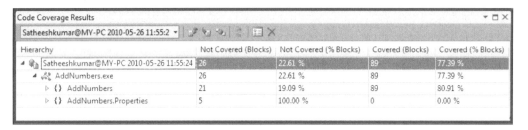

The result window also provides an option to directly open the source code associated with the listed blocks, and methods to easily navigate and fix.

Overview of files used for test settings and testing in Visual Studio 2010

There are several types of configuration and settings used for testing an application in VS 2010 and each type of test uses its own type of file to store the test related information.

- **Test Metadata file**: This file stores the tests and lists of categories for the tests in an XML format under the file with the extension `.vsmdi`. Whenever you create a new test project, this file is created under the `Solution Items` folder. The file name is the same as the solution name.

- **Test Results file**: This file contains the results of the tests that were run. This file is created automatically by Visual Studio when any test is run. It has the extension of `.trx`

- **Test Run Configuration file**: This file contains the settings required for the test run. Using these settings we can define the Data and Diagnostics information to be collected during the test run, deployment files, scripts for setup and cleanup activities before and after the test runs, and the required settings for the Web and unit test runs. This file is created under the solution with the extension `.testsettings`.

- There are other XML files for different test types with some specific extensions such as `.webtest`, `.loadtest`, `.orderedtest`, and `.generictest`.

Microsoft Test Manager

This is the new standalone product but it is not part of Visual Studio 2010 Premium. It is part of Visual Studio Test Professional and Visual Studio Ultimate. This is the functional testing tool which provides the ability to create and execute the Manual tests and collect the results. This tool works without Visual Studio but does require a connection to the Team Foundation Server and the Team Project. **MTM (Microsoft Test Manager)** contains:

- **Testing Center**: This is used for creating Test Plans and creating Test Suites and Test cases for the Test Plans. We can also associate the requirements to the Test Plans. The other features such as running the manual test, capturing the test results and defects, tracking the test results using existing queries and creating custom queries, organizing the test cases and shared steps for test cases, and maintaining the test configurations are supported by Testing Center.
- **Lab Center**: This is used to set up and create lab environments for the test execution. The environments are created using Physical and Virtual machines with a certain set of configurations. Later on, the environment is deployed so that the test is conducted using the environment.

Connecting to Team Project

MTM should be connected to the TFS Team Project to create the Test Plans and test cases. The first task on opening MTLM is to connect to the TFS Team Project from the Team Project collection.

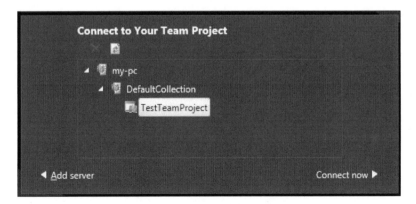

Test Plans, Suites and Test Cases

The Test Plan window in the Testing Center allows for the creation of new Test Suites, test cases, and adding test cases based on the requirements. Any number of Test cases can be created or added and configured through this window. The first step is to create the Test Plan and Test Suite. Each Test Plan contains a set of Test Suites which helps us to plan the testing effort. For example, we can create a Test Plan for each sprint if we are using agile methodology for the software development. The following screenshot has one Test Plan (*MyTestPlan*) with Two Test Suites, **Add Numbers test** and **Second Test Suite**.

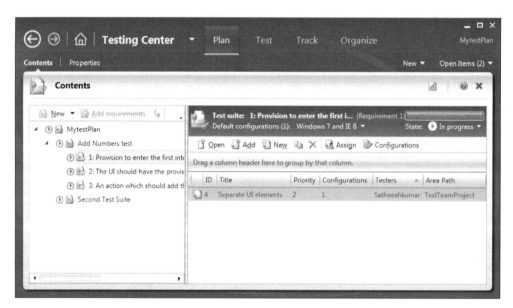

The next step is to create or add Test cases to the Suite. The requirements can be added to the plan and then test cases can be associated with the requirements. In the above example, three requirements are added to the first Test Suite, **Add Numbers test**, and new test cases are associated with the requirements. These requirements are available in TFS under the Team Project. If we followed the Application lifecycle management and tools available in TFS then we should have the requirements created as part of the requirements phase already.

Define test cases

The creation of a test case involves defining a lot of properties for the test case. Each testing step and the expected result should be defined. The user scenarios, links, and attachments can be associated to the test cases. The test case can be classified under the specific Area path and iteration path for the Team Project in TFS. Other properties such as **Assigned To**, **State**, **Priority**, and **Automation Status** can be set for the test case.

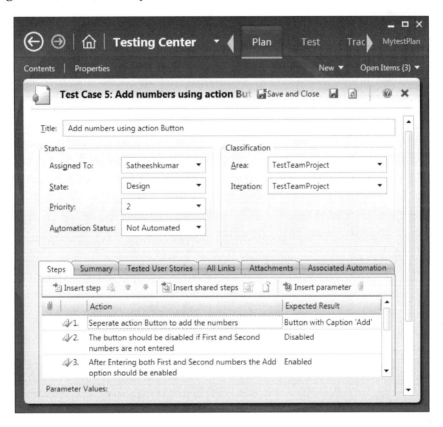

Lab Center

The Lab center in MTM helps us to create and configure different virtual/ physical environments for the test runs, test settings such as defining the roles and configuring the data and diagnostics information for the selected roles, configuring the Test Controllers required for the test, and configuring the test library to store the environment information. The following screenshot shows the Lab Center without any environment:

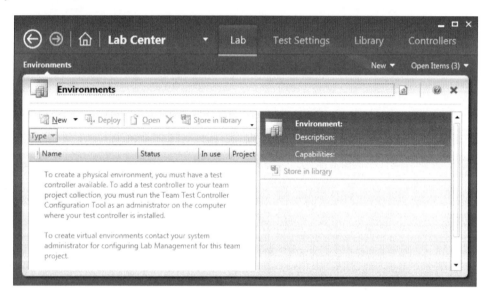

We can see the details of these configurations later in *Chapter 13, Test and Lab Center*, which explains the features of Testing Center and Lab Center.

Summary

There are lots of new testing features added to Visual Studio 2010, particularly coded UI testing and manual testing using the Test Manager standalone tool. Manual testing is very well structured with lots of options handled separately using the MTM tool. The MTM tool contains Testing Center and Lab Center which help us to maintain the test cases, test configurations and testing environments to simulate the actual user load to test the application performance. This chapter provides the high level information on the tools and techniques available and the new techniques added to Visual Studio 2010. Each of these testing techniques is explained in detail in forthcoming chapters with detailed examples.

2

Test Plan, Test Suite, and Manual Testing

Manual testing, as described earlier, is the simplest type of testing carried out by the testers without any automation tool. Manual test type is the best choice to be selected when the test is too difficult or complex to automate. Prior to TFS 2010, most of the manual test cases were created and managed using applications such as Microsoft Excel or Microsoft Word. As most of the testing was done manually, Microsoft introduced many new features for manual testing and test management with a separate testing framework and user interface with no dependency on Visual Studio. This new UI, Microsoft Test Manager, is the main entry point for test case authoring, management, execution, and tracking. Accessing the requirements, raising defects, and defect reporting has become much easier for the testers. This stands alone from Visual Studio and provides an independent testing environment for testers without having Visual Studio IDE but only needs a connection to the Team Project repository in Team Foundation Server This chapter covers the following topics in detail:

- Creating Test Plan, Test Suite, and Test Cases
- Types of Test Suites
- Executing Manual Tests and Action Recording
- Shared steps creation and action recording for shared steps
- Parameterising the Manual Test

Test Plan

Test Plans are the testing strategies documented by the testing team just like the requirement documents and design documents. The Test Plan should contain the test schedule, In-Scope and Out of Scope, testing methods, verification methods, process, and practices to be followed to effectively verify the quality of the product as per the functional specification and requirements.

The Microsoft Test Manager tool provides the flexibility for the testing team to create Test Plans and Test cases. Testers can organize Test cases, configuration, test runs, and results. The Test Manager tool should be connected to the Team Foundation Server and the Team Project under which the application related artifacts are maintained. Once Microsoft Test Manager is connected to the Team Project, Test Plans and Test cases can be associated with the requirements and design documents and other specifications.

The following screenshot shows the Testing Center from Test Manager with which the new Test Plan can be created. Click on **Add** and provide the name for the new Test Plan. For our examples, we have created a new Test Plan **Employee Maintenance Testing**.

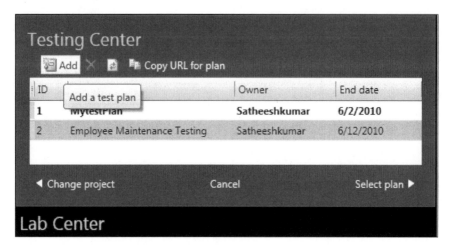

Selecting the plan opens the **Testing Center** console where Test Suites and test cases can be created and associated with the Test Plan.

Test Suite and Test Suite Types

Test Suites are used for grouping and organizing test cases under the Test Plan. Grouping test cases under a Test Suite helps Testing Teams to run and report all the tests in a particular Test Suite. After creating the Test Plan, a default Test Suite is added as a root node to the plan with the same name as Test Plan. This node contains all the other Test Suites.

A new Test Suite can be created in different ways:

- Requirement based Test Suite
- Query based Test Suite
- Static Test Suite

After creating the Test Suite, we can also customize the order of the Test Case in the Test Suite. Test Suites can also be copied from another Test Plan in the team project.

Requirement-based Test Suite

Every project has the requirements in one form or another documented as specified in the documentation which can be referred and verified during the Design, Construction and testing phases. In Visual Studio 2010, these requirements are collected as work items, often as Requirements (in MSF or CMMI) or user stories (under MSF for Agile Software Development) and saved under the corresponding Team Project. These user stories then on used during the testing phase to create test cases for the requirement and linked to the user stories. This group of test cases, linked to the requirement, are created as a Test Suite by adding the requirement to the Test Plan.

The following screenshot shows the first step, which involves the creation of test cases. On the right side of the test manager tool you can find the **New** option with multiple sub options such as Bug, Issue, Task, Test case, User Story, and shared steps. Select the Test case option and keep creating the test cases with test steps.

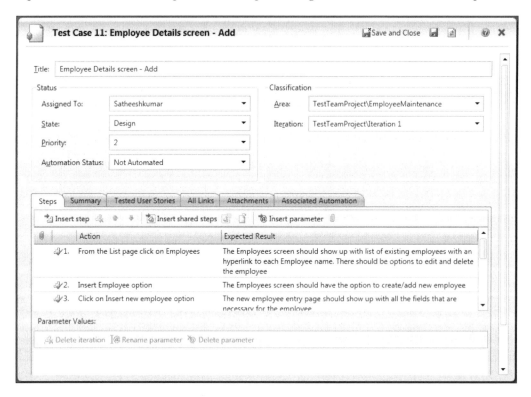

After creating the test cases and the test steps, the test case can be linked to the corresponding requirement specification. These requirements would have been created during the initial stages of the project while collecting the requirements from the users if we are following the regular Waterfall method and the Agile methodology. The requirement would be collected and decided on release. Select the fourth tab, **All Links,** from the available tabbed page and click on **Link to** from the tab page which opens the **Add link to test case** window as shown:

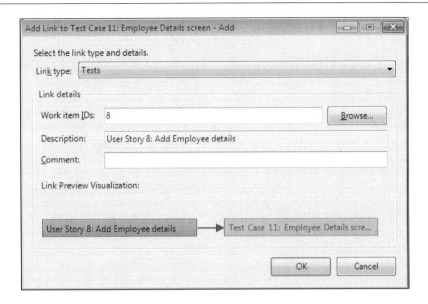

The image shows the test case already linked to the requirement. Select the **Link type** and then click on the **Browse...** option to search for the requirement and then select it for linking. One of these requirement selections is shown as follows:

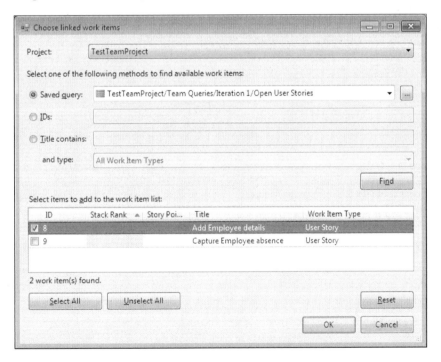

Now we have the test case linked to the User story and the requirement. Go back to the Test Plan and choose the **Add requirement** option which opens the **Add existing requirements to this test plan** to search for the requirement and add it to the plan. Build the query with the known information about the requirement such as the Team Project, area path, and work item category, and then run the query. This lists requirements available for the given query condition. Select the requirement for which we have the test cases defined and which needs to be added to the Test Plan.

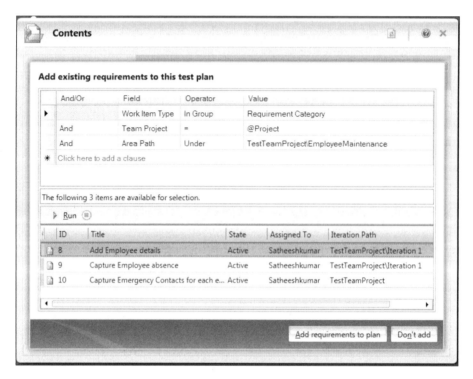

Select the requirement from the list and click on the **Add requirements to plan** option which adds the selected requirement to the Test Plan as a new Test Suite. This new Test Suite will be added under the root Test Suite node. You can also see the test cases which are linked to the requirement listed on the right.

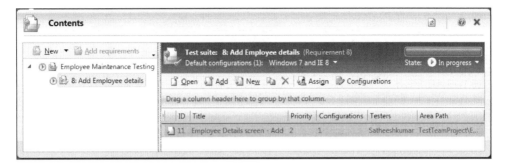

The test can be modified or can be assigned to the tester who needs to test the application as per the test case definition.

Query-based Test Suite

This is similar to the requirement based Test Suite with the difference that the selection of test cases is by query instead of requirement. To add test cases, we need to define the Query, first based on the property of test cases such as name or priority. Choose the options **Add** and **Query-Based Test Suite** from the Test Plan window which opens the **Create a Query-Based Test Suite** window. Now, build a query to fetch all priority two test cases from the available list of test cases. In the following screenshot, we have two test cases available for the query defined. Provide a name for the Query and then choose the **Create test suite** option.

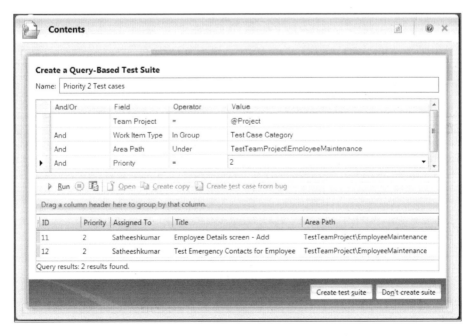

The new Test Suite is created with the name provided, while defining the query and the resulted test cases from the query makes them added to the Test Suite in the Test Plan. These test cases can be edited, assigned, and configured based on requirements.

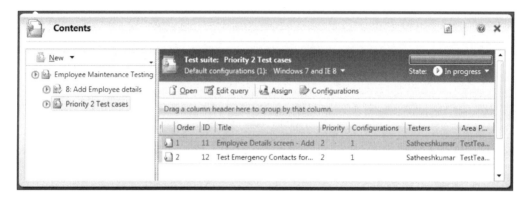

Static Test Suite

This is the Test Suite holding the hierarchy of the Test Suite, which is created by selecting the test cases from the list of available test cases from the Team Project. Choose the **Suite** option under **New** and provide a name for the new Test Suite. On the right we can see the option to Add existing test cases and Create new test cases to be added to the Test Suite. Choose the option, **Add,** if you have the test cases defined already. This brings up the **Add Test cases to Suite** window, which provides the flexibility to search for test cases and selects the required test cases from the result and selects the **Add** test cases option which adds the test cases from the result to the Test Suite.

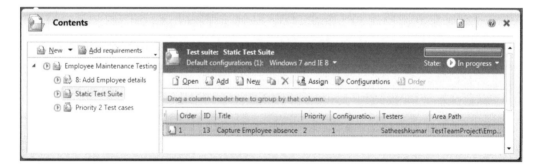

After adding, the test cases can be assigned to the testers.

In the case of a static Test Suite, there is an additional option to edit the Query directly from here.

For all the Test Suite test cases, there are additional options such as Open, Assign, and Configuration:

- **Open**: used to open the test case and modify the test case information.

- **Assign**: used for assigning testers to the test cases so that they take care of executing the test case and take full ownership of the test case.

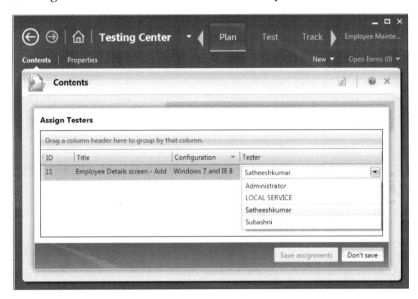

- **Configure**: used to update the default assignment of test configurations to test cases in each Test Suite. Test configurations can be selected from the list of all configurations available for the Test Project.

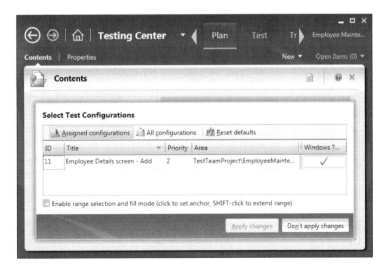

The assigned configuration option is used to view the currently assigned configuration for the selected test case.

- The All Configurations option displays all the available configurations in the Team Project so that we can select the required configuration and assign it to the test case.

- The Reset configuration clears the changes and resets the default configuration.

If there are a lot of changes to make, select the option **Enable range selection and fill mode** to mark a range and start marking the range. After completing the configurations choose **Apply changes** to save the changes made.

Run Manual Tests

The tests cases created under **Plan** can be executed under **Test** or run through the manual test runner. Running the tests is not only for verifying functionality as per the requirement, but for a lot of other test result information which can be captured during the test. Information such as defects, connectivity issues, security issues, test outcome, screen shot images, and other comments can be captured along with the test run.

1. Open **Microsoft Test Manager** and then **Testing Center**.

2. Select **Plan** from the main menu bar in **Testing Center** to create or verify all the test cases.

3. To Execute/Run the test cases created, Select **Test** from the main menu bar in **Testing Center** to open the **Run Tests** window. This window shows the list of all Test Suites and test cases that we have created. We can select all the tests under the Test Suite or select the individual test from the Test Suite and run them separately.

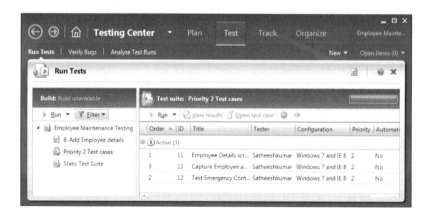

4. The filter option on the left is used for filtering the tests suites based on tester or other configurations for testing based on the current environment. Select the test suite or a particular test and run the test. Running the Test Suite opens the tests in the Test Runner and lists the test case steps for the first test in the list.

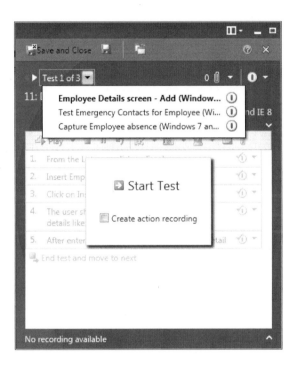

The Selected Test Suite in the Test Runner shows three tests in total as we have added three tests to the selected Test Suite and the first in the list is for testing the Employee details screen. The window also displays the test steps in the first test. You can find another small window which has the option to start the test run and to create action recording. If you choose to enable Action recording, the testing actions will be captured and recorded and can be replayed at any point of time to verify the functionality of the test case and Action recording is also used for generating the code and reusing the recording in other tests if needed. This is very useful in case of multiple similar tests or common test steps, which are also called **Shared Test Steps**.

Click on **Start Test** and follow the test steps and start testing the application manually. The following screenshot shows both the test runner with the test and the application for which the test case is written. The first step in the test runner shows what to test in the application and what the expected result from the application is. The tester should follow the steps and verify the expected result with the actual output.

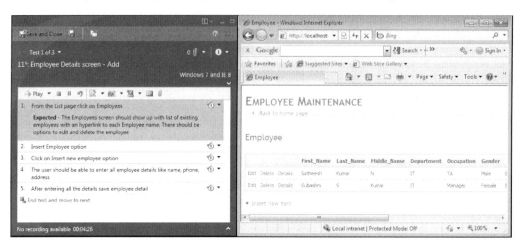

After verifying the result, the tester can make the test step as either Pass or Fail based on the output. The test runner has the option to the right of the test step to make it pass or fail. The following screenshot shows three steps passed successfully and the fourth step in progress.

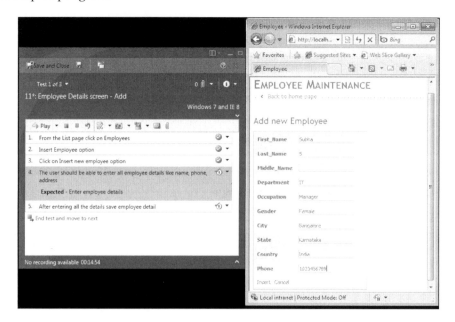

Once all the steps are tested and completed, you can end the current test and move to the next test in the Test Suite using the option below the Test Runner. After completing all the tests, click on the **Save and Close** option to close the test runner and go back to the Test Manager which will show the final status of the test run. To see the details of each test run in the Test Suite, select the test case from the right pane of the Testing Center and choose the Test case. After selecting the test case, open the test result window using the menu option **View Results**. The result window shows the details for the selected test case such as test summary, test analysis details, test steps status, attachments, and result history.

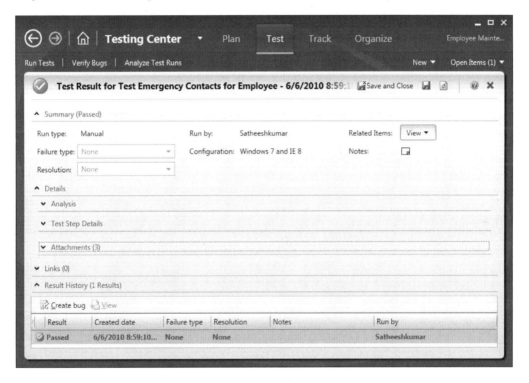

Going back to the Test Suite, select the test from the list and rerun the test. Let us see the behavior in case of test failure.

The Employee absence screen accepts all values from the user. But there are couple of fields (**Max_Casual_Leave** and **Max_Previlege_Leave**) which should be read-only and should not accept any value from the user. As per the result, the read only fields are accepting the values from the user which is a potential defect and this needs to be logged as a defect by the testers and to be fixed.

The test runner has an option to create a test defect immediately after the test step. Click on the **Create bug** option from the toolbar in Test runner. This opens the create bug screen with the preloaded information of the test case and the step details with the status of each step along with the linked work items such as requirement linked work items. To complete the defect logging, the testers need to fill in other details such as **Title, Assigned To, Area, Iteration, Priority,** and **Severity** and if any screen shot to validate the defect can be attached in the **Attachment** tab.

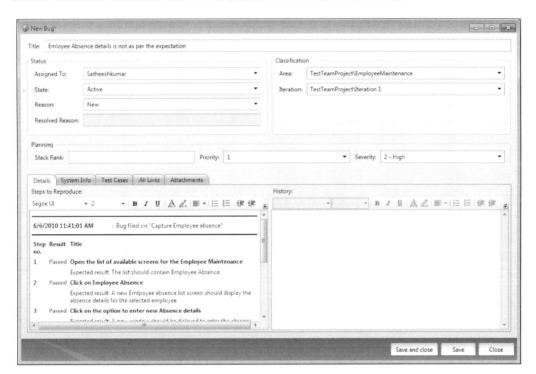

Action Recording

The test runner has the option to record the manual test steps so that it can be played back later or used in other tests action recording can be activated during the course of manual testing. Later on we can run the test and play the recording. The test steps will run automatically based on the recording.

Select the option **Create Action recording** before starting the test run in the Test Runner window. Then choose the option **Mark test case result a**s shown in the following screenshot. Follow the steps and mark the test results and then end the result.

The following screenshot shows the test with all the steps having action recording. This is denoted by the orange color coding at the right end of each test step. You can also see a message at the bottom of the Test Runner window which says recording is already available. Recording can be overridden by choosing the recording option again while running the test next time.

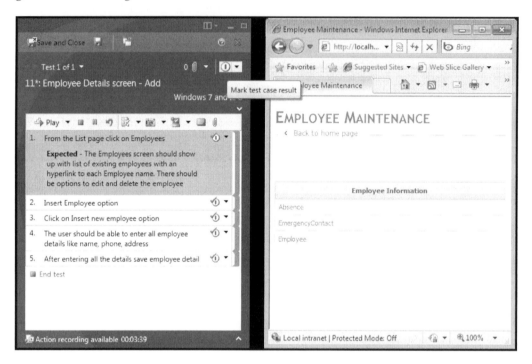

Next time, while running the test, select the play option in the Test Runner toolbar to run the test step automatically using the recorded action from the last test run. The details entered during the last run are used for the action this time.

The **Play** option in the toolbar will play the action for the current step that was selected in the test case. Multiple steps can be selected by clicking the **Play** option to run as a group or batch. The **Play All** option below the play option will play all recorded actions for the current test case.

If there is any error during the playback of the test due to unavailability of the application or any other error, the test runner will throw an error message similar to the one below. It gives an option either to Replay the action or Skip the current step and continue further if it's a Group/Batch run and has an option to create a bug as well.

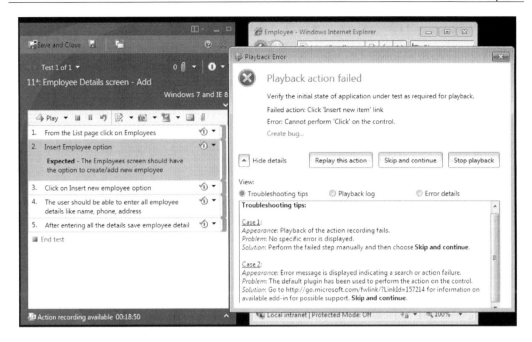

Along with the test result we can also capture the screenshot image of the current screen area or the error message, add additional documents or files as attachments to the test step, take a current environment snapshot in case of only virtual environment, and add a comment to the test to provide additional information. All these options are available under the **Test Runner** toolbar. The following screenshot shows the attachment, image, and a comment added to the test step.

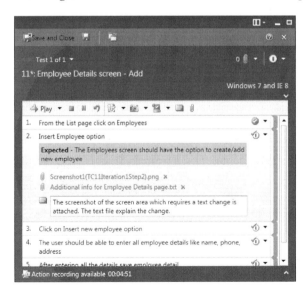

Shared steps and action recording for shared steps

Shared steps are common test steps which are shared across multiple manual tests to avoid recreating the test steps for multiple manual tests. For example, the employee maintenance application might have several test cases for which the tester has to enter the Employee details for every test case run. To avoid the repeated step and to avoid the time and effort, that particular step can be made as a shared step and make use of the shared step in multiple test cases wherever it is required.

Creating shared steps

Creating shared steps is similar to creating a normal test step but the Test Manager provides a different option to create the shared step within the Test case creation window. The following screenshot shows the Test Suite with two test cases, both having the same test step to enter employee details but the testing is for different purposes.

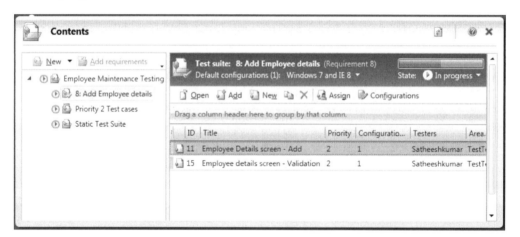

The shared step can be created while we are adding the test steps for the test cases. For example, the first test case for Employee details has several test steps and one of these steps is entering the employee details which can be made as shared steps. The test case creation window has the option to create test steps. Along with this there are two more options, **Insert Shared Step** and **Create Shared Step and insert at the current insertion point.**

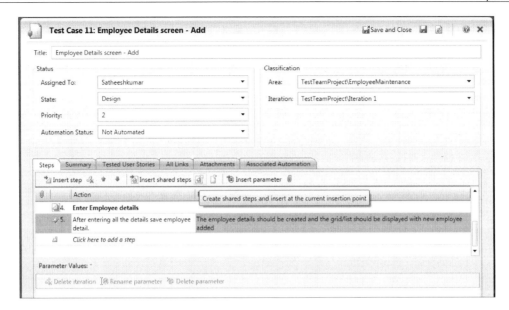

You need to select one or more steps which are already available and then make it create a shared step. The **Create shared step** option would ask for a shared step name and then replace the selected steps with the new name. The shared step will have the details of the steps which got replaced. In the preceding screenshot **Enter Employee details** is a shared step which contains the common test steps which can be reused in multiple other tests.

To modify or update the shared step, use the option **Open Shared Steps** from the toolbar. This opens a new window which contains the details of the shared test step as shown in the following screenshot:

We can keep adding the required test steps and update the properties, but keep in mind that this is a common test step which is going to be shared by multiple test cases.

Now that the shared step was created it's ready to be reused in multiple test cases. Open the second test case which requires the same step and insert the shared step at the required place as shown in the following screenshot. We do not have to write the steps but just reuse the shared step which is already available.

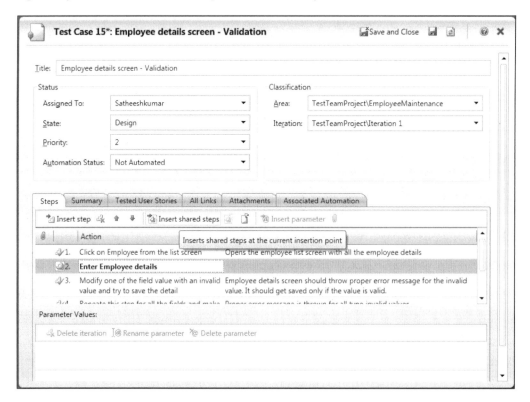

Action recording for Shared steps

Shared step actions are recorded along with the test case actions recording to which the shared step is part of the test steps. Run the Test Suite or the test case from the Test manager. The Test runner will load the test steps including the shared step which is part of the test. Choose the **Create Action recording** option and then start the test as we did before in the regular test steps scenario.

The shared step will have two additional steps:

- Start the shared test
- Start and record the test

Choose the second option and enter all the details so that it is recorded as part of shared test.

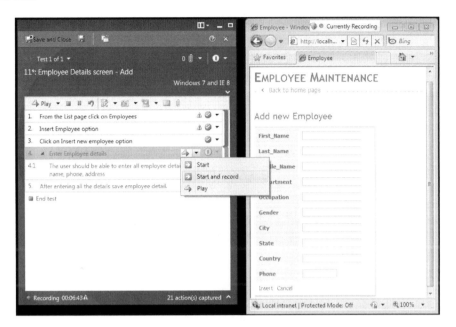

After entering all the details, make the test as pass and End the Shared test recording using the option below the test step. Complete remaining steps and save the test result.

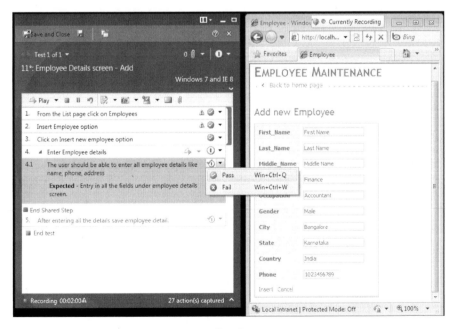

Now the shared step as well as the shared step recording is also ready. This action recording will be available to all the tests which are using this shared test.

Add Parameters to Manual Tests

Parameters are useful for running the manual test multiple times without creating the test case multiple times. We can add parameters to the actions or expected results for any test step. You can select the test step for the test case and keep adding the parameters. The other options available are to rename the parameter and delete the parameter. The following screenshot shows the test step for which the parameters are added:

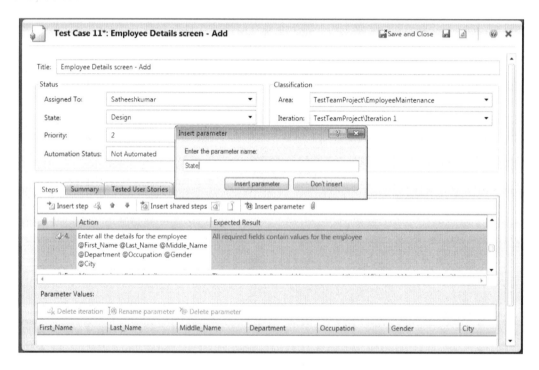

After entering the parameter we can keep adding the values for the parameters. These parameter values are validated against the fields while running the test in the test runner. Save the details and close the test case and open the Test tab to run the test.

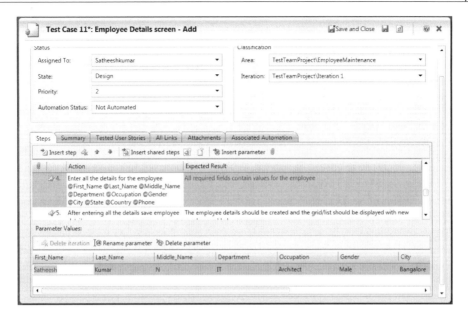

Run the test as we did before in the previous steps and continue the test steps in the test runner until we reach the test step where we added the parameters and values. The test step displays the parameters and values against each parameter. We can select the parameter value to copy and paste it to the fields accordingly. Each parameter acts as a separate test step. You can mark the test as pass or fail after testing the entire step and end the test. Save the test and close the test runner.

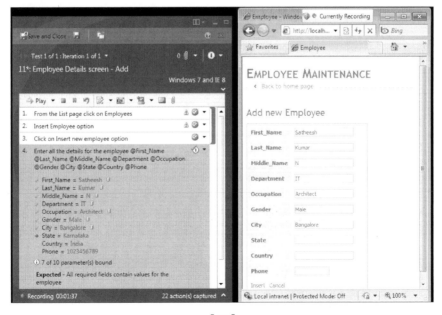

The test result shows the details of the test with the parameters and the values used for testing.

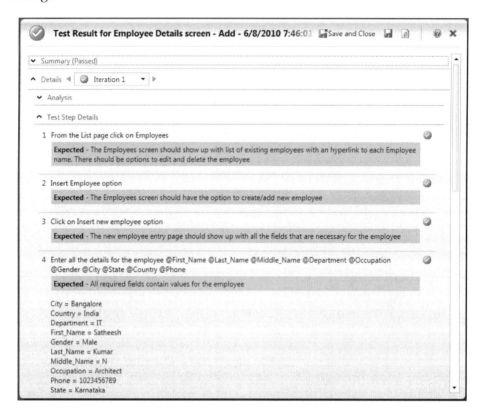

In the case of multiple tests for the same step, you can add multiple sets of parameter values as per the number of tests required. With the use of data binding to parameters, we are automating the test to run without expecting any input from the tester except initiating the test with the play button.

Summary

Manual testing has changed in many ways in VS 2010 compared to the previous version of Visual Studio. Testers can now use the Microsoft Test Manager application and start testing applications without even having Visual Studio installed on their machine. Shared steps and recording tests are great advantages for the manual tests because of their usage as a common step across multiple tests. Test Manager provides three different ways of creating the Test Suites using requirements, Queries, and Static suites. Adding parameters and binding them to the data helps us to reuse the same test case for multiple scenarios with different sets of data. Directly creating the defect from the test result will make the tester's job easier and maintaining the traceability is also easier by linking the different work items such as linking the Test case with requirement or defect with the test case.

3
Automated Tests

Automated Testing is the new simplified form of automating manual testing and automating user interface testing and controls. Validating the controls and testing the functionality of user interfaces is made simpler in Visual Studio 2010. These tests are also called coded UI tests. The existing manual tests, test cases, and the action recordings of the user interface tests are reused for generating the automated tests and the code files in managed code (C# or VB.NET). And then the UI controls can be added to the coded UI test, and properties and values of the controls can be verified using the Coded UI Test Builder feature (built-in recorder in Visual Studio 2010). To have the same test performed with multiple sets of data and test the UI functionality, the coded UI test is created as a data driven test by adding a data source to the test method. The test method is then called for each set row of data in the data source. The coded UI test can be run directly from Visual Studio, Microsoft Test Manager, or Team Foundation Build., The coded UI test can be linked to the requirements to determine the number of automated tests for each requirement.

Coded UI Test from Action Recording

Action recording is useful for manual testing to record the user action and to play back the test multiple times instead of repeating the same test manually. Recording the action is done by using the Test Runner. The details of creating and recording user actions are covered as part of *Chapter 2, Test Plan, Test Suite, and Manual Testing,* which talks about Test Plan and manual testing. This section explains the details of creating the coded UI test from the existing action recording.

The following screenshot shows the successful completion of the action recording for the manual test:

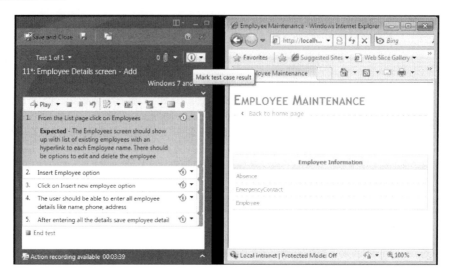

In Visual studio, select the test project that you want to test from the solution explorer if it already exists in the solution and then add a new test to the project. Otherwise select the **New Test** option from the Test menu and then select **Coded UI Test** from the available list of options.

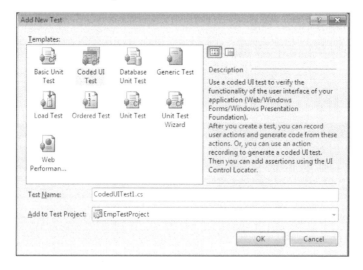

The selected Coded UI test option will add the code file to the test project. The code file will contain only the class with the CodedUITest attribute, a test method named CodedUITestMethod1 with the attribute TestMethod and a test context. All these methods are empty as we have not generated the code yet.

After selecting the coded UI test, we need to select the option to generate the code to the coded UI test file for the current test. There are two options available:

- To record the actions and edit UI Maps or add assertions
- To use an existing action recording for the manual test

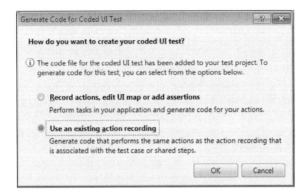

Let us select the second option to use the existing action recording which was recorded already as part of a Manual Testing chapter run in Microsoft Test Manager. After choosing the second option we need to select the manual test case and the action recording for which we need the coded UI test to be generated. Select the work item using the Work item picker screen, which is displayed after selecting the action recording option.

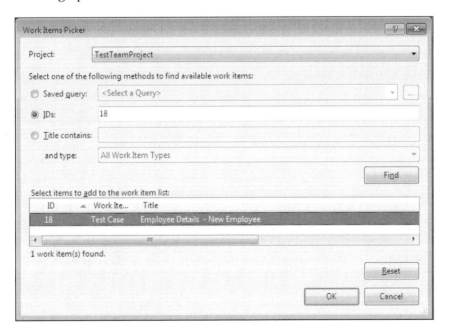

Selecting the test case from this window generates the code based on the action recording that we have for that test case. You can see that there are some additional files such as `UIMap.uitest`, `UIMap.cs`, and `UIMap.Designer.cs` created and modified at the time of code generation. The main method `CodedUITestMethod1()` in the `CodedUITest1.cs` file will contain the method calls for each action in the action recording. The corresponding method definition is created in the `Designer.cs` file by the Coded UI Test Builder itself. The following code contains the action methods generated under the `CodedUITestMethod1()`:

```
// Sample code - generated based on action recording
public void CodedUITestMethod1()
{
  // To generate code for this test, select "Generate Code for Coded
  UI Test" from the shortcut menu and select one of the menu items.
  // For more information on generated code, see
  http://go.microsoft.com/fwlink/?LinkId=179463
  this.UIMap.FromtheListpageclickonEmployees();
  this.UIMap.InsertEmployeeoption();
  this.UIMap.ClickonInsertnewemployeeoption();
  this.UIMap.EnterallthedetailsfortheemployeeFirst_NameLast_
  NameMiddle_NameDepartmentOccupationGenderCityStateCountryPhone
  Params.UIFirst_NameEditText = TestContext.DataRow["First_Name"].
  ToString();
  this.UIMap.EnterallthedetailsfortheemployeeFirst_NameLast_
  NameMiddle_NameDepartmentOccupationGenderCityStateCountryPhone
  Params.UILast_NameEditText = TestContext.DataRow["Last_Name"].
  ToString();
  this.UIMap.EnterallthedetailsfortheemployeeFirst_NameLast_
  NameMiddle_NameDepartmentOccupationGenderCityStateCountryPhone
  Params.UIMiddle_NameEditText = TestContext.DataRow["Middle_Name"].
  ToString();
  this.UIMap.EnterallthedetailsfortheemployeeFirst_NameLast_
  NameMiddle_NameDepartmentOccupationGenderCityStateCountryPhone
  Params.UIDepartmentEditText = TestContext.DataRow["Department"].
  ToString();
  this.UIMap.EnterallthedetailsfortheemployeeFirst_NameLast_
  NameMiddle_NameDepartmentOccupationGenderCityStateCountryPhone
  Params.UIOccupationEditText = TestContext.DataRow["Occupation"].
  ToString();
  this.UIMap.EnterallthedetailsfortheemployeeFirst_NameLast_
  NameMiddle_NameDepartmentOccupationGenderCityStateCountryPhone
  Params.UIGenderEditText = TestContext.DataRow["Gender"].ToString();
  this.UIMap.EnterallthedetailsfortheemployeeFirst_NameLast_
  NameMiddle_NameDepartmentOccupationGenderCityStateCountryPhone
  Params.UICityEditText = TestContext.DataRow["City"].ToString();
```

```
    this.UIMap.EnterallthedetailsfortheemployeeFirst_NameLast_
    NameMiddle_NameDepartmentOccupationGenderCityStateCountryPhone
    Params.UIStateEditText = TestContext.DataRow["State"].ToString();
    this.UIMap.EnterallthedetailsfortheemployeeFirst_NameLast_
    NameMiddle_NameDepartmentOccupationGenderCityStateCountryPhone
    Params.UICountryEditText = TestContext.DataRow["Country"].
    ToString();
    this.UIMap.EnterallthedetailsfortheemployeeFirst_NameLast_
    NameMiddle_NameDepartmentOccupationGenderCityStateCountryPhone
    Params.UIPhoneEditText = TestContext.DataRow["Phone"].ToString();
    this.UIMap.EnterallthedetailsfortheemployeeFirst_NameLast_
    NameMiddle_NameDepartmentOccupationGenderCityStateCountry
    Phone();
    this.UIMap.Afterenteringallthedetailssaveemployeedetail();
}
```

The coded UI test code generation creates several files and adds them to the test project. We will see the details of each file generated to support the coded UI test.

Files generated for the Coded UI Test

When we create a coded UI test, the coded UI Test Builder generates five different files to map the user interface, test methods, parameters, and assertions for all tests.

CodedUITest1.cs

The name of this file is generated based on the name of the test that we created. This file can be modified any time. This file contains one public class with the name CodedUITest1 with the CodedUITest attribute added to the class so that this class can be recognized as a test class.

The class also contains two additional default properties, TestContext and UIMap.

```
    /// <summary>
    ///Gets or sets the test context which provides
    ///information about and functionality for the current test run.
    ///</summary>
    public TestContext TestContext...
    private TestContext testContextInstance;

    public UIMap UIMap...

    private UIMap map;
}
}
```

There are two additional optional methods which are commented by default.

```
#region Additional test attributes

// You can use the following additional attributes as you write your tests:

////Use TestInitialize to run code before running each test
//[TestInitialize()]
//public void MyTestInitialize()
//{
//      // To generate code for this test, select "Generate Code for Coded UI Test" from the shortcut menu and select one of the menu items.
//      // For more information on generated code, see http://go.microsoft.com/fwlink/?LinkId=179463
//}

////Use TestCleanup to run code after each test has run
//[TestCleanup()]
//public void MyTestCleanup()
//{
//      // To generate code for this test, select "Generate Code for Coded UI Test" from the shortcut menu and select one of the menu items.
//      // For more information on generated code, see http://go.microsoft.com/fwlink/?LinkId=179463
//}

#endregion
```

The `MyTestInitialize()` method is called once before any other test method. This is useful for initializing the tests. This is identified as the initializer using the attribute `TestInitialize`. Similarly the `MyTestCleanup()` method is called once after each test has been called and this method is identified using the attribute `TestCleanup()`.

UIMap.Designer.cs

The Coded UI Test Builder automatically creates the code in this file when a test is created. And when the test changes, you may not have to generate the code manually as it gets recreated automatically after each change. The file is recreated whenever the test changes. This file contains a `UIMap` class which has the attribute, `GeneratedCode`, which is also there for all the other classes in this same file. The `UIMap` class contains the definition of all the methods identified during the recording. The following are some of the methods captured from the recording:

```
public void FromtheListpageclickonEmployees()
public void InsertEmployeeoption()
public void ClickonInsertnewemployeeoption()
public void Afterenteringallthedetailssaveemployeedetail()
```

Each method follows a defined structure. The structure contains the summary of the method, a region at the top which defines the variables, and then the method calls and properties are defined. The following code shows the definition for one of the method calls:

```
/// <summary>
/// FromtheListpageclickonEmployees - Test Case 18 - Use
'FromtheListpageclickonEmployeesParams' to pass parameters into this
method.
```

```
///  </summary>
public void FromtheListpageclickonEmployees()
{
  #region Variable Declarations
  HtmlHyperlink uIEmployeeHyperlink =
  this.UIBlankPageWindowsInteWindow.UIEmployeeMaintenanceDocument.
  UIEmployeeHyperlink;
  #endregion
  // Go to web page 'http://localhost:3062/' using new browser
  instance
  this.UIBlankPageWindowsInteWindow.LaunchUrl(new
  System.Uri(this.FromtheListpageclickonEmployeesParams.
  UIBlankPageWindowsInteWindowUrl));
  // Click 'Employee' link
  Mouse.Click(uIEmployeeHyperlink, new Point(19, 8));
}
```

UIMap.cs

This file contains the *Partial* UIMap class but does not contain any properties or methods initially. But we can include our custom code in the UIMap class to customize the functionality or add new functionality.

UIMap.uitest

This is an XML file which represents the structure of the coded UI test recording. It includes the actions, properties, and methods of the classes. The UIMap.Designer. cs file contains all the code that is generated by the coded UI Builder. Always use the Coded UI builder to modify the test which automatically modifies the UIMap.uitest and UIMap.Designer.cs files. Editing the file directly is not allowed and not advisable.

Data Driven Coded UI Test

The coded UI Test that we created previously is for given data during test recording. Later we might want to run the test not only for one set of data but for different sets of data and multiple times. To achieve this, we can parameterize each field to get data from a data source during testing. Each row of data in the data source is an iteration of the coded UI test. When we generate methods or assertions for the coded UI test, all constants in the recorded methods are parameterized into parameter classes. In our example, there is a method, FromtheListpageclickonEmployees as shown:

```
public void FromtheListpageclickonEmployees()
{
```

```
#region Variable Declarations
HtmlHyperlink uIEmployeeHyperlink =
this.UIBlankPageWindowsInteWindow.UIEmployeeMaintenanceDocument.
UIEmployeeHyperlink;
#endregion
// Go to web page 'http://localhost:3062/' using new browser
instance
this.UIBlankPageWindowsInteWindow.LaunchUrl(new
System.Uri(this.FromtheListpageclickonEmployeesParams.
UIBlankPageWindowsInteWindowUrl));
// Click 'Employee' link
Mouse.Click(uIEmployeeHyperlink, new Point(19, 8));
}
```

For the preceding method the coded UI test builder creates the class as follows and adds fields to the class for every constant value that we used while recording:

```
/// <summary>
/// Parameters to be passed into 'FromtheListpageclickonEmployees'
/// </summary>
[GeneratedCode("Coded UITest Builder", "10.0.30319.1")]
public class FromtheListpageclickonEmployeesParams
{
    #region Fields
    /// <summary>
    /// Go to web page 'http://localhost:3062/' using new browser
    instance
    /// </summary>
    public string UIBlankPageWindowsInteWindowUrl =
                                  "http://localhost:3062/";
    #endregion
}
```

Now we have created the required test and test files. Let us create a data source in the form of a `.csv` file and use it for the coded UI test. The sample data in the `.csv` file is shown here:

	A	B	C	D	E	F	G	H	I	J	K
1	First_Name	Last_Name	Middle_Name	Department	Occupation	Gender	City	State	Country	Phone	
2	Satheesh	Kumar	N	IT	Architect	Male	Bangalore	Karnataka	India	1112223334	
3	Subashni	S	S	IT	Manager	Female	Bangalore	Karnataka	India	1112223335	
4	Subha	S		IT	Sr Manager	Female	Bangalore	Karnataka	India	1112223336	
5											

Open the **Test View** window from the **Test** menu option. All tests in the current test project including the coded UI Test will be shown in the **Test View** window.

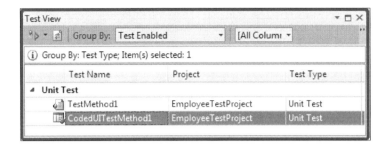

Select the coded UI Test, right-click and select **Properties**. The property window displays all the properties for the selected test. One of the properties is the Data Connection String of the data provider for the data driven test. Click the ellipsis (**...**) button next to the Data Connection property which opens the new test data source wizard. Select the type of data source from the available list of data sources such as Database, CSV File, and XML File.

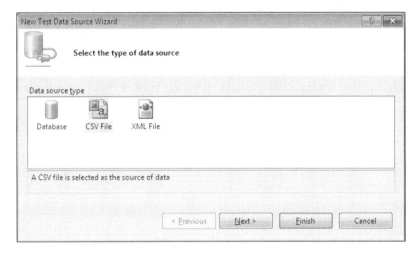

Using the wizard, select the .csv data source file that we created earlier. Once we select the file, we can see that the Data Provider name is set to Microsoft. VisualStudio.TestTools.DataSource.CSV and the Data table name is set to EmpData#csv. You can choose the file to be part of the deployment items so that it is included and deployed along with the files during the deployment of this project.

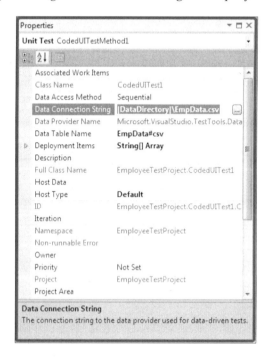

All the properties that we set in the test property window are saved in the CodedUITest1.cs file. If we check the CodedUITestMethod1, the attributes of the method contain the data source and the deployment items information set along with the attribute as shown in the following code:

```
[DeploymentItem("EmployeeTestProject\\EmpData.csv"),
DataSource("Microsoft.VisualStudio.TestTools.DataSource.CSV",
"|DataDirectory|\\EmpData.csv", "EmpData#csv", DataAccessMethod.
Sequential), TestMethod]
public void CodedUITestMethod1()
{
    // To generate code for this test, select "Generate Code for Coded
        UI Test" from the shortcut menu and select one of the menu items.
    // For more information on generated code, see http://go.microsoft.
        com/fwlink/?LinkId=179463
    this.UIMap.FromtheListpageclickonEmployees();
    this.UIMap.InsertEmployeeoption();
```

The data source is added to the method but we need to map the fields to the corresponding UI controls so that the data value from the data row is assigned to the controls automatically during runtime. To do this, we have to modify the code or use the tool itself to map the fields. The following code shows two of the fields mapped to the columns to pick the values from the data row and assign it to the field during the test run.:

```
this.UIMap.EnallthedetailsfortheemployeeFirst_NameLast_NameMiddle_
NameDepartmentOccupationGenderCityStateCountryPhoneParams.UIFirst_
NameEditText = TestContext.DataRow["First_Name"].ToString();
            this.UIMap.EnallthedetailsfortheemployeeFirst_NameLast_
NameMiddle_NameDepartmentOccupationGenderCityStateCountryPhoneParams.
UILast_NameEditText = TestContext.DataRow["Last_Name"].ToString();
```

If we run the *CodedUITest1* test now, the test runs for each row in the data source. As we have three rows in the data source the test runs three times. If one of these tests fails, the entire test result fails.

Adding controls and validation to the Coded UI Test

We always have some kind of validation to the UI controls. For example, some of the controls in the UI should not be null. We can use the Coded UI Test builder to generate code for the validation method that uses an assertion for a UI Control. We can add the UI control to the existing UI map file and generate the code to the existing coded UI test file:

1. Open the test project and the coded UI test file which is named `CodedUITest1.cs`. In the code file place the cursor on `CodedUITestMethod1()`, right-click and select the option **Generate Code for Coded UI Test** and then choose **Use Coded UI Test Builder...**.

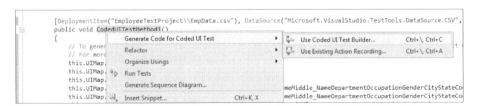

The coded UI Test builder is opened and ready for adding the controls and validations. Open the application and the UI page for which we need to add the validation logic to the controls. Keeping the UI open, drag-and-drop the crosshair from the Test Builder to the control on the UI. The other option is to select the control and keep the mouse pointer on the UI Control and then click Windows Logo Key+*I* to select the control at the mouse pointer.

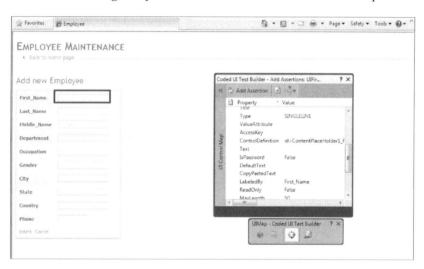

2. After selecting the control, the **Add assertion** screen opens for the selected control. The window displays all the properties of the selected control. We can add the validations and test assert for the control. Select the property of the control to be validated and then click on the **Add Assertion** option. The following screenshot shows the window to select the assertion type and to add the **Comparison Value** for the validation.

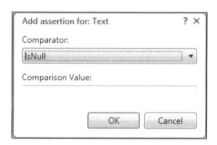

3. Just for testing purposes let's add the `IsNull` assertion type for the First Name UI control. Click **OK** to add the assertion to the test. We can keep adding the assertions for all the validations that we require. After adding all the assertions, click on the **Generate code** option in the **Test Builder** and then provide a name for the assert method. This option will automatically create the code for the assertions and add the method definition and method call to the corresponding files.

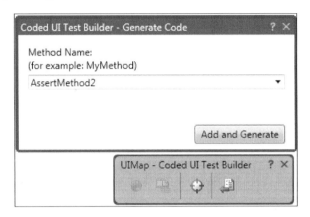

All assertion method definitions will be added to the `UIMap.Designer.cs` file and the method is called from the main method `CodedUITestMethod1()` in the `CodedUITest1.cs` file. The following snippet shows the code for the assertion generated in the designer file:

```
public void AssertMethod1()
{
  #region Variable Declarations
  HtmlEdit uIFirst_NameEdit = this.UIEmployeeWindowsInterWindow.
  UIEmployeeDocument1.UIFirst_NameEdit;
  #endregion
  // Verify that 'First_Name' text box's property 'Text' is not
      equal to 'null'
  Assert.IsNotNull(uIFirst_NameEdit.Text, "The First Name is Not
                  null");
}
```

4. Now select **CodedUITest1** from the **Test View** window and run the test. As we have three rows in the data source, three iterations of the test will run and all tests will fail because the First name has a value in all data rows. Our test is checking for a null value in the **First Name** field. So the entire test result will fail because of the test's failure.

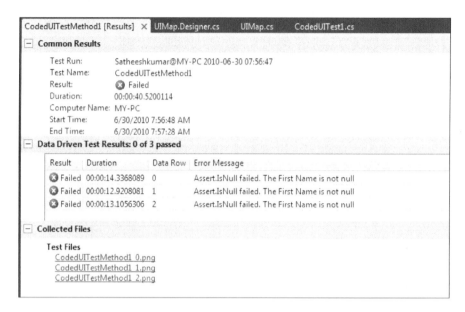

Now we can see that the required coded UI testing is successful. One difficulty in this type of code generation is the code maintenance. As we know that all the assertion code and the validation methods are added to the UIMap class, there is a chance of this class file growing to a larger size if we keep on adding the controls and methods. To avoid this situation, we can have *multiple* UIMap files generated.

The application can be grouped into modules or logical subsets and map each UIMap file to one particular logical subset of the application. This logical grouping also helps the tester to work on the individual module without affecting the other areas of the application. To create the logical grouping, we can first create a folder under the test project. Then select the folder and create a new item of type **Coded UI Test Map** from the available templates.

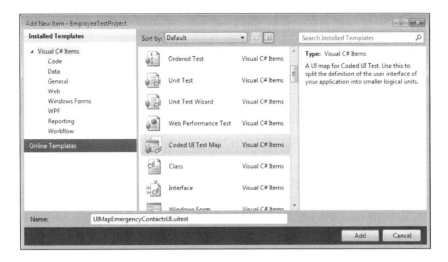

5. Click on **Add** after providing a meaningful name for the new Map file. Now the Coded UI Test Builder window appears after minimizing the Visual Studio window. Using the Test Builder we can keep recording the actions and creating the validations for the UI controls. Make sure you add the controls and validation specific to the module for which you are creating the map file. Generate the code using the option in the test builder after completing the recording. You can see the new `.uitest` file and `designer.cs` files added to the test under the new folder. The following screenshot shows two new UIMap files created for two different UI screens in the application:

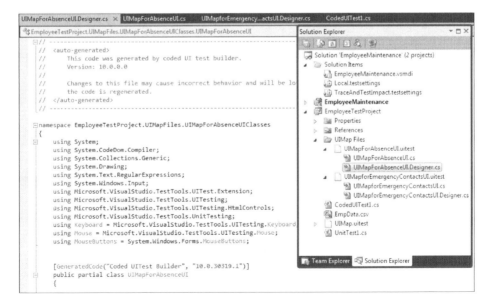

For any mapping that we create there are certain best practices to follow for easy maintenance and successful test results:

- Do not modify the `UIMap.Designer.cs` file as it is meant only for the test builder to modify
- Always use Coded UI Test Builder and create all assertions using Coded UI Test Builder and limit the recording to a few user actions
- Use meaningful names for the UIMap files and the assertion methods to easily identify and maintain the code and tests
- Always rerecord the user actions in case of changes to the user interface

Summary

This chapter has provided information on the new features added to Visual Studio 2010 Automated Testing. It was supported in the previous release of Visual Studio but only to a certain extent. But now we can use the user action recordings to create the coded UI tests and generate the code directly based on the actions and executed with the Test Builder. The new Test builder tool provides a lot of new functionality to add the UI controls to the test and to add assertions for validating the UI data without having the developer write code. Automating the test with multiple sets of data from a data source is an added extra advantage for coded UI testing.

4
Unit Testing

Unit Testing is the technique used by developers to confirm that the piece of code is producing the result as expected. In project development, there may be many modules and each module comprises a set of code or functionalities. Identifying the piece of code in the module that causes the defect is always a time consuming task and the cost involved is also more. It is always better to test the code in units and confirm the functionality before integrating the code into module(s). Requiring all code to pass the unit tests before they can be integrated ensures that the functionality always works. Developers have to make sure each unit of code is written for one piece of functionality so that the result produced by each unit test is for a single functionality. Every time a defect is fixed or code is modified, we don't have to manually retest the unit and other related functionalities by spending a lot of time and money. The automated unit test will help us make sure the functionality is unaffected.

Visual Studio 2010 is used for generating the unit test for the methods irrespective of whether they are public or private. Unit test is another class file similar to any other class and methods but having additional attributes to define the test class and the test method. The unit tests can be created either by manually writing the code or by generating the unit test code using the **Create Unit Tests** option from the context menu in VSTS.

The generated unit test class contains special attributes assigned to the class and methods in it. Test classes are marked by the attribute `TestClass()` and each test method is marked with the attribute `TestMethod()`. Apart from these two, there are many other attributes used for unit testing. After generating the unit test class and methods, we can use the `Assert` method to verify the produced result with the expected value.

All the unit test classes and methods are defined in the namespace, `Microsoft.VisualStudio.TestTools.UnitTesting`. Whenever we create a new unit test in Visual Studio, we have to include this namespace to the class file. One of the main properties of the test classes in unit testing is the `TestContext` which holds all the information about tests. This chapter covers the following topics in detail:

- Creating Unit Tests
- Naming and General Settings
- Assert Statements and Type of Asserts
- String Asserts and Collection Asserts
- Unit Tests and Generics
- Data Driven Unit Tests
- Code Coverage for Unit Tests

Creating unit tests

There are two different ways of creating a unit test. One is the manual way of writing the code and the other is to generate the unit test code for the class using the option in Visual Studio. To see how a test class is generated, let us consider the following class library which is a very simple example of total price calculation:

1. To create a new class library, open Visual Studio and select **New Project** under the **File** menu option and select **Class Library** from available templates.

```csharp
using System;
using System.Collections.Generic;
using System.Linq;
using System.Text;

namespace TestLibrary
{
  public class Class1
  {
    public double CalculateTotalPrice(double quantity)
    {
      double totalPrice;
      double unitPrice;

      // Todo get unit price. For test let us hardcode it
      unitPrice = 16.0;

      totalPrice = unitPrice * quantity;
      return totalPrice;
```

```
        }

        public void GetTotalPrice()
        {
          int qty = 5;
          double totalPrice = CalculateTotalPrice(qty);
          Console.WriteLine("Total Price: " + totalPrice);
        }
      }
    }
```

2. Now within the class file, right-click on the method for which we want to create the unit test. In the preceding code, we have `CalculateTotalPrice` and `GetTotalPrice` methods. Right-click on the `CalculateTotalPrice` method, which will show up the dialog for creating unit testing:

3. Once the **Create Unit Tests...** option is selected, we can see the window that displays all the projects and all the methods within the class from where we selected the method. The selected method will be checked in the list leaving the other methods unchecked which means that the unit test will be generated only for the selected method in the list. We can select and deselect any number of methods in the list based on our requirements. The Output project's drop-down lists the option for creating a new test project either in C#, Visual Basic, or C++. The dropdown also lists the existing test projects if the current solution already has some test projects. Choose the required option and provide a new name for the test project if the selected option is for a new project.

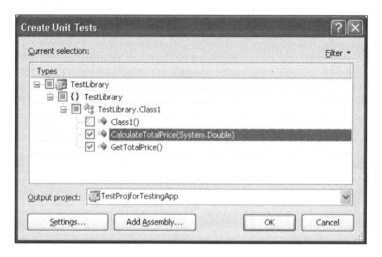

The Output project will allow the tester to create a new project if no project exists already.

4. Let us select both the methods **CalculateTotalPrice(System.Double)** and **GetTotalPrice()**. Now Visual Studio creates a new class file for the selected method's class. We can see the class name as **Class1** in the preceding screenshot. So the test class created for this would be **Class1Test**. Visual Studio takes the same class name with the word Test added to it for the test class name.

While creating the unit test, we can change the settings using the option in the **Create Unit Tests** window. These settings are used for changing the way of creating the unit tests by changing the file name, unit test class names, and the method name generation, also enabling and disabling some of the standard code and method attributes that is generated by default for all the unit test code.

The following two sections explain in detail about the settings that may be used during the unit test code generation.

Naming settings

The following are the fields under the **Name settings** section of the **Test Generation Settings** dialog:

- **File Name**: This is to modify the way the file name is generated. The **[Class]** will be replaced with the actual class name at the time of generating the code. If required, we can add our own text in addition to the name.

- **Class Name**: By default, the unit test class is generated with a name which is the actual class name with a **Test** string added. We can customize the class name if we don't like the default name suggested by the tool.

- **Method Name**: This is similar to the **Class Name** and the **File Name**. By default, Visual Studio assigns the actual method name followed by the text, **Test**. The **[Method]** is replaced with the actual method name at the time of code generation.

General settings

These are the general settings applicable for the default basic code generated for each unit test. Using this we can enable or disable some of the common code generated for the classes:

- **Mark all test results Inconclusive by default**: When this option is enabled, the `Assert.Inconclusive` statement is added to all the methods in the unit test class which means that the method is incomplete as we have not added any test code yet and we just generated the test method. The method only contains the skeleton of the auto generated test method. Later on, once we add the actual test code to the method, we can safely remove this `Assert.Inconclusive` call:

```
Assert.Inconclusive("Verify the correctness of this test
                     method.");
```

- **Enable generation warnings**: If there are any unexpected errors during the test method generation, the code generator will add the error message as a comment within the test method body. This will help us resolve the issue and add the code later on.

- **Globally qualify all types**: This is to resolve the conflict between the same type name used in multiple classes. The unit test code may contain multiple class file test methods. Sometimes the same type may be used in different class files. So to make sure the types are unique across the test, the namespaces are added to all the types in the test.

- **Enable documentation comments**: This is to generate the comments for each method. The comments are in XML format by default. The default comments can be modified or added with more comments describing the test method. If this option is disabled, the comments will not be generated for the test methods.

```
/// <summary>
///A test for GetuserDetails
///</summary>
```

- **Honor InternalsVisibleTo Attribute**: This attribute will make all the internal attributes visible to the assembly, and we will be able to call this just like any other public method.

  For example, if we have an internal method like this:

```
// Sample method for generating unit test for Internal
// method
internal static bool MethodforInternalExample(string str)
{
  bool result = false;
```

```
    if (str == "return true") result = true;
    if (str == "return false") result = false;
       return result;
}
```

The unit test generated for this internal method would be just a public method like any other method:

```
/// <summary>
///A test for MethodforInternalExample
///</summary>
[TestMethod()]
public void MethodforInternalExampleTest()
{
   string str = string.Empty; // TODO: Initialize to an
               // appropriate value
   bool expected = false; // TODO: Initialize to an
                   // appropriate value
   bool actual;
   actual = Class1.MethodforInternalExample(str);
   Assert.AreEqual(expected, actual);
   Assert.Inconclusive("Verify the correctness of this
                       test method.");
}
```

- **Add assembly**: This option in the **Create Unit Tests** dialog is used for adding additional assemblies for generating the unit tests. The **Add assembly** option helps us select the assembly to be added and then displays the methods and classes from the assembly. We can select the methods from the tree view and then generate the unit test.

Generated unit test code

The following is the unit test code generated for the selected methods and the class with all the default attributes set for each method. You may also notice that the `Assert.Inconclusive` call is added to all the methods by default, based on the settings. Visual Studio also adds the default start up and cleaning methods which we can make use of for testing. The following are the list of attributes used for the test class and test methods:

Attributes	Description
TestClass()	To identify the unit test class within the file
ClassInitialize()	The method with this attribute is used for preparing the class for the test; for example, setting up the environment or collecting details which are required for testing are handled within this method; the method with this attribute is executed just before the first test in the class; each test class can have only one method as the class initializer.
ClassCleanup()	The method with this attribute is used for cleaning or destroying the objects used in the test; this method is executed after all the tests in the class are run. Test class can contain only one method as the ClassCleanup method.
TestInitialize()	The method with this attribute is used for initializing or running the code before each test.
TestCleanup()	This method is run after each test in the class; this is similar to the ClassCleanup but the difference here is that the method is executed once after each test.
TestMethod()	This attribute identifies the method to be included as part of the test; this method has the unit test code for the method in the original class file.

In the following code, we can see many attributes and properties set to the class and methods. Visual Studio by default creates some methods with special attributes which are commented. If these methods are required for testing, we can uncomment it and make use of it.

```
using TestLibrary;
using Microsoft.VisualStudio.TestTools.UnitTesting;
namespace TestProjforTestingApp
{
  /// <summary>
  ///This is a test class for Class1Test and is intended
  ///to contain all Class1Test Unit Tests
  ///</summary>
  [TestClass()]
```

```csharp
public class Class1Test
{
  private TestContext testContextInstance;
  /// <summary>
  ///Gets or sets the test context which provides
  ///information about and functionality for the current test
  ///run.
  ///</summary>
  public TestContext TestContext
  {
    get
    {
      return testContextInstance;
    }
    set
    {
      testContextInstance = value;
    }
  }
}

#region Additional test attributes
//
//You can use the following additional attributes as you
//write your tests:
//
//Use ClassInitialize to run code before running the first
//test in the class
//[ClassInitialize()]
//public static void MyClassInitialize(TestContext testContext)
//{
//}
//
//Use ClassCleanup to run code after all tests in a class
//have run
//[ClassCleanup()]
//public static void MyClassCleanup()
//{
//}
//
//Use TestInitialize to run code before running each test
//[TestInitialize()]
//public void MyTestInitialize()
//{
//}
//
```

```
//Use TestCleanup to run code after each test has run
//[TestCleanup()]
//public void MyTestCleanup()
//{
//}
//
#endregion

/// <summary>
///A test for CalculateTotalPrice
///</summary>
[TestMethod()]
public void CalculateTotalPriceTest()
{
  Class1 target = new Class1(); // TODO: Initialize to an
                  appropriate value
  double quantity = 0F; // TODO: Initialize to an appropriate value
  double expected = 0F; // TODO: Initialize to an appropriate value
  double actual;
  actual = target.CalculateTotalPrice(quantity);
  Assert.AreEqual(expected, actual);
  Assert.Inconclusive("Verify the correctness of this test
                    method.");
}

/// <summary>
///A test for GetTotalPrice
///</summary>
[TestMethod()]
public void GetTotalPriceTest()
{
  Class1 target = new Class1(); // TODO: Initialize to an
                  appropriate value
  target.GetTotalPrice();
  Assert.Inconclusive("A method that does not return a value cannot
                    be verified.");
}

/// <summary>
///A test for MethodforInternalExample
///</summary>
[TestMethod()]
public void MethodforInternalExampleTest()
{
```

```
        string str = string.Empty; // TODO: Initialize to an appropriate
                    value
        bool expected = false; // TODO: Initialize to an appropriate
                      value
        bool actual;
        actual = Class1.MethodforInternalExample(str);
        Assert.AreEqual(expected, actual);
        Assert.Inconclusive("Verify the correctness of this test
                        method.");
    }


    }
}
```

It is recommended to use the `TestCleanup` and `ClassCleanup` methods instead of the `Finalizer` method for all the test classes. The exceptions thrown from the `Finalizer` method will not be caught, which will result in unexpected results. The cleanup activity should be used for bringing the environment back to its original state. For example, during testing we might have updated or inserted more records to the database tables or created lot of files and logs. This information should be removed once the testing is complete and the exceptions during this process should be caught and rectified.

Assert statements

The assert statement is used for comparing the result from the method with the expected result and then passing or failing the test based on the match. Whatever may be the result produced by the method, the end result of the test method depends on the return value of the assert method. The assert statement establishes the result. There are different statements supported by the `Assert` class to set the return value to `Pass`, `Fail`, or `Inconclusive`. If the assert statement is not present in the test method, the test method will always return a `Pass`. If there are many assert statements in the test method, the test will be in `Pass` state until one of the assert statements returns `Fail`.

In the preceding example, the test method, CalculateTotalPriceTest, has two assert statements, Assert.AreEqual and Assert.Inconclusive. Assert.AreEqual has two parameters, one as expected which is the expected value that should be returned by the CalculateTotalPrice method. The parameter actual is the actual value returned by the method. The Assert.AreEqual statement, which is explained in detail in the next section, compares these two values and returns the test result as Pass if both the values match. Returns Fail if there is a mismatch between these two values:

```
[TestMethod()]
  public void CalculateTotalPriceTest()
  {
    Class1 target = new Class1(); // TODO: Initialize to an
                   //appropriate value
    double quantity = 0F; // TODO: Initialize to an appropriate
                          value
    double expected = 0F; // TODO: Initialize to an appropriate value
    double actual;
    actual = target.CalculateTotalPrice(quantity);
    Assert.AreEqual(expected, actual);
    Assert.Inconclusive("Verify the correctness of this test
                        method.");
  }
```

The test method also has the Assert.Inconclusive statement to return the result as Inconclusive if the test method is not complete. We can remove this line if the code is complete and we do not want the test result to be Inconclusive. In the previous code, if we run the test without setting the value for quantity and expected, the return would be Inconclusive. Now set the value for quantity and expected as:

```
double quantity = 10F;
double expected = 159F;
```

The result returned would be a Fail because the actual value returned by the method would be 160, while our expected value is 159. If you change the expected value to 160 then the test would pass. We have seen only one type of assert statement. There are many other asserts which we can use in test methods for passing or failing the test.

Types of asserts

The Assert classes in VSTS contain the comparison and conditional testing capabilities. The namespace `Microsoft.VisualStudio.TestTools.UnitTesting` in VSTS contains all these asserts. The actual and the expected values are compared based on the type of assert used and the result decides the test pass or failure.

Assert

The assert class has many different overloaded methods for comparing the values. Each method is used for a specific type of comparison. For example, an assert can compare a string with a string, or an object with another object, but not an integer with an object. Overloaded methods are the additional or optional parameters to the method in case we want custom messages or additional functionality to be added. For example, the assert method provides an overloaded method to compare the values within a specified accuracy, which we will see in detail when comparing double values.

Let us consider a simple Item class with three properties each with different data types:

```
public class Item {
  public int ItemID { get; set; }
  public string ItemType { get; set; }
  public double ItemPrice { get; set; }
  }
```

The code shown here is a sample which creates a new Item object with values set for the properties:

```
public Item GetObjectToCompare() {
  Item objA = new Item();
  objA.ItemID = 100;
  objA.ItemType = "Electronics";
  objA.ItemPrice = 10.99;
  return objA;
}
```

Generate the unit test for the preceding method and set the properties for the local expected object similar to the one shown here:

```
[TestMethod()]
 public void GetObjectToCompareTest()
{
  Class1 target = new Class1();
  Item expected = new Item();
```

```
    expected.ItemID = 100;
    expected.ItemType = "Electronics";
    expected.ItemPrice = 10.39;
    Item actual;
    actual = target.GetObjectToCompare();
    Assert.AreEqual(expected, actual);
}
```

With the preceding sample code and the unit test we will look at the results of each overloaded method in the Assert class.

Assert.AreEqual

This is used for comparing and verifying actual and expected values. The following are the overloaded methods for Assert.AreEqual() and the result for the preceding code samples:

Method	Description
Assert.AreEqual(Object, Object);	Verifies if both the objects are equal
	The test fails because the actual and the expected are two different objects even though the properties are the same.
	Try setting expected = actual just before the assert statement and run the test again; the test will pass as both the objects are the same now.
Assert.AreEqual(Object, Object, String)	Used for verifying two objects and displaying the string message if the test fails; for example, if the statement is like this:
	`Assert.AreEqual(expected, actual, "Objects are Not equal")`
	The output of the test would be **Assert.AreEqual failed. Expected:<TestLibrary.Item>. Actual:<TestLibrary. Item>. Objects are not equal**.

Method	Description
`Assert.AreEqual(Object, Object, String, Object[])`	Used for verifying two objects and displaying the string message if the test fails; the formatting is applied to the displayed message; for example, if the assert statement is like this: `Assert.AreEqual(expected, actual, "Objects {0} and {1} are not equal", "ObjA", "ObjB")` The displayed message if the test fails would be **Assert. AreEqual failed. Expected:<TestLibrary.Item>. Actual:<TestLibrary.Item>. Objects ObjA and ObjB are not equal**.
`Assert.AreEqual(String, String, Boolean)`	Used for comparing and verifying two strings; the third parameter is to specify whether to ignore casing or not; If the assert statement is like this: `Assert.AreEqual(expected.ItemType, actual.ItemType, false)` The test will pass only if both the values are the same including the casing.
`Assert.AreEqual(String, String. Boolean, CultureInfo)`	Used for comparing two strings specifying casing to include for comparison including the culture info specified; for example, if the assert is like this: `Assert.AreEqual(expected.ItemType, actual.ItemType, false, System. Globalization.CultureInfo. CurrentCulture.EnglishName)` If the property value for `expected` is `.ItemType="electronics"`, then the result would be: **Assert.AreEqual failed. Expected:<electronics>. Case is different for actual value:<Electronics>. English (United States)**.
`Assert.AreEqual(String, String, Boolean, String)`	Used for comparing two strings specifying casing to include for comparison; display the specified message if the test fails; for example if the statement is like this: `Assert.AreEqual(expected.ItemType, actual.ItemType, false, "Both the strings are not equal")` The test result would be **Assert.AreEqual failed. Expected:<electronics>. Case is different for actual value:<Electronics>. Both the strings are not equal**

Method	Description
`Assert.AreEqual(String, String, Boolean, CultureInfo, String)`	Used for comparing two strings specifying casing and culture info to include for comparison; displays the specified message if the test fails; the following is an example: `Assert.AreEqual(expected.ItemType, actual.ItemType, false, System. Globalization.CultureInfo. CurrentCulture.EnglishName, "Both the strings {0} and {1} are not equal", actual.ItemType, expected.ItemType)`
`Assert.AreEqual(String, String, Boolean, String, Object[])`	Used for comparing two strings specifying the casing; the specified message is displayed with the specified formatting applied to it; for example if the statement is like this: `Assert.AreEqual(expected.ItemType, actual.ItemType, false, "Both the strings '{0}' and '{1}' are not equal", actual.ItemType, expected. ItemType);` The test result if the test fails would be **Assert.AreEqual failed. Expected:<electronics>. Case is different for actual value:<Electronics>. Both the strings 'Electronics' and 'electronics' are not equal**
`Assert.AreEqual(String, String, Boolean, CultureInfo, String, Object[])`	Used for comparing two strings specifying casing and culture information to include for comparison; displays the specified message if the test fails; the specified formatters are applied to the message to replace it with the parameter values. The following is an example: `Assert.AreEqual(expected.ItemType, actual.ItemType, false, System. Globalization.CultureInfo. CurrentCulture.EnglishName, "Both the strings '{0}' and '{1}' are not equal", actual.ItemType, expected. ItemType);` If the test fails, it displays the message with the formatters {0} and {1} replaced with the values in `actual.Itemtype` and `expected.ItemType`.

Method	Description

`Assert.AreEqual(Double, Double, Double)`
 	
`Assert.AreEqual(Double, Double, Double, String)`
 	
`Assert.AreEqual(Double, Double, Double, String, Object[])`
	These are the three different overloaded assert methods for comparing and verifying the `Double` values; the first and second parameter values are the expected and actual values, the third parameter is to specify the accuracy within which the values should be compared. The fourth parameter is for the message and fifth is the format to be applied for the message; for example, if the assert is like this:
	
	`Assert.AreEqual(expected.ItemPrice, actual.ItemPrice, 0.5, "The values {0} and {1} does not match within the accuracy", expected.ItemPrice, actual.ItemPrice);`
	
	The test would produce a result of: **Assert.AreEqual failed. Expected a difference no greater than <0.5> between expected value <10.39> and actual value <10.99>. The value 10.39 and 10.99 does not match within the accuracy.** Here the expected accuracy is 0.5 but the difference is 0.6.

`Assert.AreEqual(Single, Single, Single)`
 	
`Assert.AreEqual(Single, Single, Single, String)`
 	
`Assert.AreEqual(Single, Single, Single, String, Object[])`
	This is very similar to the `Double` value comparison as shown previously but the values here are of type `Single`; this method also supports the message and the formatters to be displayed if the test fails.

`Assert.AreEqual<T>(T, T,)`
 	
`Assert.AreEqual<T>(T, T, String)`
 	
`Assert.AreEqual<T>(T, T, String, Object[])`
	These overloaded methods are used for comparing and verifying the generic type data; the assertion fails if they are not equal and displays the message by applying the specified formatters; for example, if the assert is like
	
	`Assert.AreEqual<Item>(actual, expected, "The objects '{0}' and '{1}' are not equal", "actual", "expected")`
	
	The test would produce the result if the test fails as **Assert.AreEqual failed. Expected:<TestLibrary.Item>. Actual:<TestLibrary.Item>. The objects 'actual' and 'expected' are not equal**

Assert.AreNotEqual

All the previously mentioned overloaded methods for `Assert.AreEqual` also applies to `Assert.AreNotEqual` but the only difference is that the comparison is the exact opposite of the `AreEqual` assert. For example, the following method verifies if the two strings are not equal by ignoring or not ignoring the casing as specified by Boolean. The test fails if they are equal and the message is displayed with the specified formatting applied to it:

```
Assert.AreNotEqual(String, String, Boolean, String, Object[])
```

The following code compares two strings and verifies whether they are equal or not:

```
Assert.AreNotEqual(expected.ItemType, actual.ItemType, false,
                   "Both the strings '{0}' and '{1}' are equal",
                   expected.ItemType, actual.ItemType);
```

If the string values are equal, the output of this would be:

Assert.AreNotEqual failed. Expected any value except:<Electronics>. Actual:<Electronics>. Both the strings 'Electronics' and 'Electronics' are equal

Assert.AreSame

The following table shows different type of overloaded assert methods for the assert type `AreSame` to check if the objects are the same or not:

Method	Description

`Assert.`
`AreSame(Object,`
`Object)`
	This method compares and verifies whether both the object variables refer to the same object; even if the properties are the same, the objects might be different; for example, the following test will pass because the objects are the same:
	
	`ArrayList A = new ArrayList(5);`
	`ArrayList B = A;`
	`Assert.AreSame(A, B);`
	
	Both the objects A and B refer to the same object and so they are the same

Method	Description

`Assert.`
`AreSame(Object,`
`Object, String)`
	This method compares and verifies whether both the object variables refer to the same object; if not, the message will be displayed; for example, the following code compares the two objects A and B:
	
	`ArrayList A = new ArrayList(5);`
	
	`ArrayList B = new ArrayList(10);`
	
	`Assert.AreSame(A, B, "The objects`
	`                are not same");`
	
	The test fails with the output **Assert.AreSame failed. The objects expected and actual are not same.**

`Assert.`
`AreSame(Object,`
`Object, String,`
`Object[])`
	This method compares and verifies whether both the object variables refer to the same object; if not, the message will be displayed with the specified formatting; for example, the following code compares the two objects A and B:
	
	`ArrayList A = new ArrayList(5);`
	`ArrayList B = new ArrayList(10);`
	`Assert.AreSame(A, B, "The objects`
	`                {0} and {1} are not`
	`                same", "A", "B");`
	
	The test fails with the output **Assert.AreSame failed. The objects A and B are not same.**

Assert.AreNotSame

This Assert is used for verifying whether the two objects are not the same. The test fails if the objects are the same. The same overloaded methods for `Assert.AreSame` apply here, but the comparison is the exact opposite. The following are the three overloaded methods applied to `Assert.AreNotSame`:

- `Assert.AreNotSame(Object, Object)`
- `Assert.AreNotSame(Object, Object, String)`
- `Assert.AreNotSame(Object, Object, String, Object[])`

For example, the following code verifies if objects A and B are not the same. If they are the same, the test fails with the specified error message with the specified formatting applied to it:

```
ArrayList A = new ArrayList(5);
ArrayList B = A;
Assert.AreNotSame(A, B, "The test fails because the objects {0} and
                {1} are same", "A", "B");
```

The preceding test fails with the message, **Assert.AreNotSame failed. The test fails because the objects A and B are same**.

Assert.Fail

This assert is used for failing the test without checking any condition. `Assert.Fail` has three overloaded methods:

Method	Description
`Assert.Fail()`	Fails the test without checking any condition.
`Assert.Fail(String)`	Fails the test without checking any condition and displays the message.
`Assert.Fail(String, Object[])`	Fails the test without checking any condition and displays the message with the specified formatting applied to the message; for example, the following code does not check for any condition but fails the test and displays the message:

```
Assert.Fail("This method '{0}' is set to fail
temporarily", "GetItemPrice");
```

The output for the preceding code would be **Assert.Fail failed. This method 'GetItemPrice' is set to fail temporarily**.

Assert.Inconclusive

This is useful if the method is incomplete and we cannot determine whether the output is true or false. We can set the assertion to be inconclusive until we complete the method for testing. There are three overloaded methods for `Assert.Inconclusive`:

Method	Description
`Assert.Inconclusive()`	Assertion cannot be verified; set to inconclusive.
`Assert.Inconclusive(String)`	Assertion cannot be verified; set to inconclusive and displays the message.
`Assert.Inconclusive(String, Object[])`	Assertion cannot be verified; set to inconclusive and displays the message with the specified formatting applied to it; for example, the following code sets the assertion as inconclusive which means neither true nor false.

```
Assert.Inconclusive("This method
'{0}' is not yet ready for testing",
"GetItemPrice");
```

The output for the preceding code would be **Assert. Inconclusive failed. This method 'GetItemPrice' is not yet ready for testing**.

Assert.IsTrue

This is used for verifying if the condition is true. The test fails if the condition is false. There are three overloaded methods for `Assert.IsTrue`:

Method	Description
`Assert.IsTrue()`	Used for verifying the condition; test fails if the condition is false.
`Assert.IsTrue(String)`	Used for verifying the condition and displays the message if the test fails with the condition false.
`Assert.IsTrue(String, Object[])`	Verifies the condition and displays the message if the test fails with the condition false; applies the specified formatting to the message.
	For example, the following code fails the test as the conditions return false.

	<pre>ArrayList A = new ArrayList(5);
	ArrayList B = new ArrayList(10);
	Assert.IsTrue(A == B, "Both '{0}' and
	'{1}' are not equal", "A", "B");</pre>

	The output message for the above test would be **Assert. IsTrue failed. Both 'A' and 'B' are not equal**.

Assert.IsFalse

This is to verify if the condition is false. The test fails if the condition is true. Similar to `Assert.IsTrue`, this one has three overloaded methods:

Method	Description
`Assert.IsFalse()`	Used for verifying the condition; the test fails if the condition is true.
`Assert. IsFalse(String)`	Used for verifying the condition; displays the message if the test fails with the condition true.
`Assert. IsFalse(String, Object[])`	Verify the condition and display the message if the test fails with the condition true and apply the specified formatting to the message.
	For example, the following code fails the test as the conditions returns true:

	<pre>ArrayList A = new ArrayList(5);
	ArrayList B = A;
	Assert.IsFalse(A == B, "Both '{0}' and
	'{1}' are equal", "A", "B");</pre>

	The output message for the preceding test would be **Assert. IsFalse failed. Both 'A' and 'B' are equal**.

Assert.IsNull

This is useful in verifying whether the object is null. The test fails if the object is not null. Given here are the three overloaded methods for `Assert.IsNull`:

Method	Description
`Assert.IsNull(Object)`	Verify if the object is null.
`Assert.IsNull(Object, String)`	Verify if the object is null and display the message if the object is not null and the test fails.
`Assert.IsNull(Object, String, Object[])`	Verify if the object is null and display the message if the object is not null; apply the formatting to the message.
	For example, the following code verifies if the object is null and fails the test if it is not null and displays the formatted message:

	`ArrayList A = new ArrayList(5);`
	`ArrayList B = A;`
	`Assert.IsNull(B, "Object '{0}' is`
	`                    not null", "B");`

	The preceding code fails the test and displays the error message **Assert.IsNull failed. Object 'B' is not null**.

Assert.IsNotNull

This is to verify if the object is null or not. The test fails if the object is null. This is the exact opposite of the `Assert.IsNull` and has the same overloaded methods.

Method	Description
`Assert.IsNotNull(Object)`	Verifies if the object is not null.
`Assert.IsNotNull(Object, String)`	Verifies if the object is not null and displays the message if the object is null and the test fails.
`Assert.IsNotNull(Object, String, Object[])`	Verifies if the object is not null and displays the message if the object is null; applies the formatting to the message.
	For example, the following code verifies if the object is not null and fails the test if it is null and displays the formatted message:

	`ArrayList B = null;`
	`Assert.IsNotNull(B, "Object '{0}'`
	`                    is null", "B");`

	The preceding code fails the test and displays the error message, **Assert.IsNotNull failed. Object 'B' is null**

Assert.IsInstanceOfType

This method verifies whether the object is of the specified `System.Type`. The test fails if the type does not match.

Method	Description
`Assert.IsInstanceOfType(Object, Type)`	This method is used for verifying whether the object is of specified `System.Type`;
	for example, the following code verifies whether the object is of type `ArrayList`:
	``` Hashtable obj = new Hashtable(); Assert.IsInstanceOfType(obj, typeof(ArrayList)); ```
	The test fails as the object `obj` is not of type `ArrayList`. The error message returned would be **Assert.IsInstanceOfType failed. Expected type:<System.Collections.ArrayList>. Actual type:<System.Collections.Hashtable>.**
`Assert.IsInstanceOfType(Object, Type, String)`	This is the overloaded method for the preceding method with an additional parameter; the third parameter is the message to be displayed in case the test fails.
`Assert.IsInstanceOfType(Object, Type, String, Object[])`	The purpose of this method is the same as that of the preceding methods; but the additional parameter is the formatter to be applied on the error message displayed if the test fails.

StringAsserts

This is another `Assert` class within the Unit test namespace `Microsoft.VisualStudio.TestTools.UnitTesting` that contains methods for the common text-based assertions. `StringAssert` contains the following methods with additional overloaded methods. Overloaded methods are the additional or optional parameters to the method in case we want custom messages.

StringAssert.Contains

This method verifies if the second parameter string is present in the first parameter string. The test fails if the string is not present. There are three overloaded methods for `StringAssert.Contains`. The third parameter specifies the message to be displayed if the assertion fails and the fourth parameter specifies the message formatter to be applied to the error message for the assertion failure. The formatters are the placeholders for the parameters values:

- `StringAssert.Contains(String, String)`
- `StringAssert.Contains(String, String, String)`
- `StringAssert.Contains(String, String, String, Object[])`

For example, the following code verifies if the string, **Test,** is present in the first string. If not, the message is displayed with the format applied to it:

```
string find = "Testing";
StringAssert.Contains("This is the Test for StringAsserts",
find, "The string '{0}' is not found in the first
parameter value", find);
```

The assertion fails with the specified error message added to its default message as **StringAssert.Contains failed. String 'This is the Test for StringAsserts' does not contain string 'Testing'. The string 'Testing' is not found in the first parameter value**.

StringAssert.Matches

As the name suggests, this method verifies if the first string matches the regular expression specified as the second parameter. These assert methods contain three overloaded methods to display the custom error message and apply formats to the message if the assertion fails:

- `StringAssert.Matches(String, Regex)`
- `StringAssert.Matches(String, Regex, String)`
- `StringAssert.Matches(String, Regex, String, Object[])`

For example, the following code verifies if the string contains any numbers between 0 and 9. If not, the assertion fails with the message specified with the formatters.

```
Regex regEx = new Regex("[0-9]");
StringAssert.Matches("This is first test for StringAssert",
                     regEx, "There are no numbers between {0} and {1}
                     in the string", 0, 9);
```

The error message would be **StringAssert.Matches failed. String 'This is first test for StringAssert' does not match pattern '[0-9]'. There are no numbers between 0 and 9 in the string.**

StringAssert.DoesNotMatch

This is the exact opposite of `StringAssert.Matches`. This assert method verifies whether the first parameter string matches the regular expression specified as the second parameter. The assertion fails if it matches. This assert type has three overloaded methods to display the error message and apply the message formatting to it which is the place holder for the parameter values in the message:

- `StringAssert.DoesNotMatch(String, Regex,)`
- `StringAssert.DoesNotMatch(String, Regex, String)`
- `StringAssert.DoesNotMatch(String, Regex, String, Object[])`

For example, the following code verifies if the first parameter string does not match with the regular expression specified in the second parameter. The assertion fails if it does match and displays the specified error message with the formatting applied to it:.

```
Regex regEx = new Regex("[0-9]");
StringAssert.DoesNotMatch("This is 1st test for StringAssert",
                      regEx, "There is a number in the string");
```

The assertion fails with the error message **StringAssert.DoesNotMatch failed. String 'This is 1st test for StringAssert' matches pattern '[0-9]'. There is a number in the string.**

StringAssert.StartsWith

This is to verify whether a string in the first parameter starts with the value in the second parameter. The assertion fails if the string does not start with the second string. There are three overloaded methods to specify the error message to be displayed and to specify the formatting to be applied to the error message:

- `StringAssert.StartsWith(String, String)`
- `StringAssert.StartsWith(String, String, String)`
- `StringAssert.StartsWith(String, String, String, Object[])`

For example, the following code verifies if the first string starts with the specified second parameter value. The assertion fails if it does not, and displays the specified error message with the specified formatting:

```
string startWith = "First";
StringAssert.StartsWith("This is 1st test for StringAssert",
                        startWith, "The string does not start with
                        '{0}'", startWith);
```

The assertion fails with the error message **StringAssert.StartsWith failed. String 'This is 1st test for StringAssert' does not start with string 'First'. The string does not start with 'First'.**

StringAssert.EndsWith

This is similar to the `StringAssert.StartsWith`, but here, it verifies if the first string ends with the specified string in the second parameter. The assertion fails if it does not end with the specified string and displays the error message. There are three overloaded methods to specify the custom error message and the formatting:

- `StringAssert.EndsWith(String, String)`
- `StringAssert.EndsWith(String, String, String)`
- `StringAssert.EndsWith(String, String, String, Object[])`

For example, the following code verifies whether the first string ends with the specified string as the second parameter. The assertion will fail and display the message with the specified formatting.

```
string endsWith = "Testing";
StringAssert.EndsWith("This is 1st test for StringAssert",
endsWith, "'{0}' is not the actual ending in the string",
endsWith);
```

The error message displayed would be **StringAssert.EndsWith failed. String 'This is 1st test for StringAssert' does not end with string 'Testing'. 'Testing' is not the actual ending in the string**.

CollectionAssert

Visual Studio provides another type of assert through the namespace `Microsoft. VisualStudio.TestTools.UnitTesting`, which helps us to verify the objects that implement the **ICollection** interface. The collections might be the system collection type or the custom collections. Using `CollectionAssert` we can compare and verify whether the objects implementing the ICollection interface return the contents as expected.

We will consider the following array lists and find out the usage of Collection Assert Statements. These array lists are used in all the collection assert samples given here in this section:

```
ArrayList firstArray = new ArrayList(3);
firstArray.Add("FirstName");
firstArray.Add("LastName");

ArrayList secondArray = new ArrayList(3);
secondArray = firstArray;
secondArray.Add("MiddleName");

ArrayList thirdArray = new ArrayList(3);
thirdArray.Add("FirstName");
thirdArray.Add("MiddleName");
thirdArray.Add("LastName");

ArrayList fourthArray = new ArrayList(3);
fourthArray.Add("FirstName");
fourthArray.Add("MiddleName");
```

The `firstArray` array list has its maximum index as three, but has only two elements added to it.

The `secondArray` array list has its maximum index as three and `firstArray` is assigned to it with an additional item `MiddleName` added to it.

The `thirdArray` array list has its maximum index as three and contains three items in the array.

The `fourthArray` array list also has three as its maximum index but contains only two items.

CollectionAssert.AllItemsAreNotNull

This assert verifies if any of the items in the collection is not null. The assertion will pass as none of the items is null in `firstArray`.

```
CollectionAssert.AllItemsAreNotNull(firstArray)
```

The assertion will fail if we add the third item as:

```
firstArray.Add(null)
```

There are three overloaded methods to display the custom error message and to specify the formatting for the message if the assertion fails:

- `CollectionAssert.AllItemsAreNotNull(ICollection)`
- `CollectionAssert.AllItemsAreNotNull(ICollection, String)`

- `CollectionAssert.AllItemsAreNotNull(ICollection, String, Object[])`

CollectionAssert.AreEquivalent

`CollectionAssert.AreEquivalent` verifies if both the collections are equivalent. It means that even if the items are in different order in the collections, the items should match:

```
CollectionAssert.AreEquivalent(thirdArray, secondArray);
```

In the example, we can see that `MiddleName` is the last item in the `secondArray` but it is the second item in the `thirdArray`. But both the collections have the same items, so the assertion will pass. The following are the overloaded methods for `Collectionassert.AreEquivalent`:

- `CollectionAssert.AreEquivalent (ICollection, ICollection)`
- `CollectionAssert.AreEquivalent (ICollection, ICollection, String)`
- `CollectionAssert.AreEquivalent (ICollection, ICollection, String, Object[])`

CollectionAssert.AreNotEquivalent

The `assert CollectionAssert.AreNotEquivalent` statement verifies if both the first and second parameter collections do not contain the same items. It means that the assert fails even if one item in the first collection is present in the second collection. In the example, if we remove or replace one of the items from any of the two collections `secondArray` or the `thirdArray`, the assertion will pass as the items will not match.

```
thirdArray.Remove("MiddleName");
thirdArray.Add("FullName");
CollectionAssert.AreNotEquivalent(thirdArray, secondArray);
```

The following are the method syntax and the overloaded methods for the `CollectionAssert.AreNotEquivalent` assert to specify the custom error message and the formatting for the message.

- `CollectionAssert.AreNotEquivalent (ICollection, ICollection)`
- `CollectionAssert.AreNotEquivalent (ICollection, ICollection, String)`
- `CollectionAssert.AreNotEquivalent (ICollection, ICollection, String, Object[])`

CollectionAssert.AllItemsAreInstancesOfType

This statement verifies if all the items in the collection are of the specified/expected type in the second parameter. The following code verifies if all the elements of the collection thirdArray is of type, string. The assertion will pass as the items are string:

```
CollectionAssert.AllItemsAreInstancesOfType(thirdArray,
                                            typeof(string))
```

The following are the syntax and the overloaded methods for the CollectionAssert.AllItemsAreInstacesOfType assert, with parameters for custom error messages and to specify the formats or the placeholders for the parameter values in the message:

- CollectionAssert.AllItemsAreInstancesOfType(ICollection, Type)

- CollectionAssert.AllItemsAreInstancesOfType(ICollection, Type, String)

- CollectionAssert.AllItemsAreInstancesOfType(ICollection, Type, String, Object[])

CollectionAssert.IsSubsetOf

This statement verifies whether the collection in the first parameter contains some or all of the elements of the collection in the second parameter. But all the items of the first parameter collection should be part of the collection in the second parameter. As per the example, the following assertion will pass as the items in the fourthArray are the subset of the items in the thirdArray:

```
CollectionAssert.IsSubsetOf(fourthArray, thirdArray)
```

The following are the syntax and the overloaded methods for the CollectionAssert.IsSubsetOf assert:

- CollectionAssert.IsSubsetOf(ICollection, ICollection)

- CollectionAssert.IsSubsetOf(ICollection, ICollection, String)

- CollectionAssert.IsSubsetOf(ICollection, ICollection, String, Object[])

CollectionAssert.IsNotSubsetOf

This statement verifies whether the collection in the first parameter contains at least one element which is not present in the second parameter collection. As per the example, the following assertion will fail as the items in the `fourthArray` are the subset of the items in the `thirdArray`. It means that there are no items in `fourthArray` which are not present in `thirdArray`.

```
CollectionAssert.IsNotSubsetOf(fourthArray, thirdArray)
```

Try adding a new element to the `fourthArray` which is not present in `thirdArray` such as:

```
fourthArray.Add("FullName");
```

Now try the same `CollectionAssert` statement. The assertion will fail as the `fourthArray` is not a subset of the `thirdArray` collection.

The following is the syntax and the overloaded methods for `CollectionAssert`. The `IsNotSubsetOf` assert is to specify the custom error message and the formats for the error message:

- `CollectionAssert.IsNotSubsetOf(ICollection, ICollection)`

- `CollectionAssert.IsNotSubsetOf(ICollection, ICollection, String)`

- `CollectionAssert.IsNotSubsetOf(ICollection, ICollection, String, Object[])`

CollectionAssert.AllItemsAreUnique

This verifies whether the items in the collection are unique. The following assertion will pass as per the same collection. The assertion fails if we add a third item, `LastName`, which duplicates the existing item:

```
firstArray.Add("LastName")
```

The syntax for this method and its two overloaded methods are given here. The additional parameters are to specify the custom error message and the formats for the error message.

- `CollectionAssert.AllItemsAreUnique(ICollection)`

- `CollectionAssert.AllItemsAreUnique(ICollection, String)`

- `CollectionAssert.AllItemsAreUnique(ICollection, String, Object[])`

CollectionAssert.Contains

This assert verifies if any of the elements of the collection specified as the first parameter contain the element specified as the second parameter. The following assert will pass as the `FirstName` is an element in the `fourthArray` collection:

```
CollectionAssert.Contains(fourthArray, "FirstName")
```

We can specify the custom error message and custom formats for the assertion failure. This assert has two overloaded methods in addition to the default method:

- `CollectionAssert.Contains(ICollection, Object)`
- `CollectionAssert.Contains(ICollection, Object, String)`
- `CollectionAssert.Contains(ICollection, Object, String, Object[])`

CollectionAssert.DoesNotContain

This is the exact opposite of the `CollectionAssert.Contains` statement. This assert verifies if any of the elements in the first parameter collection is not equal to the value specified as the second parameter:

```
CollectionAssert.Contains(fourthArray, "Phone Number")
```

We can specify the custom error message and custom formatters for the assertion failure. This assert has two overloaded methods in addition to the default method:

- `CollectionAssert.DoesNotContain(ICollection, Object)`
- `CollectionAssert.DoesNotContain(ICollection, Object, String)`
- `CollectionAssert.DoesNotContain(ICollection, Object, String, Object[])`

CollectionAssert.AreEqual

This method verifies if both the collections are equal. The following assertion fails as the number of items added to the `firstArray` is different from the `thirdArray`.

```
CollectionAssert.AreEqual(firstArray, thirdArray)
```

The assertion will pass if we add the same items from `firstArray` to the `thirdArray` or assign the `firstArray` to `thirdArray` which makes both the arrays equal:

```
thirdArray = firstArray;
```

This assert type has six overloaded methods:

- `CollectionAssert.AreEqual(ICollection, ICollection)`

- `CollectionAssert.AreEqual(ICollection, ICollection, IComparer)`

- `CollectionAssert.AreEqual(ICollection, ICollection, IComparer, String)`

- `CollectionAssert.AreEqual(ICollection, ICollection, IComparer, String, Object[])`

- `CollectionAssert.AreEqual(ICollection, ICollection, String)`

- `CollectionAssert.AreEqual(ICollection, ICollection, String, Object[])`

The parameter `String` and `Object[]` can be used when we need a custom error message and formatters for the error message in case of assertion failure.

`IComparer` can be used if we have the custom objects in the collection and if we want to use a particular property of the object for comparison. For example, if a collection contains a list of Employee objects, having the `FirstName`, `LastName`, and `EmployeeID` of each employee, we may want to sort the elements in the collection based on the `FirstName` of the employees. We may want to compare the two collections containing the employees list based on the `FirstName` of the employees. To do this, we have to create the custom comparer.

Consider the following `Employee` class, which has a `EmployeeComparer` class that compares the `FirstName` in the `Employee` implemented from the `IComparable` interface:

```
public class Employee : IComparable
{
  public string FirstName { get; set; }
  public string LastName { get; set; }
  public int ID { get; set; }
  public Employee (string firstName, string lastName, int
                   employeeID)
  {
    FirstName = firstName;
    LastName = lastName;
    ID = employeeID;
  }
  public int CompareTo(Object obj)
  {
    Employee emp = (Employee)obj;
    return FirstName.CompareTo(emp.FirstName);
```

```
  }
  public class EmployeeComparer : IComparer
  {
    public int Compare(Object one, Object two)
    {
      Employee emp1 = (Employee)one;
      Employee emp2 = (Employee)two;
      return emp1.CompareTo(two);
    }
  }
```

Now create two collections of the type `ArrayList` and add employees to the lists.
The first names of the employees are the same in both the lists but the last names and
the IDs vary.

```
ArrayList EmployeesListOne = new ArrayList();
EmployeesListOne.Add(new TestLibrary.Employee("Richard", "King",
                     1801));
EmployeesListOne.Add(new TestLibrary.Employee("James", "Miller",
                     1408));
EmployeesListOne.Add(new TestLibrary.Employee("Jim", "Tucker",
                     3234));
EmployeesListOne.Add(new TestLibrary.Employee("Murphy", "Young",
                     3954));
EmployeesListOne.Add(new TestLibrary.Employee("Shelly", "Watts",
                     7845));
ArrayList EmployeesListTwo = new ArrayList();
EmployeesListTwo.Add(new TestLibrary.Employee("Richard", "Smith",
                     4763));
EmployeesListTwo.Add(new TestLibrary.Employee("James", "Wright",
                     8732));
EmployeesListTwo.Add(new TestLibrary.Employee("Jim", "White",
1829));
EmployeesListTwo.Add(new TestLibrary.Employee("Murphy", "Adams",
                     2984));
EmployeesListTwo.Add(new TestLibrary.Employee("Shelly", "Johnson",
                     1605));
```

Now, in the test method, use `CollectionAssert.AreEqual` to compare the
preceding collections.

```
CollectionAssert.AreEqual(EmployeesListOne, EmployeesListTwo, "The
                          collections '{0}' and '{1}' are not equal",
                          "EmployeesListOne", "EmployeesListTwo");
```

This assertion will fail because the objects in the collection are not the same. Even if you update the employee object properties to be the same in both the collections, it will fail because the objects are not the same. The error message will be the specified custom message with the specified formatters. But we can use the custom comparer we created to compare the collection objects based on the `FirstName` element which is used in the comparer. We can create the custom comparer on any of the object properties:

```
TestLibrary.Employee.EmployeeComparer comparer = new
                            TestLibrary.Employee.EmployeeComparer();
CollectionAssert.AreEqual(EmployeesListOne, EmployeesListTwo,
                    comparer, "The collections '{0}' and '{1}'
                    are not equal", "EmployeesListOne",
                    "EmployeesListTwo");
```

The assertion will pass now as the comparison is done on the first name of the elements in both the collection.

CollectionAssert.AreNotEqual

This is similar to `CollectionAssert.AreEqual` but this will verify if the collections are not equal. This assert type also has multiple overloaded methods similar to the `CollectionAssert.AreEqual`:

- `CollectionAssert.AreNotEqual(ICollection, ICollection)`
- `CollectionAssert.AreNotEqual(ICollection, ICollection, IComparer)`
- `CollectionAssert.AreNotEqual(ICollection, ICollection, IComparer, String)`
- `CollectionAssert.AreNotEqual(ICollection, ICollection, IComparer, String, Object[])`
- `CollectionAssert.AreNotEqual(ICollection, ICollection, String)`
- `CollectionAssert.AreNotEqual(ICollection, ICollection, String, Object[])`

AssertFailedException

This is to catch the exception thrown when the test fails. This exception is thrown whenever there is a failure of the assert statement.

The following code verifies if the **fourthArray** contains the string, **Phone Number**. The assertion fails and the exception, **AssertFailedException,** is caught using the **catch** block. For this example, we will add the exception message and a custom message to the test trace.

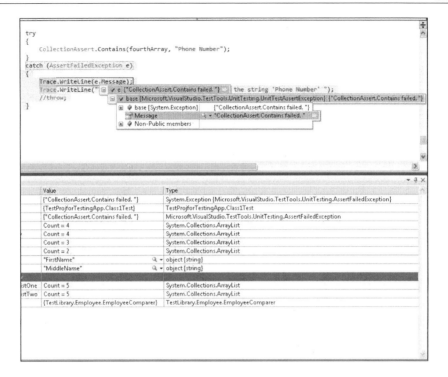

The preceding code shows that the code has thrown the exception,
`AssertFailedException`, and is caught by the exception code block. Now the test
will pass as the expected exception is thrown by the test. The test result details will
show the details of tracing. The following screenshot depicts the test result with the
trace:

UnitTestAssertionException

This is the base class for all unit test exceptions. If we have to write our own custom `Assertion` class, we can inherit the class from the `UnitTestAssertionException` class to identify the exceptions thrown from the test.

The code debug image with the exception shown in the previous section shows `AssertFailedException` which is derived from `UnitTestAssertException`.

ExpectedExceptionAttribute

This attribute can be used to test if any particular exception is expected from the code. The attribute expects the exact exception that is expected to arise out of the code to be specified as the parameter. Let's discuss this step-by-step with the help of an example. The following code shows the custom exception which is derived from the application exception. This custom exception does nothing but just sets a message:

```
namespace TestLibrary
{
  class MyCustomException : ApplicationException
  {
    public string CustomMessage { get; set; }
    public MyCustomException(string message)
    {
      CustomMessage = message;
    }
  }
}
```

The class contains a method which returns the total price but throws the custom exception with a message, if the total price is less than zero.

```
public double GetTotalItemPrice(int count) {
  double price = 10.99;
  double total;
  total = count * price;
  if (total < 0)
  {
    throw new TestLibrary.MyCustomException("the total is less than
                                     zero");
  }
  return total;
}
```

Create a unit test method for the preceding method by choosing the **Create Unit Test** option from the context menu. The following code shows the unit test method for the preceding code that returns the total item price:

```
[TestMethod()]
public void GetTotalItemPriceTest()
{
  Class1 target = new Class1();
  int count = 0;
  double expected = 0F;
  double actual;
  actual = target.GetTotalItemPrice(count);
  Assert.AreEqual(expected, actual);
}
```

To test the preceding method set the count to a value less than zero and run the test from the **Test view** window. The assertion will fail. For example, for a value of -1 the assertion will fail with the following message which says the application thrown by an exception is of type **MyCustomException**:

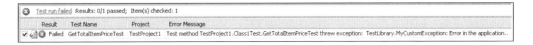

This is not what we want here. This is the application we are going to use for testing the expected exception.

Now we have to test the method `GetTotalItemPrice` for `MyCustomException`. To do this, add the `ExpectedException` attribute to the test method as shown here and run the test by setting different values for the variable count.

```
[TestMethod()]
[ExpectedException(typeof(TestLibrary.MyCustomException))]
public void GetTotalItemPriceTest()
{
  Class1 target = new Class1();
  int count = -1;
  double expected = 0F;
  double actual;
  actual = target.GetTotalItemPrice(count);
  Assert.AreEqual(expected, actual);
}
```

The preceding test will pass as the method throws `MyCustomException`, which means that the method resulted in an exception because of its total value, which is less than zero.

We can include any exception as an attribute to the test method and verify the actual method if it actually throws an exception. This is very useful in the case of very complex methods where there is a high possibility of getting exceptions such as divide by zero, File IO, or file/folder access permissions.

Unit tests and generics

Before going into the actual testing of generics, let us understand the use of generics. Generics in .NET Framework help us to design the classes and methods without any specific parameter types but allow us to realize type safety at compile time. It means that we can continue working with the class in a type safe way, but we don't have to force it to be of any specific type. Generics help us to reuse the code and increase the performance. Generics are mostly used with the collections such as Array List, Linked List, Stacks, Queues, and other collections. This is because the collections can hold any type of items, for example, an array list can be a list of integers or it can be a list of strings. The following is an example of a generic method, which just accepts two generic values and copies the first one into the second one:

```
public static void CopyItems<T>(List<T> srcList, List<T> destList)
{
  foreach (T itm in srcList)
  {
    destList.Add(itm);
  }
}
```

Here, you can see that the type is not specified anywhere. It is generic, which is denoted by <T>. It can be an integer or string or any type that is identified when the method is called. The following code shows the example for using the CopyItems generic method. The first time the CopyItems is called, the listSource collection passed as the first parameter contains String items. The second time the CopyItems method is called the listSrc collection passed as the first parameter contains the items of type Employee object.

```
static void Main(string[] args)
{
  List<string> listSource = new List<string>();
  listSource.Add("String1");
  listSource.Add("string2");
  List<string> listDestination = new List<string>();
  Console.WriteLine("Items count in listDestination before copying
                   items: {0} ", listDestination.Count);
  CopyItems(listSource, listDestination);
```

```
Console.WriteLine("Items count in listDestination after copying
                   items: {0} ", listDestination.Count);
Console.WriteLine("");
List<Employee> listSrc = new List<Employee>();
listSrc.Add(new Employee(1001, "Employee 1001"));
listSrc.Add(new Employee(1002, "Employee 1002"));
listSrc.Add(new Employee(1003, "Employee 1003"));
List<Employee> listDest = new List<Employee>();
Console.WriteLine("Items count in listDest before copying items:
                   {0} ", listDest.Count);
CopyItems(listSrc, listDest);
Console.WriteLine("Items count in listDest after copying items: {0}
                   ", listDest.Count);
}
```

The result would be the copy of the objects in the destination collection which is the second parameter to the generic method. The output of the method after calling the generic method would be as shown in the following screenshot:

The unit testing for the generic method can be generated in a similar way to any other method. Now right-click on the **CopyItems** generic method and select the **Create Unit Tests** option and select the option for the project. You can see that Visual Studio generates two methods for the selected generic method, one as a helper method and the other one as the test method. The generics can contain one or more type constraints so that the type arguments satisfy the constraints. For example, the GenericSample shown as follows has a constraint where T : Employee which should be satisfied by the arguments.

```
public class GenericSample<T> where T : Employee
{
  // code
}
```

The test method calls this helper method with the constraint to make sure the method under test works as expected.

The unit test for the generic method `CopyItems` example would be:

```
public void CopyItemsTestHelper<T>()
  {
     List<T> srcList = null; // TODO: Initialize to an // appropriate
                        value
     List<T> destList = null; // TODO: Initialize to an //appropriate
                        value
     Program.CopyItems<T>(srcList, destList);
     Assert.Inconclusive("A method that does not return a value cannot
                        be verified.");
  }
  [TestMethod()]
  public void CopyItemsTest()
  {
   CopyItemsTestHelper<GenericParameterHelper>();
  }
```

Let us try customizing the preceding generated unit test code to pass the collection with employee type items and see the output:

```
public void CopyItemsTestHelper<T>()
  {
    List<Employee> srcList = new List<Employee>();
    srcList.Add(new Employee(1001, "Employee 1001"));
    srcList.Add(new Employee(1002, "Employee 1002"));
    srcList.Add(new Employee(1003, "Employee 1003"));
    List<Employee> destList = new List<Employee>();
    Program.CopyItems<Employee>(srcList, destList);
    Assert.AreEqual(3, destList.Count);
  }

  [TestMethod()]
  public void CopyItemsTest()
  {
    CopyItemsTestHelper<GenericParameterHelper>();
  }
```

The assertion for the test method will pass because `destList.Count` would contain three items after calling the `CopyItems` method which equals the expected value. We can create collections with any type of items and use the same generic method to copy the items.

Data-driven unit testing

This type of testing is useful in carrying out the same test multiple times with different input data from a data source. The data source can have any number of records or data rows for which we want the test to be carried out.

Instead of passing each data row value to the test application and executing an entire test for each data row, we can link the test method to the data source. So when the test is run, the test method will retrieve the data rows one by one from the data source and will carry out the test for that number of times with different input values.

This is similar to the Web Performance Testing or Load Testing with a data source attaching to the web method parameters. This could be used in the case of testing number of user scenarios with different user logins to check the access permission or to see the validation based on the user roles, if anything is applicable to the application.

There are two different ways of configuring the data source or attaching the source to the test method. Let us consider one simple example of a method which takes two parameters as quantity and unit price. The result of the method would be to return the multiplied value of these two values and apply a percentage of tax to it.

```
public double CalculateTotalPrice(double uPrice, int Qty)
{
    double totalPrice;
    double tax = 0.125;
    totalPrice = uPrice * Qty + (uPrice * tax * Qty); //
    return totalPrice;
}
```

Create a unit test for the preceding example. The unit test code would contain the following code for the preceding method:

```
[TestMethod()]
public void CalculateTotalPriceTest()
{
    Class1 target = new Class1();
    double uPrice = 0F;
    int Qty = 0;
    double expected = 0F;
    double actual;
    actual = target.CalculateTotalPrice(uPrice, Qty);
    Assert.AreEqual(expected, actual);
}
```

Before setting the properties we have to create the data source. The data source can be of a different format such as CSV, XML, Microsoft Access, Microsoft SQL Server Database, or Oracle Database, or any other database. For this example, we will consider a CSV file which has five records and each record has values for **UnitPrice**, **Quantity**, and **ExpectedTotalPrice**. These are the values required in the test method:

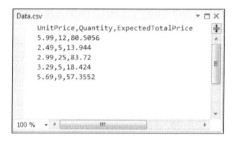

Now the new unit test would also be listed in the **Test View** and **Test List Editor**. Open the **Test View** or **Test List Editor** using the **Test** menu option from the IDE. Select the test method from the list and open the **Properties** window. From the list of properties for the unit test, select the connection property, and choose the option to open the **Data Source** wizard. From the wizard, select the data source type as a CSV file from the options. Select the CSV file we created from the location. This will show the preview of the data too. Now the property of the test should look like the window shown as follows:

- **Data Provider Name**: This property is disabled as we have selected the file directly and made the connection. Visual Studio automatically assigns the **Data Provider Name** as **Microsoft.VisualStudio.TestTools.DataSource.CSV**.

- **Data Table Name**: After making the connection, we can see the tables listed from the database. The table that we select from the list will be the source of data for the testing.

- **Data Access Method**: This can be *Sequential* or *Dynamic*. This is the method which will be used for retrieving the data from the data source for the test.

We can see the properties added as attributes to the test method when we change the properties of the test:

```
[DeploymentItem("TestProject\\Data.csv"),
        DataSource("Microsoft.VisualStudio.TestTools.DataSource.CSV",
        "|DataDirectory|\\Data.csv", "Data#csv",
        DataAccessMethod.Sequential), TestMethod()]
public void CalculateTotalPriceTest()
{
}
```

The data source which is a CSV file is added as the deployment item. The other attributes specify the method of data access and the namespace used. These are the method level attributes set for the test run.

To set the value of the data from the data source to the test method, modify the test method a little bit as follows. `testContextInstance.DataRow` is used to fetch the value from the current row for the current instance of the test. For example, if we have five rows in the data source there would be five different instances of tests, one for each row.

You can see the custom error message added to the assert to get the actual and expected values if the test fails:

```
[DataSource("Microsoft.VisualStudio.TestTools.DataSource.CSV",
            "|DataDirectory|\\Data.csv", "Data#csv",
            DataAccessMethod.Sequential),
            DeploymentItem("TestProject1\\Data.csv"), TestMethod()]
public void CalculateTotalPriceTest()
{
  Class1 target = new Class1();
  double uPrice = 0F;
  int Qty = 0;
  double expected = 0F;
  double actual;
```

```
expected = Convert.ToDouble(testContextInstance.
        DataRow["ExpectedTotalPrice"]);
actual = target.CalculateTotalPrice(Convert.ToDouble
                    (testContextInstance.DataRow["UnitPrice"]),
Convert.ToInt32(testContextInstance. DataRow["Quantity"]));
Assert.AreEqual(expected, actual, "The expected value is {0} but
            the actual value is {1}", expected, actual);
Trace.WriteLine("Expected:" + expected + "; Actual:"+ actual);
}
```

Now open the **Test View** window and select the test method listed in the window:

On running the test, we can see the test execution happening for each row in the data source. Once the test has been completed for all of the rows in the data source, we can see the test result based on the results of all individual tests. Even if one test fails, the end result of the test run will be a failure. To get the test run to pass, all of the individual tests within the selected test run should pass.

The output for the preceding test with the data source having five records in it, as shown in the previous screenshot, would be:

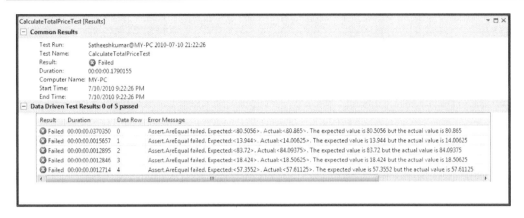

We can see the total time taken for each test and the row picked for each test from the preceding result. All five tests fail and you can see the custom error message displayed with the expected and actual values applied to the formatters. The entire test fails because of the calculation mistake in the actual method. The data source contains the expected values based on the tax value as 0.12 but the actual method has the value as 0.125. If you change the value to 0.12 in the method `CalculateTotalPriceTest` and rerun the test, the test will pass.

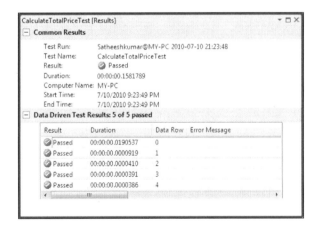

The **Test Run** details window shows the status of each test run for each row in the data source.

Unit testing an ASP.NET application

Creating the unit test for an ASP.NET web site or application is similar to how we created one for the normal class library. The ASP.NET unit test is used for testing the methods or the business logic used for the ASP.NET site. The only difference is the additional attributes added to the methods to identify the URL and the Host. The ASP.NET unit test can be run using IIS web server or the development web server. If it is on the IIS server, we can choose the user identity with which the unit test should run. The default identity depends on the version of the IIS server and the operating system.

Let us consider a simple user registration page created using ASP.NET using Visual Studio. The following is the UI for the user to get registered.

This web application runs on the local development server. The application has two methods. One is to get the user details from the user interface and create a new user object and the other is to just display the user name on the screen after submit. The application also has a class file for the user information.

```
protected void BtnSubmit_Click(object sender, EventArgs e)
{
    User usr = new User();
```

```
    GetUserDetails(usr);
    LabelOutput.Text = "Hello " + usr.FirstName + " " + usr.LastName +
                        " you are successfully registered with the site";
}

public User GetUserDetails(User user)
{
    user.FirstName = TextBoxFirstName.Text;
    user.LastName = TextBoxLastName.Text;
    user.MiddleName = TextBoxMiddleName.Text;
    user.Address = TextBoxCity.Text;
    user.Street = TextBoxStreet.Text;
    user.City = TextBoxCity.Text;
    user.Country = TextBoxCountry.Text;
    user.Email = TextBoxEmail.Text;
    user.Phone = TextBoxPhone.Text;
    return user;
}
```

Before generating the unit test for the web application, let us build and run the application once to make sure it runs as expected.

Now to generate the unit test, open the code file of the web page, right-click and select the **Create Unit Tests...** option which identifies all the classes and the methods for which the unit test can be generated as shown in the following screenshot:

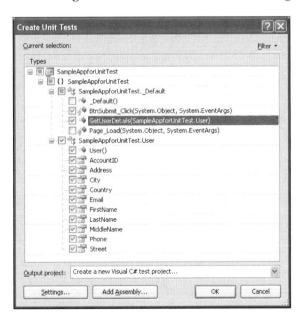

Select the methods and the user class for which the unit test can be generated and tested. Now Visual Studio creates the unit test class file for the new test with the required attributes and the base code for the test. The unit test code for the two methods of the web page would be:

```
[TestMethod()]
[HostType("ASP.NET")]
[AspNetDevelopmentServerHost("C:\\Workspace\\UnitTest\\
                   SampleAppforUnitTest\\SampleAppforUnitTest", "/")]
[UrlToTest("http://localhost:11961/")]
[DeploymentItem("SampleAppforUnitTest.dll")]
public void BtnSubmit_ClickTest()
{
  _Default_Accessor target = new _Default_Accessor();
  // TODO: Initialize to an appropriate value
  object sender = null; // TODO: Initialize to an //appropriate value
  EventArgs e = null; // TODO: Initialize to an appropriate //value
  target.BtnSubmit_Click(sender, e);
  Assert.Inconclusive("A method that does not return a value cannot
                       be verified.");
}


/// <summary>
///A test for GetUserDetails
///</summary>
[TestMethod()]
[HostType("ASP.NET")]
[AspNetDevelopmentServerHost("C:\\Workspace\\UnitTest\\
SampleAppforUnitTest\\SampleAppforUnitTest", "/")]
[UrlToTest("http://localhost:11961/")]
public void GetUserDetailsTest()
{
  _Default target = new _Default(); // TODO: Initialize to //an
                       appropriate value
  User user = null; // TODO: Initialize to an appropriate
                //value
  User expected = null; // TODO: Initialize to an //appropriate value
  User actual;
  actual = target.GetUserDetails(user);
  Assert.AreEqual(expected, actual);
  Assert.Inconclusive("Verify the correctness of this test method.");
}
```

There are different attributes added to the unit test methods:

- `TestMethod`: attribute to identify whether a method is a unit test method
- `HostType`: the type of the host that takes care of running the unit test. In this case it is ASP.NET
- `AspNetDevelopmentServerHost`: this specifies the settings to be used when the development server is used as the host for the unit testing
- `UrlToTest`: specifies the application URL to be used for the test context
- `DeploymentItem`: this is to specify the items such as files and folders to be deployed before the test

After creating the test and setting the environment, set the expected values and include the required assert method for comparing the values and passing the test. For example, change the `GetUserDetailsTest` method as follows:

```
[TestMethod()]
[HostType("ASP.NET")]
[AspNetDevelopmentServerHost("C:\\Workspace\\UnitTest\\
                 SampleAppforUnitTest\\SampleAppforUnitTest", "/")]
[UrlToTest("http://localhost:11961/")]
public void GetUserDetailsTest()
{
  _Default target = new _Default();
  User user = new User();
  User expected = new User();
  expected.FirstName = "Subha";
  expected.LastName = "S";
  User actual;
  actual = target.GetUserDetails(user);
  Assert.AreEqual(expected.FirstName, actual.FirstName);
}
```

The test will pass if the value of the `FirstName` and `LastName` properties of the expected object and the actual object returned by the method are equal. Right-click on the method and select **Run Tests...**.

We can use the different assert methods and test all the different scenarios of the unit test with different expected values.

Unit testing web services

Web services are similar to any other method in the web application. We have to just add the reference of the web service and call the method, as we call any other method of the web application. All the methods and attributes required for testing the web service are available under the namespace **Microsoft.VisualStudio. TestTools.UnitTesting.Web**.

Similar to the web application, the web service can be hosted using IIS server or the local development server. If it is hosted in the IIS, just add the reference to the unit test application and call the web service method just like calling the method in the web application. If it is available on the local machine but not hosted on the web server, just add the attributes required to start the development server. This attribute takes care of hosting the service locally.

Let us create a simple web service which returns values based on the input parameter value that is passed to the web method. Given is the sample code:

```
public class Service1 : System.Web.Services.WebService
{
  [WebMethod]
  public string HelloWorld()
{
  return "Hello World";
}

[WebMethod]
public string GetuserDetails(int id)
{
  string name = "";
  if (id == 100)
    name = "Subha";
  if (id == 200)
    name = "Satheesh";
  return name;
  }
}
```

After creating the web method, right-click on the method and select **Create Unit Tests...** This will create the unit test with the attributes required for the web service test.

```
[TestMethod()]
[HostType("ASP.NET")]
```

```
[AspNetDevelopmentServerHost("C:\\Workspace\\UnitTest\\
                    SampleAppforUnitTest\\WebService1", "/")]
[UrlToTest("http://localhost:15558/")]
public void GetuserDetailsTest()
{
    Service1 target = new Service1();
    int id = 100;
    string expected = "User Name";
    string actual;
    actual = target.GetuserDetails(id);
    Assert.AreEqual(expected, actual);
}
```

The preceding unit test method for the web method is very similar to the method for the ASP.NET application. This web service runs on a local development server. If it has to run on the IIS server, we can change the configuration settings.

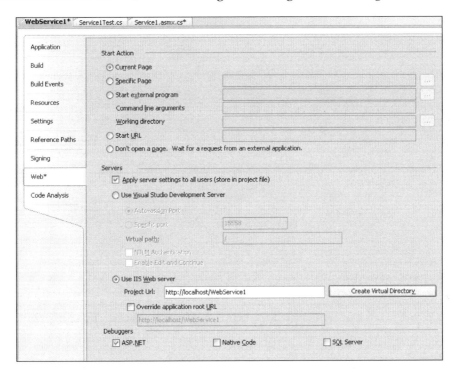

This is the property set for the **Web Service** project. The servers are by default set as **Visual Studio Development Server**. To change it to run on the IIS server, select the second option, **Use IIS Web server,** and create, virtual directory. Now the if we generate the unit test, the URL used for the unit test would be `http://localhost/WebService1`.

Just run the test similar to the other test by changing the expected value and using the required assert methods. Sometimes the test may fail because of unavailability of the web server or the server may not be running. In that case we can use the `TryUrlRedirection` method of `WebServiceHelper` to try connecting to the URL before testing. The sample code for redirection would be

```
Assert.IsTrue(WebServiceHelper.TryUrlRedirection(target,
              testContextInstance, "MyServer"),
          "Redirection failed.");
```

Code coverage unit test

This is to see the methods or the code that has been covered by the unit test. This is the property we can set on the project level before starting the unit testing. Open the settings file, **local.testsettings** file, under the solution. If there is a new settings file then open the corresponding settings file. Select **Data and Diagnostics** from the list shown on the left side. Now you need to select the **Role** listed on the right. The roles are associated to the agents used for testing. On selecting the **Role**, the corresponding diagnostics types are listed so that the required diagnostics can be enabled or disabled from the list. Check the option to enable **Code Coverage**.

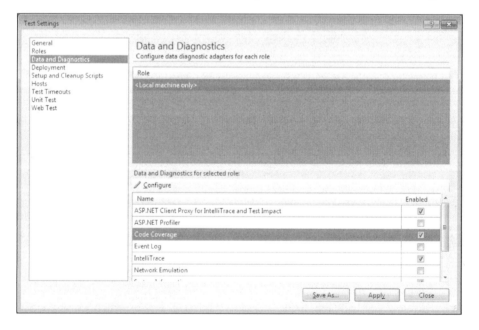

Select **Code Coverage** and then click on **Configure** to choose the projects for collecting the diagnostic information. Now you can see the list of projects or artifacts to instrument options. Select the project for which the code coverage has to be turned on and select **OK** and close the dialog.

Now select the test and run the test again. Once the test is complete we can see the code coverage details from the **Code Coverage** window which can be opened using the option in the **Test** menu option.

The **Code Coverage** window shows the coverage details collected from the last test run. The following is the sample of the **Code Coverage Result**:

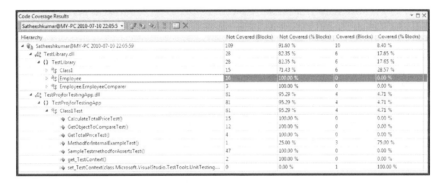

If we know the fix for the test to complete 100% coverage of the method, we can just right-click on the particular method and select **go to source code** which will take us to the source code of the particular method. We can fix the code and rerun the test until the code is completely covered by the test. To get more details on the code coverage, add additional columns or remove existing columns to the output window and collect more details on the code coverage.

Summary

This chapter went through some common statements in unit test projects such as assert statements and explained the different ways of unit testing the class library application, ASP.NET web application, and the web services created using Visual Studio. We have also seen the data-driven testing method which helps us to test the class methods using the data collected in a data source and attaching that to the test application. This chapter also covered the different settings and configurations that we can make on the application configuration file to get the basic code to be generated by default for the method and class under the unit test. Different Assert methods and the usage of different assert methods are also explained in detail in this chapter. Lastly we have seen the method of collecting and analyzing the code coverage results for the unit tests.

So far we have seen the different ways of testing code developed by the developers. The next chapter concentrates on testing the actual web application using different features supported by Visual Studio Team System.

Web Performance Testing

This chapter concentrates on different ways of verifying website responses for each request and responses in multiple scenarios such as slow network speed, rendering on different browsers, or with different numbers of users at a given point in time. All these factors affect the website performance and response time. Web Performance Testing helps us verify if website produces the expected result within the expected response time. This helps us to identify the problems and rectify them before they happen in the actual production environment. Web Performance Testing also helps in finding out if the hardware can handle the maximum expected amount of requests at a time or needs additional hardware to handle the traffic and respond to multiple user requests.

Discussed here are some of the main testing highlights that are performed on web applications for better performance and availability:

- **Validation and verification test**: It helps to verify the inputs or the expected entries that satisfy the requirements. For example, if a field requires a date to be entered, the system should check for the date validation and should not allow the user to submit the page until the correct entry is made.

- **Web page usability test**: It is the method of simulating the user's way of experience the application in production, and testing the same as per requirement. This could be something like checking help links, contents in the page, checking menu options and their links, think times between the pages and message dialogs in the pages.

- **Security Testing**: It helps us to verify the application response for different end users based on the credentials and different other resources required from the local system or a server in the network. For example, this could be writing/reading the log information file in the network share.

- **Performance Testing**: It verifies web page responses as per expectations based on the environment. This also includes stress testing and Load Testing of the application with multiple user scenarios, and the volume of data that is explained in detail in the *Chapter 7, Load Testing*.

- **Testing web page compatibility**: It is the method of testing multiple browsers based on user requirements. The web page presentation depends on how well the components are used and supported on all the different browsers that end users may choose.

- **Testing a web application using different networks**: This is because of the user location that varies based on where the user is accessing the system from. The performance and the accessibility of the application are based directly on the network involved in providing the web pages to the user. This is also part of performance testing. For example, it could be a local intranet or an internet with a lower network speed.

There are many other types of testing that can be performed as part of Web Performance Testing such as using different operating systems, using different databases, or installing different versions of an operating system.

All these tests with many additional capabilities are supported by Microsoft Visual Studio 2010. Dynamic web pages can be created by any of the supported .NET languages by Visual Studio using the ASP.NET web project and web page templates. Custom services, components, and libraries are used in the web application to get the functionality and make it more dynamic. Other scripting languages and technologies such as JavaScript, Silverlight, and Flash are used in the web pages for validations and making the presentation better. Once we are ready with the web application, we need to test it and deploy it to check if the website functionalities and qualities are satisfied as per requirements. To get there, Microsoft Visual Studio 2010 provides tools for testing a web application. There are different ways of using the tool to test the application. One is to use the user interface to record and then add the validation rules and parameters to make it dynamic. The other way is to record the requests and then create the coded Web Performance Test for the recorded Web Performance Test and customize it using the code.

This chapter explains the basic means of Web Performance Testing using Visual Studio 2010 but also of using features such as adding rules and parameterization of dynamic variables. Microsoft Visual Studio 2010 provides many new features to Web Performance Testing such as adding new APIs to the test results, Web Performance Test results in a separate file, looping and branching, new validation and extraction rules, and many more. This chapter will provide detailed information on the following listed features:

- Creating a new Web Performance Test
- Web Performance Test Editor and properties
- Web Requests properties, validations, and Transactions
- Toolbar options and properties
- Performance Session for Test
- Debugging and Running Web Performance

Creating Web Performance Test

The Web Performance Test activates the web performance test recorder to record all the actions that are performed while browsing websites and adds it to the performance test. The recorder comes by default with Visual Studio Ultimate. Creating a performance Web Performance Test is similar to creating any other test in Visual Studio. There are three different ways to create a new web performance test:

1. Select the test project, right–click, and choose **Add**.

2. Select the menu option **Test** and choose **New Test...** which opens the **Add New Test** window containing the different test type templates.

3. Select the menu option **Test** and choose **Windows** and then select **Test View**, which opens the **Test View** window listing all available tests. Right-click on the surface of the **Test View** window to open the context menu. Choose the **New Test** option, which opens the **Add New Test** window.

4. After selecting one of the above three, select the **Web Performance Test** template from the list of different test types.

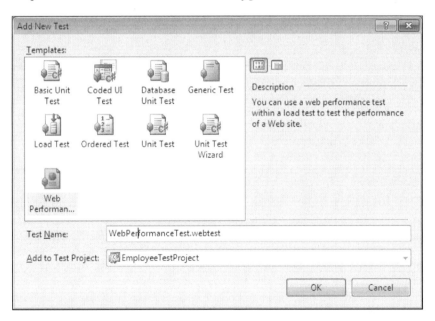

Once you select the **Web Performance Test** and click **OK**, a new test is created under the selected test project and a new instance of a web browser opens. The left-pane of the browser contains the **Web Test Recorder** for recording the user actions.

Recording a test

The web test recorder is used mainly to record all the actions performed while browsing web pages. The recorder records all requests and responses and helps us to find out if the request produces the expected result as per the requirement with different scenarios.

The user can request web pages to record and create the test scenario. Once the scenario is created, we can build the scenario or customize it to make it more dynamic using parameters and a dynamic data source.

As stated above, after starting the Web Performance Test, a new browser window opens with the web test recorder. The recorder has five different options as follows:

- **Record**: This is to start recording the web page requests.
- **Pause**: This is used to pause the recording. In some cases, we may not want to record all requests in the web application. But we would have first identified the pages for which we may have to pause the recording and restart the recording for the forthcoming pages.
- **Stop**: This is to stop the recording session. As soon as we click on the **Stop** button, the browser will close and the session will stop.
- **Add a Comment**: This option is used for adding any additional comments to the current request in the recording.
- **Clear all requests**: This is to clear out all the requests in the recording. Sometimes, if we make mistakes in the recording, or if the web application we are testing is not the correct one, then we can clear all the requests and start from the beginning.

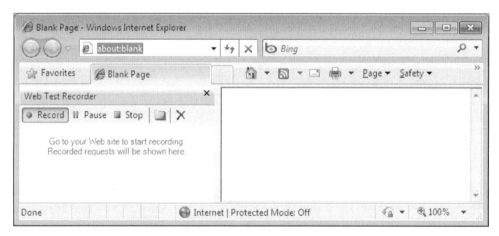

Before we proceed to Web Performance Testing, let us create a sample web application for testing. Let's consider a new employee creation page in which the user has to provide information such as **First Name**, **Last Name**, **Middle Name**, **Occupation**, and **Address**. This information is required to keep track of user activity in the website, which is common in most websites. For our example, let us consider only this simple page. It contains a **Save** option which collects all the information entered by the user and saves it to the database table. The user entries are validated as per the requirement, which we will see in the examples in the subsections. The database is the SQL Server Express database with one table for storing all the information. The following is the database table for the sample application:

The sample application web page user interface is shown here with some required fields such as those to show the validation error messages and the **Insert** option to send the request with the details:

The application can be tested when it is hosted on a web server or when it is running on the local development web server within Visual Studio 2010. The examples given in this chapter are based on the local Visual Studio 2010 development server. The approach is the same for hosted application on a web server.

As we are using the Visual Studio 2010 local development web server, build the new web project and keep it running. Get the web address from the running web application so that we have the web address with a dynamic port assigned to it.

First, let us look at the features of the Web Performance Test and then we can go into the details of collecting information from the test and the actual testing.

Create a new web performance test so that you get the new web test browser recorder window. The Web test tool opens the Microsoft Internet Explorer browser for the recording as IE is the default web browser for testing. Now in the **Address** bar, enter the web page address and hit *Enter*. In this case it is going to be `http://localhost:3062/Employee/Insert.aspx` (this is a test address using the local web server and will vary based on the dynamic port assigned to it). If you are planning to test the application from the hosted server, then record the test by browsing the web pages from the hosted server. Whether it is hosted on a server or a local development server, the web application should now be up and running for testing. Once you get the web page, enter all the required details and click on **Insert** to save the new employee details. You can see each row getting added to the tree view below the recorder toolbar. All request details will get recorded till we hit the **Stop** button or the **Pause** button. To get the test scenario right, enter all the required fields and perform a positive test so that there are no error messages displayed. After getting the scenario, we can perform invalid entries and test the application.

After entering the URL and hitting *Enter* in the **Address** bar you can see the page loaded on the right, while the request is captured on the left.

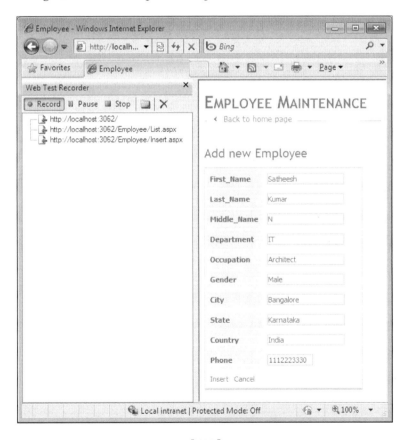

Enter all request details and then click on the **Insert** button. As soon as the web page is submitted, we can see the second request captured by the recorder with its details and this is shown in the tree view.

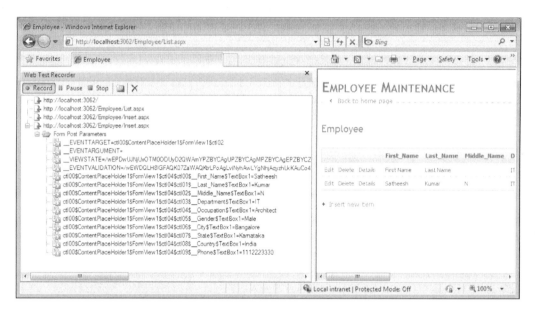

We had three requests during the recording: one for main page displays to select the employee details page, a second one to select the insert option to enter new employee details, and the third option to save the employee details and display the mail screen. The details of these requests are displayed in the tree view. If you expand the third root node in the tree view, you can find different values or strings passed by the web application on clicking the **Insert** button captured under the folder **Form Post Parameters**. You will also note that the event took place on clicking the **Insert** button in the web page. All other details are the parameter values posted by the request.

There are different protocols used for sending these requests: HTTP-GET, HTTP-POST, and SOAP:

- **HTTP-GET (Hypertext Transfer Protocol-GET)** protocol appends the query strings to the URL. The Query string is the name and the value pair that is created out of the parameters and the data.

- **HTTP-POST (Hypertext Transfer Protocol-POST)** protocol passes the name and value pairs in the body of the HTTP request message.

- **SOAP** protocol is an XML-based protocol used for sending structured information. This is mostly used by the web services.

From the recording details you can see that only the independent requests (GET or POST) are recorded, not the dependent requests such as requests for getting the images and other such requests. These requests will be reported only when the test is run, but during recording it will neither be shown nor captured.

When the web application is run, the application dynamically generates data such as session ID and is sent through Query String parameter values and Form Post parameter values. The Web Performance Test uses these generated parameter values by capturing them from the HTTP response using an extraction rule and then binding them to the HTTP request. This is known as the promotion of dynamic parameters. Detecting dynamic parameters happens immediately after finishing the web performance testing recording. On a click of the **Stop** button in the recorder window, you can see a dialog window with the message, Detecting Dynamic Parameters, and the progress bar. The dialog displays a message, Did not detect any dynamic parameters to promote. If dynamic parameters are detected, the Promote Dynamic Parameters to Web Test Parameters dialog box appears.

Adding comments

While recording the web page requests, we may need to add some comments about the page or the test. This comment could be any text with additional information for our reference. This is similar to the comments that we add to our code during development. Sometimes we may need to add information about the steps to be followed during the test. Basically, comments are there to record the information about the task that we may have to do during the test, but could easily forget to do. These comments can be added by just clicking the **Add Comments** button in the **Web Test Recorder** toolbar.

Cleaning the Recorded Tests

In the web test recording we might have requested many pages, but at the end of the recording we may not need all of the requests to be part of testing. This is because we might have forgotten to stop and restart the test, or we might have stopped and restarted the test at the wrong place. To remove the unwanted recording of the requests we have to edit the recording. We should go through each recorded request and delete the requests that are not required.

Copying the requests

In some situations, we may need the same requests to be tested multiple times, for example, page refresh. To simulate this, we can copy the recorded requests and place them into the recording list. We can copy a request any number of times. We need to select the request from the list in the tree view, right-click and select **Copy** or use (*Ctrl + C*) and then select the destination folder, right-click and choose **Paste**.

 By copying the requests we are also changing the order of testing. This is an easy way to change the order. Instead of copying, we can also cut and paste the requests to a different place just to change the order. But we should be careful in changing the order that the dependent requests are not affected. For example, if request B is dependent on request A, then we should not move request B before A. We should take care while copying and changing the order of tests.

Web Performance Test editor

After completing all requests recording, click on the **Stop** option in the **Web Recorder** pane which will stop recording and close the browser window. Now you can see the **WebTest** editor window open and the recording details in the **WebTest** editor.

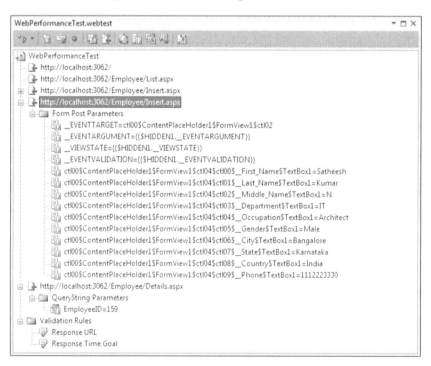

The editor shows the tree view of all the requests captured during recording. This editor also exposes the different properties of requests and the parameters for each request. We can set not only the properties, but also the **Extraction** and **Validation** rules using this editor. There are different levels of properties that we can set using the **WebTest** editor on the recorded requests:

- Properties at **WebTest** root level, which applies to the entire Web Performance Test, for example, setting the user credentials and giving a description to the test.

- Request level properties that apply to individual requests within the web test. For example, we can set the timeout, think times, and recording results properties on each request level.

- Properties for a request parameter apply to the requests using HTTP-POST or HTTP-GET protocol. Each parameter in the request contains parameters such as URL encodes, value, and name.

- Setting the extraction and validation rules for the responses to make sure the request gets the expected results and that they are validated.

Apart from all these the Web Performance Test editor has a toolbar that provides different functionalities such as running the test, adding a new data source, and setting the credentials and parameters, which are explained in detail in the coming sections.

Web Test Properties

The following are the different **Properties** of the **WebTest** that we can set using the editor:

Property	Description
Description	To specify the description for the current test
Name	Name of the current **WebTest** application
User Name	This is to specify the username of the user for this test, if we are using a user credential; we can also associate this with a data source of any type such as CSV file, XML file, or a Database
Password	This field is useful in the case of the use of any specific credentials for the test; this is the password for the username specified in the **Username** field
PreAuthenticate	This is a Boolean filed, which indicates whether the page has to be authenticated on every request or not; only if this property is set to true, the authentication header is sent for each request, otherwise headers are sent, if required; the default is **True**

Property	Description
Proxy	In some cases, the requested web pages in the test might be outside the firewall which has to go through the proxy server; so we can use this field to set the proxy server name to be used by the test
Test ID	This is the unique ID to identify the test; this ID is auto generated when we create the test; this can be used to define the test in a coded Web Performance Test; this property gets the unique identifier when implemented in the derived class
Stop On Error	This is useful to inform the application whether to stop the test or continue in case of any errors; if this value is true, the execution of the complete test will stop in the first occurrence of the error; the default is **True**.

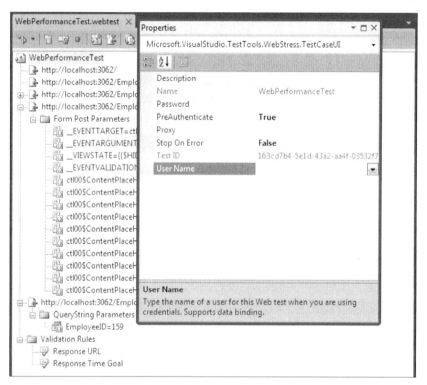

Web Performance Test request properties

The following are the properties of the requests within the Web Performance Tests. If you select any request from the tree view and open the properties, you can find these properties for each request:

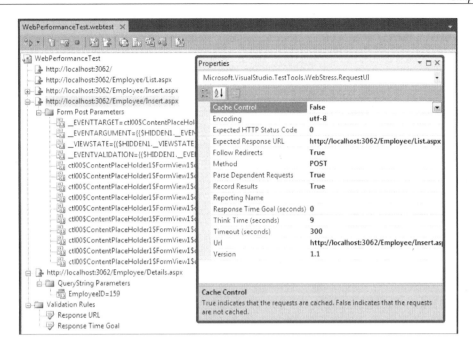

Property	Description
Cache Control	This property is to simulate the caching property of the web pages. The value can be true or false. If it is set to true, it means that caching is turned on, which means that the dependent requests are retrieved only once for subsequent requests. For example, an image file used in all the web pages is retrieved from the source only once and kept in cache and re-used for all further requests.
	If we turn caching off, then the dependent requests are retrieved from the source for every web page request. If it is an image, then the same image file will be retrieved for every request even though it is the same image. This property is very useful when testing performance by turning the caching on and off. Based on the performance we can see whether to cache the data or not.
	This property is set to the main request but not to dependent requests of the main requests. An image embedded within the web page is one of the best examples of a dependent request.
	The default value for this property is **False**.
Encoding	This is defaulted to **utf-8** as most of the HTTP requests are utf-8 encoding. It can be changed if we need a different encoding for the texts.

Property	Description
Expected HTTP Status Code	We can set this to the expected status code for the request. For example, if we don't want this request to be found on the server then we set this value to 404. The error code 404 denotes that the resource cannot be found. The default is set to **0** which returns pass if the return status is in the 200 or 300 range and returns fail if the return status is in the 400 or 500 range.
Expected Response URL	This is set to the final URL response that we expect after the current request and redirects, if any, are made. This is to validate the response. The expected response is validated using the validation rule.
Follow Redirects	This is set to true or false based on whether we want to allow the page redirects made by the request to follow or not. If set to true, then the request continues to its redirected web page and verifies if the status is the code entered for **Expected HTTP Status Code**. If it is false, the redirects are not followed.
	For example, if the value of the **Expected HTTP Status Code** is set to any value between 200 and 300, and the **Follow Redirects** is set to **True**, then the end result status of the request after all redirects should be a success.
	Status code with 200 or 300 level is a pass while status level with 400 or 500 is a failure.
Method	This property is used to set the request method used for the current request. It can either be GET or POST.
Parse Dependent Requests	This property can be set to True or False to parse the dependent requests within the requested page. For example, we may not be interested in collecting the details for the images loaded in the web page. So we can turn off the requests for loading images by setting this to False. Only the main request details will be collected.
	We should not get confused with this property and the Cache control property. Cache is to disable the dependent requests after caching the first occurrence of the request, but this property is to completely switch off the dependent requests or to completely turn them on.
Record Results	This is a Boolean value which can hold true if the performance data has to be collected for this HTTP request. It is false if the data is not required to be collected
Response Time Goal(Seconds)	There are situations where users need the application to respond quickly without any delay. To test this scenario, we can set this property to the expected maximum response time and then test the pages to find out the ones which do not meet the requirement. This value is specified in seconds. The default value is **0**, which means the property is not set

Property	Description
Think Time(Seconds)	This is set for the think time required by a user between pages. This is not the exact time that the user can spend thinking, but is a rough estimation. Also, this property is not very useful for the normal single user Web Performance Test. This is very useful in the case of a Load Test where we can predict the load including the think time of the user between the pages. The recorder automatically records the think times at the same time as recording the test
Timeout (Seconds)	This is the expiry time for the request. This is the maximum time for the request to respond back. If it doesn't return within this limit, then the page gets timed out with an error.
Version	This is to set the HTTP version to use for the request, which can be 1.0 or 1.1. The default is **1.1** which is the normal or the latest of the HTTP versions.
Url	This is the URL address for the request.

Other request properties

Each request in the Web Performance Test has its own properties, and there may be many dependent requests for each main request. We can get and set some properties even at the dependent request level. This is based on the request submit method GET or POST used for the request. We can set the values for the parameters used in the request. Also, there are some validation rules and extraction rules that can be used to extract the information from the request response.

Form POST parameters

These are the parameters sent along with the request if the method used for the request is POST. All field entries made by the user in the web page are sent to the server as Form POST Parameters. After recording we can check the actual values of the parameters that were sent during the request.

- **Name** denotes the name of the component used for collecting the data.
- **Recorded Value** is the value entered by the user during recording. This is a read-only field which is assigned while recording.
- **URL Encode** determines whether the **Name** and **Value** of the parameter should be URL encoded or not. The default is **True**.

- **Value** is the actual parameter value which should be used during testing. Initially, it is set to the same value as the recorded value, but the user can change it. This property also has the flexibility to be bound to a different data source such as a Database or XML file or a CSV File. This is very useful in the case of testing for different sources of information and multiple test runs with different sets of data. The next section covers more on how to add the new data source and point to the fields.

In the following screenshot, the **Middle Name** field was not entered by the user before submitting the form, so it contains nothing. The tester can change the parameter value by selecting the form parameter property and changing the value field.

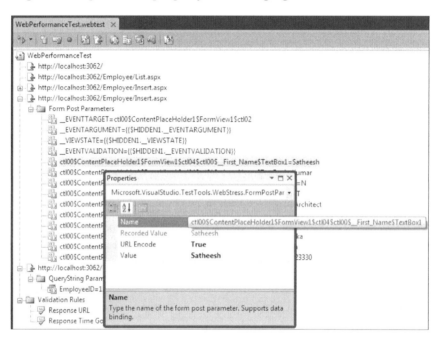

Sometimes, there are additional properties based on the type of control we use on the web page. In that case, we may have to set those properties as well. For example, if we use the **File Upload** control, we may have to set the type of file that can be uploaded.

QueryString parameters

This is very similar to **Form POST Parameters**. These query string parameters are listed under the request which uses the `QueryString` method for the request.

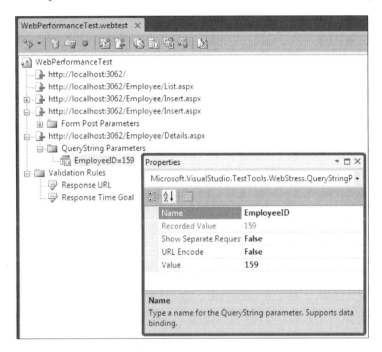

The properties and the usage of **QueryString Parameters** are the same as **Form Post Parameters** properties, except for an additional property which is **Show Separate Request Result**. This property is used for grouping the requests based on the value of this query string parameter. This is very useful when Load Testing for grouping a bunch of requests based on this field value. The default is **False**.

Extraction rules

Extraction rules are useful for extracting data or information from the HTTP response. Normally in any web application, the web forms are interdependent. This means that the request is based on the data collected from the previous request's response. Each request from the client in the web receives some kind of response from the server with the expected data within it. The data from the response has to be extracted and then passed on to the next request by passing the values using query strings or values persisted in the `ViewState` object, or using **Hidden** fields.

In previous examples, we used the new employee creation page where the user can enter details to create new employee details, or the user can select the employee from the list page and get the employee details displayed, or select the emergency contacts or absence details for the employee. In this case, once the user selects a particular employee from the list, we have to validate the user and pass on the user information to the next `absence.aspx` or `emergencycontacts.aspx` page where the absence details and emergency contact details are displayed.

This validated user information is hidden somewhere in the request using **ViewState** or **Hidden** fields. In this case, we can use the extraction rules to extract the user information and pass it on to the next request, or to further requests. We can extract the information and store it in the context parameter and use it globally across all requests following this.

Visual Studio 2010 provides several built-in types of extraction rules. This helps us to extract the values based on the HTML tags or different type of fields available in the web form. If we need additional extraction behavior, which is not supported by the existing one, then we can go for the custom rules. The following are the existing Extraction rule types.

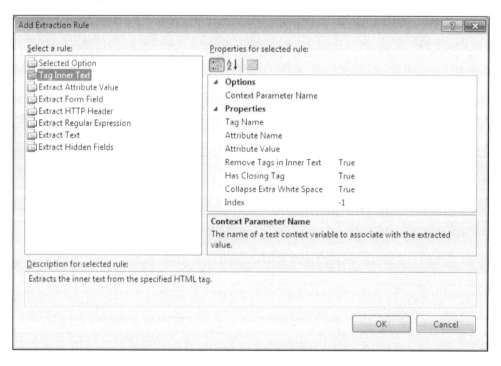

Rule Type	Description
Tag Inner Text	To extract the inner text from the specified HTML tag. We can use the attribute name and value parameters to find the exact match of the attribute and then find the inner text from the matching attribute.
Extract Attribute Value	This is to extract the attribute value from the request page based on the tag and the attribute name; we can also use the optional matching attribute name and value within the same tag to find out the required attribute easily; the extracted value will be stored in the context parameter
Extract Form Field	This is to extract the value from one of the Form fields in the response; the field name is identified here
Extract HTTP Header	This is to extract the HTTP message header value in the response page
Extract Regular Expression	This extracts the value using the regular expression to find the matching pattern in the response
Extract Text	This is to extract the text from the response page; the text is identified based on its starting and ending value with text **Casing** as optional
Extract Hidden Fields	This extracts all hidden field values from the response and assigns them to the context parameter

The screenshot below shows the sample image added to the employee maintenance web pages. The image source is highlighted in the following screenshot of the code:

```
<form id="form1" runat="server">
<h1 class="DDMainHeader"> 
    <img alt="Employee Details" class="style1" longdesc=""
        src="Images/Image1.gif" /> Employee Maintenance </h1>
<div class="DDNavigation">
    <a runat="server" href="~/"><img alt="Back to home page" r
</div>
```

Now let us add an extraction rule for the image that we have for the employee maintenance web pages. The following screenshot shows how to set the properties of the **Extraction Rules**. This extraction rule is created for a sample HTML image used on the page. The extraction rule type is an **Attribute Value** rule to find the image source URL used for the image.

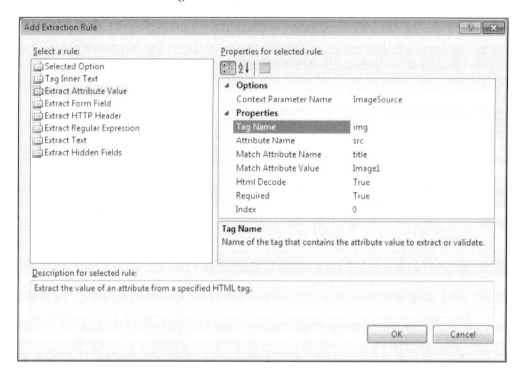

We can add as many rules as we want, but should make sure that the **Context Parameter Names** are unique across the application. It is like a global variable used in the application, which is referred to in all the forms.

By default, Visual Studio adds extraction rules for hidden fields automatically. The references to the hidden fields are also automatically added to the **Form POST Parameters** and **Query String Parameters**.

For coded Web Performance Tests we can create a custom extraction rule by deriving from the ExtractionRule class.

Validation rules

Every application has some sort of validation done on the input and output data, for example, a valid e-mail address, a valid username without any special characters, or a valid password which is not less than six letters. All these validations are performed using the validation rules against the fields as per expectation.

Validation rules are simply defining criteria which the information contained in the response has to pass through. All the data collected from the response is validated against the set of defined rules. If it passes it means that the response is validated, otherwise the test fails. For example, if the user has to enter a specific value or if the user has to select a value from a set of values then we can define these validations as rules and use them against the values returned in the response fields.

Visual Studio 2010 provides a set of predefined rules for validations. These rules are used for checking the text returned by the response.

To add the validation rules, just right-click on the request and select the **Add Validation Rule** option which opens the validation rules' dialog. Select the type of validation rule required and fill in the parameters required for the rule.

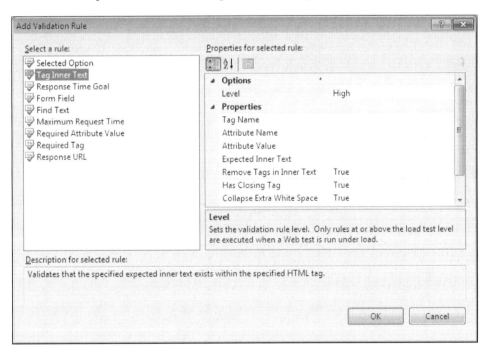

Validation Rule Type	Description
Selected Option	Validates that the specified option in the HTML 'select' tag is selected. The parameters are:
	Select Tag Name
	Expected Selected Option
	Index
	Ignore Case
Tag Inner Text	Validates if the specified expected inner text exists within the specified HTML tag
Response Time Goal	Validates if the response time for the request is less than or equal to the response time goal as specified on the request
Form Field	The existence of the form field name and value is verified using this; the parameters are:
	Form Field Name
	Expected Value
Find Text	This is to verify the existence of a specified text in the response; the parameters used for this are:
	Find Text
	Ignore Case
	Use Regular Expression
	Pass If Text Found
Maximum Request Time	This is to verify whether the request finishes within the specified maximum request Time
	Max Request Time (milliseconds)

Validation Rule Type	Description
Required Attribute Value	This is similar to the attribute used in the Extraction rules; in extraction rules we just extract the value of the specific attribute using the tag and the other attribute within the tag; but here in validation rules, we use the same tag to find out whether the attribute is returning the expected value; the parameters used here are the same as the ones used in extraction rules with an additional field to specify the expected value. The properties are:
	Tag Name
	Attribute Name
	Match Attribute Name
	Match Attribute Value
	Expected Value
	Ignore Case
	Index
	The index is used here to indicate which occurrence of the string to validate; if the index is set to **-1**, then it checks any form field value in the form and passes the test if any one match is found
Required Tag	To verify if the specified tag exists in the response; we can also set the minimum occurrence if there is a chance of getting the same tag many times in the response; the parameters are:
	Required Tag Name
	Minimum Occurrences
Response URL	This is to verify whether the URL is the same as the Expected URL; the property is the level for the response URL; the level can be High, Medium, or Low

We can keep adding as many number of validation rules as we want, but as the number grows, the performance or the time taken for the test will also grow. So we should decide which one is the most important for Load Testing. These rules will affect the time taken for the test.

In all the above rule types, we have a special parameter known as the **Level** that can be set to **Low**, **Medium**, or **High**. As mentioned earlier, the Load Test performance is affected directly by the number of validation rules we have. So to control the execution of rules in a request during the Load Test, we can use the Level property. The level does not mean the priority for the rule, but it defines when it should get executed based on the Load Test property. The Load Test also has properties of **Low, Medium**, or **High.**

Based on the following Load Test property, the rules with the corresponding levels will get run during the Load Test:

- **Low** — All validation rules with level **Low** will be run
- **Medium** — All validation rules with level **Low** and **Medium** will be run
- **High** — All validation rules with level **Low**, **Medium**, and **High** will be run

Based on the importance of the Load Test, we can set the properties of the rules.

We will see more details about this in the chapter which talks about Load Test

Transactions

Transactions are very useful when grouping a set of activities. In this case, we can group a set of requests so that we can track the total time taken for this set of requests for our analysis. This is also helpful in collecting the timing of the individual requests.

We simply need to state the starting request and the ending request for the transaction so that all the requests in between will be part of the transaction, including these two requests.

To add a transaction, select the starting request and right-click and choose the **Insert Transaction** option.

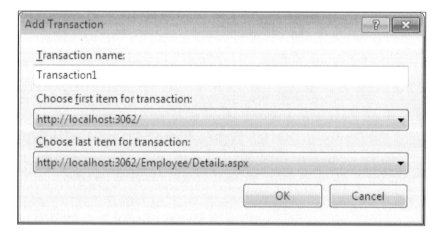

The Transaction dialog requires a name for the transaction and then the requests for the first item and the last item of the transaction. When you choose both and say **OK,** the transaction is added before the first item is selected for the transaction and all the other requests between the first and last item including the first and last are part of the transaction as shown here:

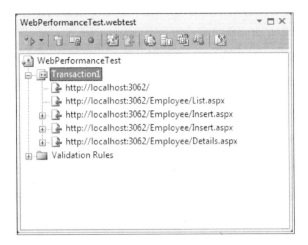

So when the test is run you can see the total time taken for all the requests under the transaction.

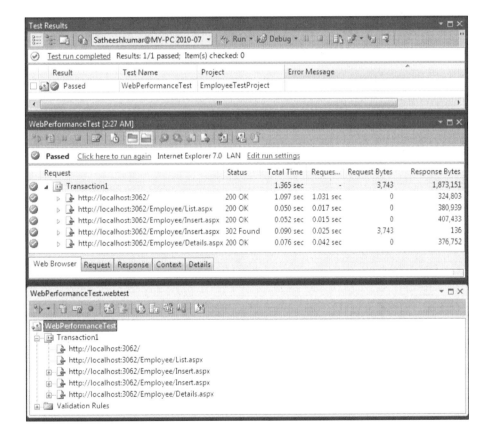

Toolbar properties

The web test editor has a toolbar to work on the Web Performance Tests. There are different options such as adding a data source, setting credentials, adding more requests recording, adding plug-ins to the test, generating code, parameterizing web servers, and creating the performance session for the test.

Add data source

We have seen the **Form POST parameters** and **QueryString parameters** and how to set the values of the parameters using the property. Now, each and every time we test the application, we have to change the property. In the case of load or web performance testing, it is difficult and time consuming to test for more users. To automate the process, we can directly link the parameters to the available data from a different data source.

Visual Studio supports different types of data sources such as CSV, SQL Server database, XML File, Access, Excel, and any other database using the OLE DB provider connection.

To add a new data source:

1. Select the **Add Data Source** button from the **Web Test** editor toolbar which opens the **New Test Data Source Wizard**.
2. Name the data source and select the type of data source (Database, CSV, XML File, and so on).
3. If you select the database, you can create a new connection using either OLE DB, ODBC, SQL Server, or the Oracle data provider. For our example here, select the CSV file as the data source and in the next screen select the CSV file from the file location.

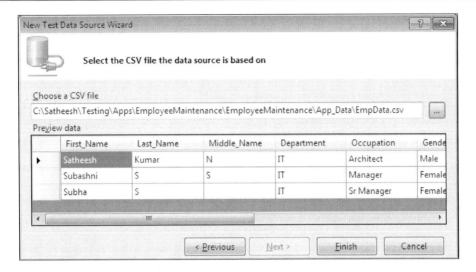

4. Once you select the file you can see the data in the Preview data grid.
5. Select **OK** to see the data source added to the test project.

You can add any number of data sources based on the requirement and on the sources of data we have for testing.

The following screenshot shows two data sources, **CSVFileDataSource** is for new user data and **XMLCountriesDataSource** is for the list of countries for the user.

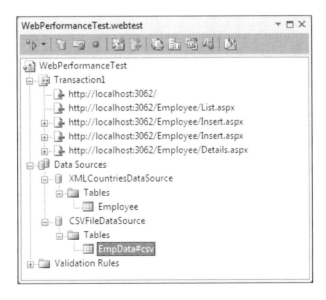

Once the data source is ready, we can change the source of the Form Post or QueryString properties. To do this, select the **Form Post Parameter** under the request, then right-click and choose **Properties**. In the **Value** property, select the data source and select the field from the data source.

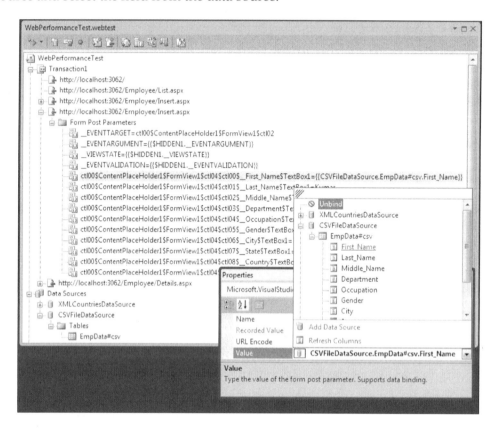

You can see the value assigned to the form post parameters. It is pointing to the field in the selected data source as in: **{{CSVFileDataSource.EmpData#csv.First_Name}}**

At runtime, this field is replaced with the exact value extracted from the CSV file and the test runs successfully.

Set credentials

This is useful for setting other user credentials to be used for the test instead of the current user credentials. You can apply this user credential to test the page, which uses basic authentication or integrated authentication. If we have multiple user credentials to be tested against this web page, and if the user credentials are stored somewhere, we can use this as a data source for credentials and bind the credentials field to these data source fields.

Credentials can be set using the option in the **Web Performance Test** editor toolbar. Click the **Set Credentials** option and enter the **User Name** and **Password** values. If you have the data source already, you can click on the **Bind...** option and choose the data source and the field for the multiple user credentials test for the test page.

Add recording

This option adds a new request recording to the existing test. Sometimes we may forget to browse certain web pages during the recording. So after recording is done, we can still add requests to the recording using this option. On clicking the option **Add Recording** in the **Web Performance Test** editor toolbar, you will see the recording window opened up for new recording. After completing the recording, this current recording will get added to the existing Web test recording. This is one of the ways to edit the recording. We can also delete a request from the existing recording and add a new one.

Parameterize web server

All Web Performance Tests are recorded and conducted using one web server. If we have to test the same test on another web server, we then have to re-record the testing on the new server and test again. But now Visual Studio provides a feature for parameterizing the web servers. It means that the web server to which all the Web Performance Test requests should point is identified at runtime using these parameters.

For example, this is required when performing the same kind of testing but with different hardware configurations. The requests in the Web Performance Test should point to different hardware every time the configuration is changed. The test scenario is the same in all these cases, but only the configuration changes based on the parameter values set at runtime. This is very useful when the application is tested for load testing, performance testing, and integration testing where only the configuration has changed.

To parameterize the web server in a Web Performance Test:

1. Select the **Parameterize Web Servers** option in the **Web Performance Test** editor toolbar, which opens the dialog that lists different web servers used by the Web Performance Test. The list contains the context parameter names and the web server URLs associated with the context parameter.

We can change the context parameter value to point to a different server by choosing the **Change...** option after selecting the context parameter name from the list. This opens the second dialog which helps us to change the name and the web server URL.

If you are planning to use the local ASP.NET development server, choose the second option, **Use ASP.NET Development Server**, and provide the local website path and the application root.

After changing the value for the new context parameter, close the **Parameterize Web Server** dialog box. Now we can see the context parameter added to the Web Performance Test under the **Context Parameters** folder. Also, we can see that the server addresses in all the request URLs of the Web Performance Tests are replaced with this new parameter, and the value is held by the context parameter.

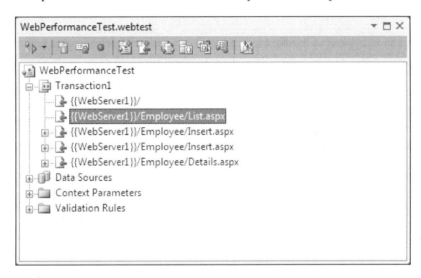

We can see that the context parameters are used in the requests within the brackets as in **{{WebServer1}}**, which is replaced by the actual value at runtime.

Context Parameters

There are different ways of creating Context Parameters:

- Context parameters can be created by right-clicking on the **Context Parameters** folder and selecting **Add Context Parameter**
- The plug-in can create the context parameter and assign the value in the event that runs before the Web Performance Test

For example, the following plug-in assembly code creates a new context parameter for the current window, **Country**, and adds the parameter to the Web Performance Test. The code also assigns the **Country** value to the existing **Form Post Parameter** field, **TextBoxCountry.**

```
// Sample plug-in assembly code to create new context parameter
```

```
public override void PreWebTest(object sender, PreWebTestEventArgs e)
{
  e.WebTest.Context["CountryParameter"] =
                          System.Environment.UserName.ToString();
  e.WebTest.Context["ctl00$ContentPlaceHolder1
     $FormView1$ctl04$ctl08$_Country$TextBox1"] =
                          e.WebTest.Context["CountryParameter"];
}
```

When the Web Performance Test is run, we can see the value assigned to the context parameter as well as the **Country Text Box** form post parameter.

We can also have the Context Parameter added to the Web Performance Test at design time and assign the value at runtime using the plug-in.

Add web test plug-in

Plug-ins are a set of external libraries or assemblies written for custom functionality which can run along with the Web Performance Test. Each plug-in runs once for every iteration of the test. For example, a currency converter could be an external service, which can be used as a plug-in to convert a currency value in the test.

To add a plug-in, we need to first create an assembly or a separate class library with a class containing the custom code. The class should inherit from **Microsoft. VisualStudio.TestTools.WebTesting.WebTestPlugin** and should implement the PreWebTest() and PostWebTest() methods. At least one of the following methods should be implemented:

- PreWebTest(): This code will run before the Web Performance Test starts execution
- PostWebTest(): This code will run after the Web Performance Testing is over

To get this namespace, we have to add the **Microsoft.VisualStudio.QualityTools. WebTestFramework** reference to the assembly. After completing the coding, add this assembly project reference to the Web Performance Test project. Then select the Web Performance Test and choose the **Add Web Test Plug-in** option from the toolbar, which will list the classes within the assembly. On selection, the class for the plug-in will get added to the test project.

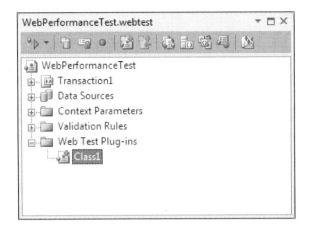

For example, if the class contains the following code, we can see the context variable with the value added to each request in the Web Performance Test. Create an assembly containing the class derived from `WebTestPlugin` and add the reference to this assembly in the test project.

```csharp
using System;
using System.Collections.Generic;
using System.Linq;
using System.Text;
using Microsoft.VisualStudio.TestTools.WebTesting;

namespace ClassLibrary1forPlugIn
{
  public class Class1 : WebTestPlugin
  {
    public override void PostWebTest(object sender,
                                        PostWebTestEventArgs e)
    {
    }
    public override void PreWebTest(object sender,
                                        PreWebTestEventArgs e)
    {
      e.WebTest.Context["TestParameter"] = "Test Value";
    }
  }
}
```

`e.WebTest.Context` contains the current context of the Web Performance Test. The `e` is the current object that fires the event. The parameters and properties for the current context can be accessed using the `e.WebTest.Context` object. Click on **Add Web Test Plug-in** in the Web Performance Test toolbar to open the dialog box that displays the available plug-ins.

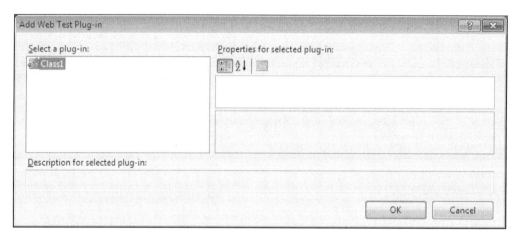

Now when the test is run, you can see the context variable added to each request's context.

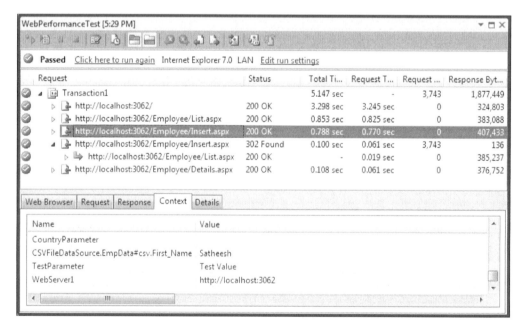

Add Request Plug-in

This is very similar to the Web Performance Test plug-in, but the only difference is that the plug-in code runs for every request in the Web Performance Test. This is the custom code written for complex functionality which should run before or after every request in the Web Performance Test.

The code assembly should reference the library, **Microsoft.VisualStudio. QualityTools.WebTestFramework**, and the class should inherit from **Microsoft. VisualStudio.TestTools.WebTesting.WebTestPlugin** and implement the `PreRequest()` or `PostRequest()` methods based on whether the code should execute before the request or after the request.

Performance session for the test

After running the test we will only see the success or failure result of the test, and the different parameter values handled in the test. To get the actual performance of the functions or method calls and the time taken for all the methods within the test, VSTS provides the option to create a performance session. This performance session uses the profiling tool that collects runtime performance data for the application.

Performance session reports various information such as method calls, memory allocations, and time spent in running the methods. To run the performance session:

1. Select the Web Performance Test and choose the option, **Create Performance Session for this Test**, which opens the **Performance Wizard**. The wizard provides four options for the session type:

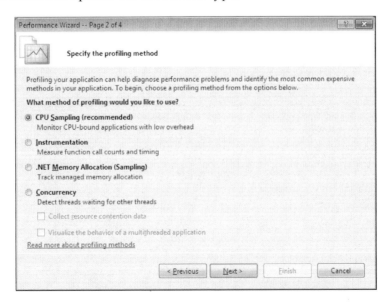

- ○ **CPU Sampling**: This technique collects information such as the CPU time taken for the methods. Moreover, the information is collected between specific time intervals. This is to identify the expensive method which takes the most CPU time to process the code.

- ○ **Instrumentation**: This technique is used in that case where more information is collected from the test and the external programs are called within the test. This method is used in the case of smaller tests, as the information collected is more than the sampling.

- ○ **.NET Memory Allocation (Sampling):** This technique collects information like type, size, and the number of objects created or destroyed. The total bytes allocated to the objects are also collected with this profiling

- ○ **Concurrency:** This technique is used for collecting information about multithreaded applications.

- ○ Resource contention occurs when threads are forced to wait until the shared resources are accessed by multiple threads. This option is used for reporting the total number of contentions and the total time spent waiting for the resource.

- ○ The concurrency visualizer provides general information about how the multi threaded application interacts with hardware, operating system, and other processes.

2. After selecting the required option, choose the current test application from the list.

Performance Explorer opens with the new performance session for the selected test. The explorer contains two folders, **Targets** and **Reports**. **Targets** is the applications under profiling. The **Report** folder contains the list of reports collected on every test run from the performance explorer.

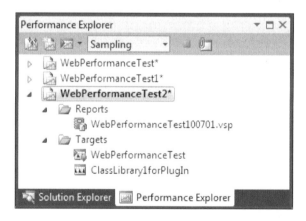

Now launch the test application from **Performance Explorer** using the options in the explorer. This starts the application at the same time the profiler starts, collecting the execution data from the running application. We need to enter the details and browse through the application UI so that the performance profiler will collect the details up until we finish working with the application. At the end of completing the application run, the profiler produces a report, with all the information collected, by grouping them based on the functionality, as shown below. This is the default summary view of the report that shows the hot path that takes most of the CPU time during the run and the functions that are performing most of the work.

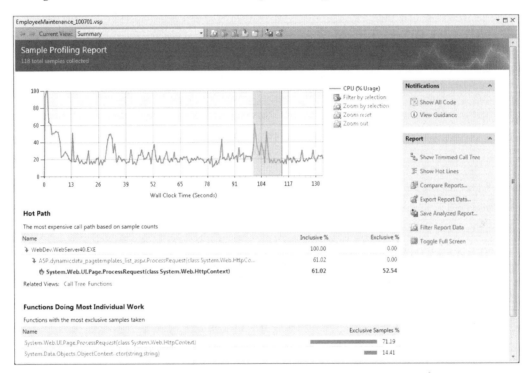

We can change the summary view to show different types of views like **Call tree**, **Modules**, **Functions**, **Processes** and so on, by selecting the different options given in the toolbar or using the link provided under the reports section in the summary view. The result can be exported for further analysis.

Performance Explorer also provides options to set or change different properties of the profiling. We can change the type of profiling and the data to be collected during data collection like clock cycles, page faults, system calls, and performance counters. We can also set properties for **CPU Counters**, **Windows Events**, and **Windows Counters**.

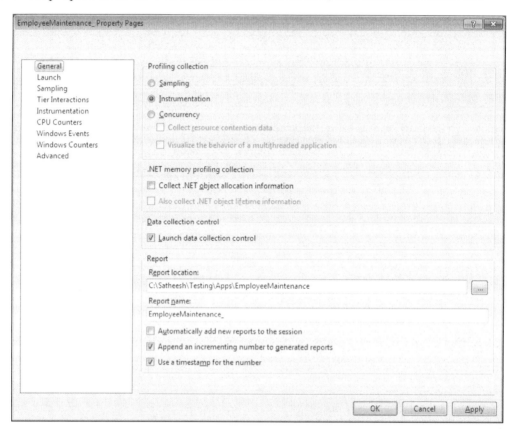

Debug/Running Web Performance Test

Once we finish recording the Web Performance Test, we can verify the test by running it once to make sure it is working fine without any errors. There are different configuration files such as .vsmdi, .testsettings that support the running and debugging of the Web Performance Test. These files are created automatically when we create a new test project.

Settings in the .testsettings file

Most of the assembly built in .NET holds a configuration file associated to it to hold the settings required for the application. Similarly, the test project creates two test settings files by default with the extension `.testsettings`. We can choose any of these settings based on the testing requirement:

- `Local.testsettings`: This runs the test locally without diagnostic data adapters

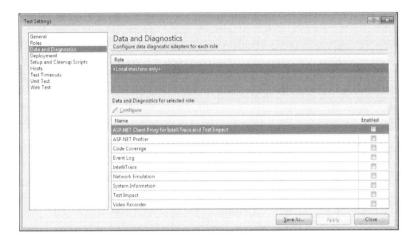

- `Traceandtestimpact.testsettings`: This runs the test locally with the diagnostic data adapters like IntelliTrace, test impact, system information to collect data from all modules, and processes.

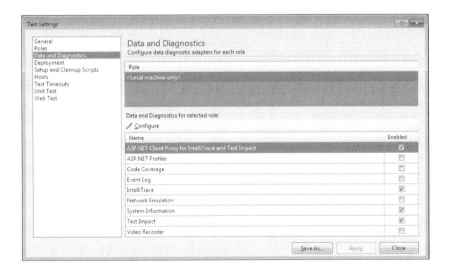

Select **IntelliTrace** from the **Data and Diagnostics for selected role** section and click on the **Configure** option to open the configuration page. We can modify the configuration data here for the IntelliTrace diagnostic data adapter.

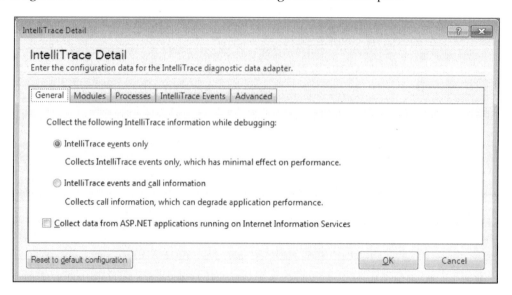

There are many other data adapters which can be used and configured. The following table shows the different data adapters:

Diagnostic data adapter	Description
ASP.NET Client Proxy for IntelliTrace and Test Impact	This data adapter allows us to collect information on the HTTP calls from the client to the server
IntelliTrace	This is used to collect specific diagnostic trace information in a trace file `.itrace`
ASP.NET Profiler	This is useful to collect performance data on the ASP.NET web application
Code Coverage	This is used to analyze how much of the code is covered by the test
Event Log	It is Useful to include the event log to log the information while testing
Network Emulation	These settings are useful to test the application under a particular network connection speed
System Information	This setting is useful to include the system information from the machine where the test is running. The system information would also be shown along with the test results.

Diagnostic data adapter	Description
Test Impact	This is useful to collect the method level information about which method code was used while testing. This can also be used to identify the tests which are affected by the code change.
Video Recorder	Video recorder settings are useful to record the session while automated testing is run. This helps to view user actions.

We can create our own test settings instead of the default and make them active for our automated tests. To create new test settings, select the solution from the solution explorer, right-click and select **Add New Item** to choose an item from the **Installed Templates**. There are three different categories of templates: **General**, **Performance**, and **Test Settings**. Choose the test settings from the category and select the test settings from the available templates.

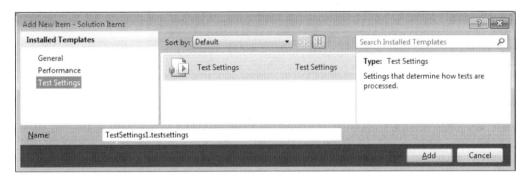

After adding the test settings, you can edit the configuration data required for testing. We may have multiple test settings created in the solution but at any point only one test setting can be active. To make the test setting the active setting, choose the **Test** menu option in Visual Studio and then select the test setting to make it active from the sub menu, **Select Active Test Setting**.

Select the active test setting and double-click to open the configuration details.

General

The **General** section contains the settings which are common to the tests they are similar to names and descriptions.

- **Name**: This is to specify a name for the configuration file.
- **Description**: This is a short description of the test configuration. In the case of maintaining multiple configuration files, we can use this field to briefly describe the changes from the previous settings.

- **Test run naming scheme**: When this test is run, the results are created and stored under a specific name in the application results folder. By default, the name is the current Windows user name followed by the @ symbol then the machine name and the current date and time. We can choose the next option, which is the user defined schema text. We can also choose to append the date-time stamp with the user-defined scheme.

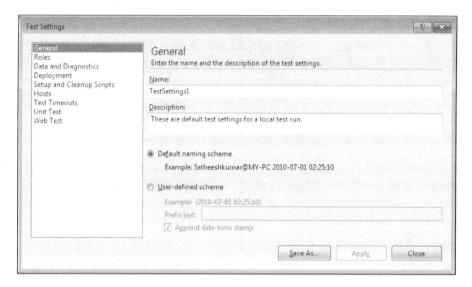

Web Performance Test

This section describes all the settings required for Web Performance Testing. These settings are applied only for Web Performance Testing. Some of the properties will be overridden when Load Testing:

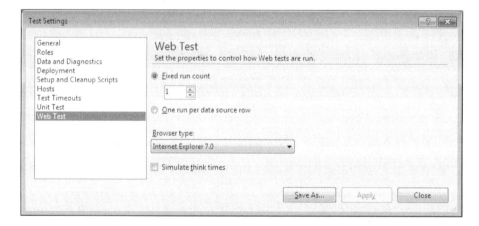

- **Number of Run Iterations**: This is to set the number of times the test has to run. There are two options for this: one is to set it to a specific number of times, which can be greater than 1. The second option is to set it to take the number of rows available in the data source associated to the Web Performance Test and run once per row. This property does not apply to Load Test as the Load Test is for the number of users and scenarios, not for iterations.

- **Browser type**: This property is to set the type of browser to use for requests. The drop-down list contains the list of different browser types to choose from. The following screenshot shows that list:

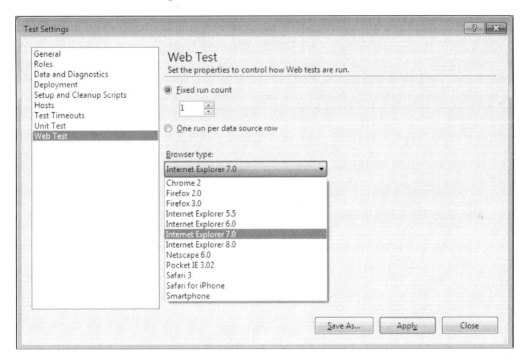

Roles

This page helps us to configure the execution and data collection location for the tests. There are three different methods of test execution.

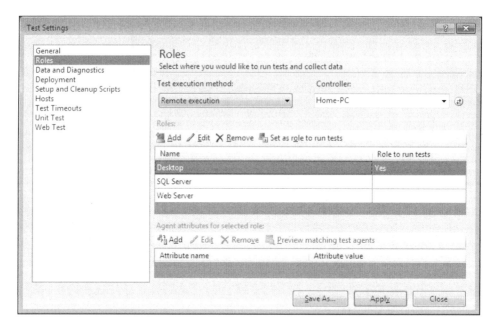

- **Local execution**: This is to run the test locally and collect the test execution data locally
- **Local Execution with remote collection**: This is to run the test locally and collect the data remotely
- **Remote execution**: This is to run the test remotely and collect the data remotely

For remote execution of the test, we need to select the controller for the test agent which will be used for testing the application remotely.

To add roles to run the test and collect the data, click on **Add** under the **Roles** toolbar and provide a name for the role. For example, **Web Server, SQL Server,** or **Desktop Client**. Select the role that you want to run the test on and then click on the option, **Set as role to run tests**. The other roles in the list will not run the test but will only be used for collecting the data.

To limit the agents that can be used for testing as a role, we can add attributes to filter the agents. Click on **Add** from the **Agent attributes for selected role** toolbar and then enter the attribute name and attribute value in the dialog box. We can keep adding any number of attributes.

Test Timeouts

Sometimes, the response for a request can take a very long time. The test application or the user in real time cannot wait that long to get the response. In this case, we can abort or mark the test as failed after waiting for a specified duration. The duration can be specified in seconds, minutes, or hours. If the execution of the test is not completed within the specified time, then the execution will be stopped and marked as aborted or failed or both based on the chosen option.

Deployment

Deployment settings specify or select the additional files or assemblies that go along with the test deployment. This is part of the configuration information for the test project. To add more files, open the test configuration file by double-clicking the file which opens in the configuration dialog. Select the additional files or folders using the **Add File** or **Add Directory** option in the dialog as shown in the following screenshot:

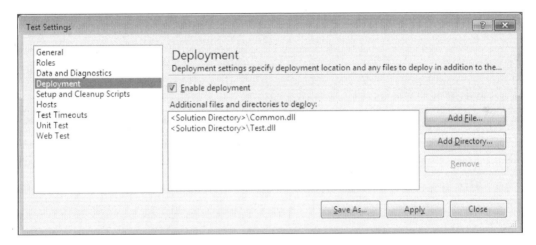

In the case of coded Web Performance Tests, the additional deployment items can be added using the `DeploymentItem` attribute. For example, the following code shows the deployment of the library files as part of deploying the test application:

```
[DeploymentItem("Test.dll")]
[DeploymentItem("Common.dll")]
public class WebTest11Coded : WebTest
{

}
```

Hosts

This specifies the default host for any test which cannot be hosted by the specified adapters. We can select either to run in the default host or not to run the test.

Setup and Cleanup scripts

This property is to specify the script files that can be used before and after the test. In some test scenarios, we might have to set the environment for the test using setup scripts while in some other cases, we might have to clean up the environment by cleaning the files created by the test or the updates made by the system. This section takes care of setting the scripts to be run. The following screenshot shows the script files that run before and after the test run. The `SetEnvironment.bat` file contains the script that takes care of setting the environment for the test. `CleanTestFolder.bat` is the file that contains the script which executes after the test completion to clean up the environment.

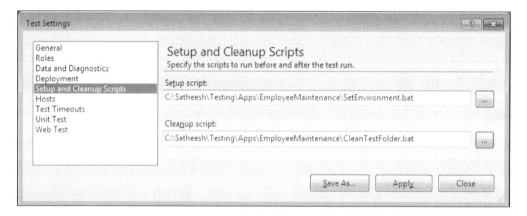

Running the test

Once we've created all the required settings and finished recording all the required requests, running the test is very easy. Before running it, we can also define the context parameters, extraction and validation rules, and add the data sources and bind the Form Post or QueryString parameters. Once we run the test, we need to verify all the results that we receive out of this test run. Use the **Run Test** option in the Web Performance Test editor toolbar to start running the test.

Now you can see the test execution and the progress of each request in the Web Performance Test window. After completing the execution, the result window displays success and failure information and marks against each request. If any one of the requests in the test fails, the entire test is marked as failed. Here, the test result window shows the end result of the testing:

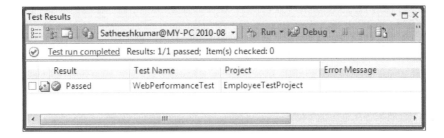

If there are multiple requests in the test, the test result details window shows the result for each request. It shows the status of the request as well as the details of the request, response, context, and the details of information gathered during the testing. These details are shown as a tabbed page with details as shown here:

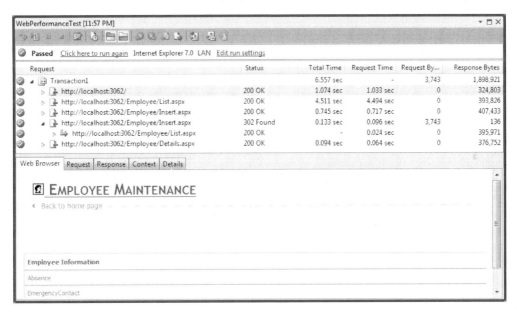

Web Browser

This is the same web page used by the request. This tab displays the entire web page used to get the view of the request.

Request

The **Request** tab contains all the information about the request such as Headers, Cookies, QueryString Parameters, Form Post Parameters. You can see the Form Post Parameters with the values assigned to them and sent to them with the request.

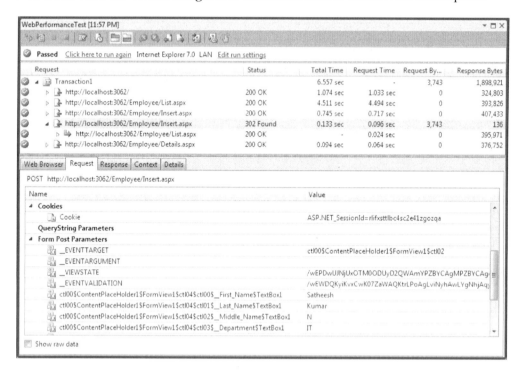

Response

This tab section shows the response for the requested web page. The result is shown as plain HTML text with the headers and body of the web response. There is also an option to view the response in an HTML editor.

Context

This section is very important as we have all the runtime details assigned to the test being captured here. Remember to add the data source in the **Add Data Source** section and to bind the Form Post Parameters to the data source fields. We added the CSV file and bound the parameters. All the values picked from the data source and the values assigned to the parameters are shown here. Also, the context parameters that we created before testing and the values assigned to the parameters during the runtime are also shown here. This is the place to visually verify all the values that are assigned to the context parameters and form fields.

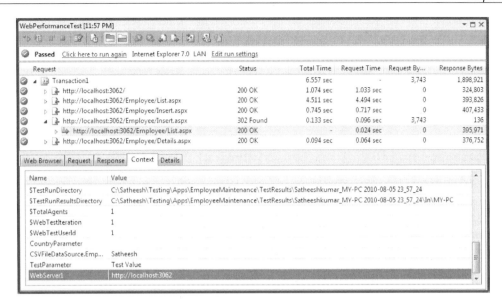

Details

The **Details** tab shows the status of the rules that were executed during the test. We can see from the following image that all the rules created as explained in the rules section got executed successfully. The details section also shows the type of the rule and the parameter values fetched during the execution of the rule.

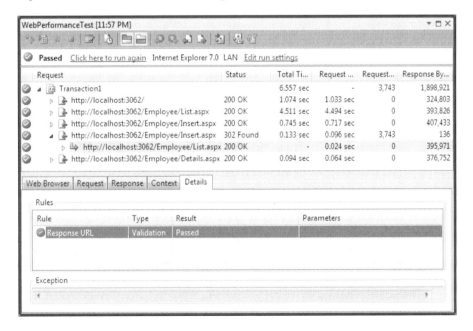

Below the toolbar in the Web Performance Test window we can see the option for running the test again. This is useful to re-run the same test and find if there are any changes to the source data or the configurations. There is another option to edit run settings. This option opens the same **Web Test Run Settings** window used by the configuration settings. This is another shortcut to change the Web Performance Test settings.

Summary

This chapter explained in detail how Web Performance Testing works, and how the recording of Web Performance Testing takes place for the web applications. We have gone through different properties of the Web Performance Tests including copying the tests, cleaning the unwanted recorded requests, and extracting the details from the request as to whether it has Form POST Parameters or QueryString Parameters. In this chapter, we also learned about setting the rules for validating details and extracting details based on different conditions. Transaction helps us to group a set of similar requests and give it a name, which we saw with an example. Many times during testing we may have to use dynamic data that we may not be aware of while recording or creating the test. We have learned how to include different data sources and map the fields to the data source fields and also parameterize fields and web server names.

At the end of this chapter, we learned how to execute the tests and collect the test results. There are some more advanced Web Performance Testing features using custom code in tests. This is covered in detail in the next chapter.

6
Advanced Web Testing

This chapter is the continuation of the previous chapter, which explained web testing. There is another way of performing web testing using Visual studio 2010. We have seen the recording of the testing scenario as explained in *Chapter 5*, *Web Performance Testing*, which explained web performance testing in detail. After the recording is completed, we can generate the code for the same tests using the **Generate Code** option in the **Web Performance Test** toolbar. Without using this option, we should be able to create the code by creating a new class file and using the namespace, `Microsoft.VisualStudio.TestTools.WebTesting`, which contains all the classes required for creating the web performance test. However it is too complex to create the test as compared to generating the code from the recording. Whether it is generated code or normal web testing using the user interface, the testing is the same. The only advantage is that we can customize the testing by using the .NET Framework language. This chapter concentrates on creating the code from the recorded test and customizing it. This chapter covers the overview on the following topics:

- Dynamic parameters in Web Performance Testing
- Creating the Web Performance Test by code in Visual Studio 2010.
- Debugging coded Web Performance Test
- Custom rules to be added to the Web Performance Test

Dynamic parameters in Web Performance Testing

Most web applications generate data dynamically and send it via the Query String Parameter or Form Post Parameter to subsequent requests. For example, the current user session ID, and connection string or parameter values to the called method are some of the dynamic data. Web Performance Test can identify and detect these dynamic parameters from the request response and then bind it to the other requests. This process is also known as **Promoting Dynamic Parameters**.

Dynamic parameters are automatically detected by Web Performance Test after the Web Performance Test recording is complete and stopped. Visual Studio Web Performance Testing keeps track of the requests and finds the hard coded values, which can be replaced by dynamic parameters. The advantage of using dynamic parameters is that we can pass different values to the parameter and verify the test. The other reason is to avoid playback failure. If we don't promote the dynamic parameters, the playback of the test may fail as the parameter values would still have the same values captured during the recording and the record would already exist in the system, or may not satisfy the current test condition.

Once Web Performance Test recording is complete, all query string values used in the web page during testing are hard-coded in the recording. So, if the values that are hard-coded are not valid during the playback of the test, then the test will fail. So the Visual Studio Web Performance Test provides the feature to extract new values from the request and use these in the dependent requests. This is the same extraction rule we saw in *Chapter 5*. But in this case, it is automatically added by the Web Performance Test. At the same time, the parameters are also added to the subsequent request.

For example, the following screenshot shows the recording of the web site, which has obtained the links to the absence and emergency contacts page by passing the query strings, and the session ID that keeps changing every time the test is run.

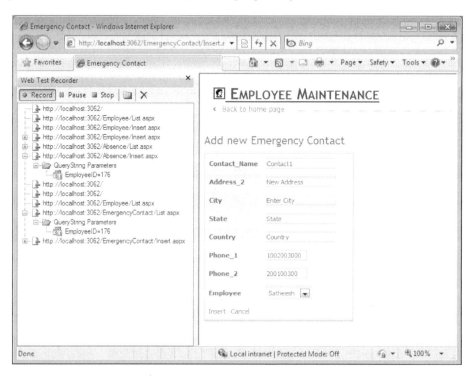

When the recording is stopped, we can see the dialog saying **Detecting dynamic parameters....** During this time, all the values that can be changed to a Web Performance Test parameter are detected and listed on the next screen.

Visual Studio lists the parameters that can be promoted to Web Performance Test parameters from normal hard-coded values and gives the choice to the tester who is recording the test. Either we can choose **OK** to promote the parameters, or we can **Cancel** the suggestion and keep it hard-coded. But if we leave the parameters as they are, the next playback of the test might fail because of the hard-coded value which may not be valid.

Visual Studio also provides the option for detecting dynamic parameters outside of the recording. It means that we can find the parameters, which can be promoted to Web Performance Test parameters after completing the recording of the test. The Web Performance Test toolbar also has this option to find out the dynamic parameters.

Now let's add an extraction rule to the web request to find the EmployeeID passed on to the request from the previous page. Before adding the rule, we need to check the format of the Employee ID which passed on the request so that we can set the extraction rule according to that. Select the **Request** from the Web Performance Test result details pages and check the **Response** tab and search for EmployeeID.

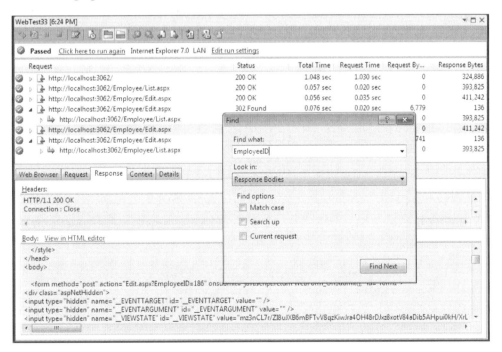

The query string **EmployeeID** will be highlighted where it contains value 186 as per the preceding image. Now let's add an extraction rule to find the value passed for **EmployeeID** and name the new parameter as `ExtractID`.

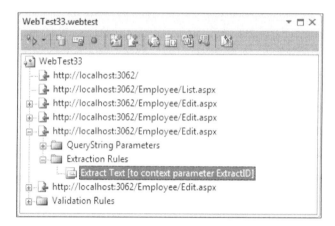

The extraction rule added to the recorded web request extracts the text value from the query string and assigns it to the parameter.

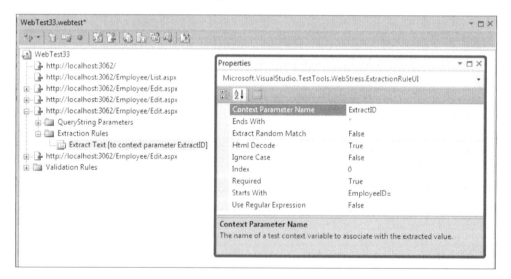

After saving the request, when the recorded test is run again, the test result details will show the value extracted for the new context variable **ExtractID** which is shown under the **Context** tab as shown in the following screenshot:

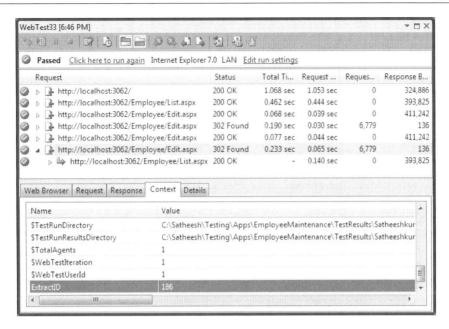

Coded Web Performance Test

All the examples in the preceding sections explain different features which are applicable to the recorded Web Performance Test. Creating the same Web Performance Test is also possible using code in Visual Studio 2010. The recorded Web Performance Test is simple, but the coded Web Performance Test gives more flexibility. The coded Web Performance Test generates the sequence of Web Performance Test requests and the main advantage is that we can add more complex features such as looping, adding more requests, or any additional logic to the test using the .NET programming languages C# and Visual Basic.

The recorded Web Performance Test can be converted to coded Web Performance Test as it is always better to record the Web Performance Test and then create the code out of it, for example, defining the data sources, extraction rules, validation rules, and binding the form post fields to the data source before creating the coded test. This is because we can let the tool generate the coding for all these tasks so that our job will be easier. We can concentrate only on customizing the generated code with additional features.

The other advantage in coded test is the full control of the test execution. It's just a class file, which is created in the language of our choice. Once the class is created we can include the required functionality and methods, whether it is a `for` loop or a different method call. We can also copy the requests and include them as many times as we want.

Creating a coded test from a recorded test

The recorded Web Performance Test is very easy to create as there is no coding involved in it. The WebTest editor provides features to create the code out of a recorded Web Performance Test. Select the recorded Web Performance Test which you want to convert and then select the option **Generate Code** from the editor toolbar which opens a dialog asking for the name for the coded Web Performance Test.

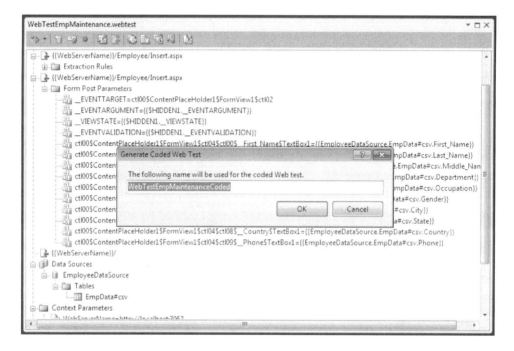

Now you can see the new code file created with the name given. The code file contains the code for the whole of the web performance test. The following is a part of the code from the generated file:

```
WebTestEmpMaintenanceCoded.cs*                                                    ▾ ☐ ×
⬚$ EmployeeTestProject.WebTestEmpMaintenanceCoded          ▾ ⬚ testPlugin0              ▾
  ⊟namespace EmployeeTestProject
   {
  ⊞    using System;
       using System.Collections.Generic;
       using System.Text;
       using Microsoft.VisualStudio.TestTools.WebTesting;
       using Microsoft.VisualStudio.TestTools.WebTesting.Rules;
       using ClassLibrary1forPlugIn;

       [DeploymentItem("employeetestproject\\EmpData.csv", "employeetestproject")]
       [DataSource("EmployeeDataSource", "Microsoft.VisualStudio.TestTools.DataSource.CSV", "|DataDirectory|\\employeetestproject\\EmpData.csv", …
       [DataBinding("EmployeeDataSource", "EmpData#csv", "First_Name", "EmployeeDataSource.EmpData#csv.First_Name")]
       [DataBinding("EmployeeDataSource", "EmpData#csv", "Last_Name", "EmployeeDataSource.EmpData#csv.Last_Name")]
       [DataBinding("EmployeeDataSource", "EmpData#csv", "Middle_Name", "EmployeeDataSource.EmpData#csv.Middle_Name")]
       [DataBinding("EmployeeDataSource", "EmpData#csv", "Department", "EmployeeDataSource.EmpData#csv.Department")]
       [DataBinding("EmployeeDataSource", "EmpData#csv", "Occupation", "EmployeeDataSource.EmpData#csv.Occupation")]
       [DataBinding("EmployeeDataSource", "EmpData#csv", "Gender", "EmployeeDataSource.EmpData#csv.Gender")]
       [DataBinding("EmployeeDataSource", "EmpData#csv", "City", "EmployeeDataSource.EmpData#csv.City")]
       [DataBinding("EmployeeDataSource", "EmpData#csv", "State", "EmployeeDataSource.EmpData#csv.State")]
       [DataBinding("EmployeeDataSource", "EmpData#csv", "Country", "EmployeeDataSource.EmpData#csv.Country")]
       [DataBinding("EmployeeDataSource", "EmpData#csv", "Phone", "EmployeeDataSource.EmpData#csv.Phone")]
  ⊟    public class WebTestEmpMaintenanceCoded : WebTest
       {
           private Class1 testPlugin0 = new Class1();

           public WebTestEmpMaintenanceCoded()
  ⊟        {
               this.Context.Add("WebServerName", "http://localhost:3062");
               this.PreAuthenticate = true;
               this.PreWebTest += new EventHandler<PreWebTestEventArgs>(this.testPlugin0.PreWebTest);
               this.PostWebTest += new EventHandler<PostWebTestEventArgs>(this.testPlugin0.PostWebTest);
               this.PreTransaction += new EventHandler<PreTransactionEventArgs>(this.testPlugin0.PreTransaction);
               this.PostTransaction += new EventHandler<PostTransactionEventArgs>(this.testPlugin0.PostTransaction);
               this.PrePage += new EventHandler<PrePageEventArgs>(this.testPlugin0.PrePage);
               this.PostPage += new EventHandler<PostPageEventArgs>(this.testPlugin0.PostPage);
           }

  ⊟        public override IEnumerator<WebTestRequest> GetRequestEnumerator()
100 % ▾ ◂                           ⫶⫶⫶                                          ▸
```

The code in the preceding screenshot uses the following namespaces, which contain the classes required for Web Performance Testing: **using Microsoft.VisualStudio. TestTools.WebTesting** and **using Microsoft.VisualStudio.TestTools.WebTesting. Rules**.

You can see the first section of the code that contains all the deployment and the data source information. This is the same information we added to the Web Performance Test using the WebTest editor. It defines the parameters for each field in the data source. The following are some of the attributes and classes that you can find in the generated code:

- `DeploymentItem`: Specifies whether the additional files should be deployed as part of the deployment. In the preceding example, there are two additional libraries, `Test.dll` and `ClassLibrary1.dll`, added as deployment items.

    ```
    [DeploymentItem("Test.dll")]
    [DeploymentItem("ClassLibrary1.dll")]
    ```

- `DataSource`: This attribute specifies if any data file or database is added as the source for dynamic data. The source can be CSV, XML, or any other database. The attribute contains the data source name, the connection string to access the data source, the location, the mode for accessing the data such as `Sequential`, `Random`, or `Unique`, and the table name to access from the source. In the case of Excel, each spreadsheet can represent a table. For example, the following code shows the data source attribute for a CSV file:

```
[DataSource("EmployeeDataSource", "Microsoft.VisualStudio.
TestTools.DataSource.CSV", "|DataDirectory|\\
employeetestproject\\EmpData.csv", Microsoft.VisualStudio.
TestTools.WebTesting.DataBindingAccessMethod.
Sequential, Microsoft.VisualStudio.TestTools.WebTesting.
DataBindingSelectColumns.SelectOnlyBoundColumns, "EmpData#csv")]
```

- `DataBinding`: This attribute denotes the fields in the data source. We can provide custom names for the fields by changing their names. For example, the following code denotes three fields, `First_Name`, `Last_Name`, and `Middle_Name`, in the above data source. The attribute contains the data source name, the table name to refer to within the source, a custom name for the field within the table, and the actual field name in the data source table.

```
[DataBinding("EmployeeDataSource", "EmpData#csv", "First_Name",
            "EmployeeDataSource.EmpData#csv.First_Name")]
[DataBinding("EmployeeDataSource", "EmpData#csv", "Last_Name",
            "EmployeeDataSource.EmpData#csv.Last_Name")]
[DataBinding("EmployeeDataSource", "EmpData#csv", "Middle_Name",
            "EmployeeDataSource.EmpData#csv.Middle_Name")]
```

- `WebTest`: This is the base class for all the Web Performance Tests. Coded Web Performance Tests are directly derived from this base class. In the example, the class `WebTestEmpMaintenanceCoded` is derived from this `WebTest` class.

- `Web Test Constructor`: The constructor is for initializing the new instance of the class. The constructor has the context variables for the test, for example the `WebServerName`. This is the main context variable which is used by all the requests within the test and replaced by the actual value during the test run. The next thing is to set the credentials for the Web Performance Test to run. We can leave them as preauthenticated or set the credentials, if the Test has to run with different credentials. All the global declaration with respect to the Web Performance Test is done at the constructor level.

- **Pre and post events for web test and requests**: The next are the `PreWebTest` and `PostWebTest` events to the test. The `PreWebTest` and `PostWebTest` events occur before and after the test. These events are mainly used for setting the environment for the test before the test run and cleaning the environment after the test is completed.

```
this.PreWebTest += new
EventHandler<PreWebTestEventArgs>(this.testPlugin0.PreWebTest);
this.PostWebTest += new
EventHandler<PostWebTestEventArgs>(this.testPlugin0.
PostWebTest);
```

- **Pre and post events for web Transactions**: The `PreTransaction` and `PostTransaction` are the `WebTestPlugin` methods which handle the events before and after the Transactions associated to the current web performance test. The `PreTransaction` callback is called just before starting the transaction in the web performance test and the `PostTransaction` callback is called just after the Transaction is complete in the Test.

  ```
  this.PreTransaction += new EventHandler<PreTransactionEventArgs
  >(this.testPlugin0.PreTransaction);
  this.PostTransaction += new EventHandler<PostTransactionEventAr
  gs>(this.testPlugin0.PostTransaction);
  ```

- **Pre and post events for Page**: `PrePage` and `PostPage` are the `WebtestPlugin` methods which handle the events before starting the web page and just after completing the page.

  ```
  this.PrePage += new EventHandler<PrePageEventArgs>(this.
  testPlugin0.PrePage);
  this.PostPage += new EventHandler<PostPageEventArgs>(this.
  testPlugin0.PostPage);
  ```

- **Pre and post Request**: `PreRequest` and `PostRequest` are the `WebtestPlugin` methods which handle the events before starting the HTTP request and after completing the HTTP request. Because these events have to fire for every request in the Web Performance Test, these methods are called from the `GetRequestEnumerator` method.

  ```
  this.PreRequest += new EventHandler<PreRequestEventArgs>(this.
  testPlugin0.PreRequest);
  this.PostRequest += new EventHandler<PostRequestEventArgs>(th
  is.testPlugin0.PostRequest);
  ```

- **Pre Request Data Binding**: `PreRequestDataBinding` is the `WebtestPlugin` method which is called just before the data binding call.

- `PreWebTest`, `PostWebTest`, `PreTransaction`, `PostTransaction`, `PrePage`, `PostPage`, `PreRequest`, `PostRequest`, and `PreRequestDataBinding` are just virtual methods. We can decide whether to implement them or not. If not implemented, the base class method is called.

The following screenshot shows all the derived methods in the `WebTestPlugin` class where the methods can be overridden:

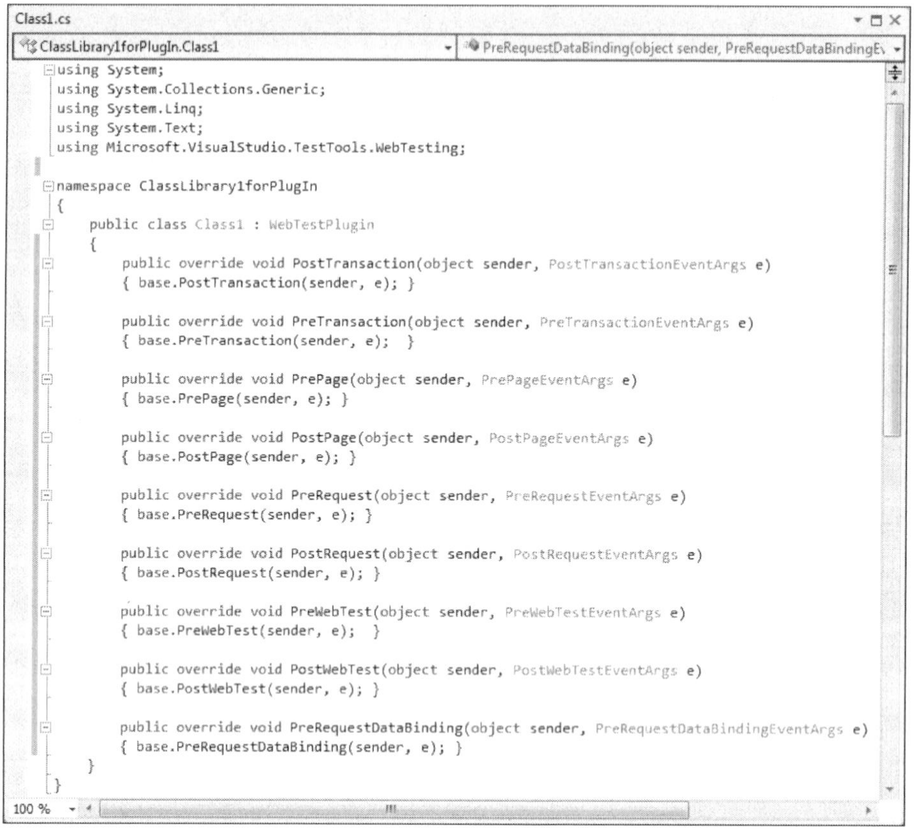


```
using System;
using System.Collections.Generic;
using System.Linq;
using System.Text;
using Microsoft.VisualStudio.TestTools.WebTesting;

namespace ClassLibrary1forPlugIn
{
    public class Class1 : WebTestPlugin
    {
        public override void PostTransaction(object sender, PostTransactionEventArgs e)
        { base.PostTransaction(sender, e); }

        public override void PreTransaction(object sender, PreTransactionEventArgs e)
        { base.PreTransaction(sender, e);  }

        public override void PrePage(object sender, PrePageEventArgs e)
        { base.PrePage(sender, e); }

        public override void PostPage(object sender, PostPageEventArgs e)
        { base.PostPage(sender, e); }

        public override void PreRequest(object sender, PreRequestEventArgs e)
        { base.PreRequest(sender, e); }

        public override void PostRequest(object sender, PostRequestEventArgs e)
        { base.PostRequest(sender, e); }

        public override void PreWebTest(object sender, PreWebTestEventArgs e)
        { base.PreWebTest(sender, e);  }

        public override void PostWebTest(object sender, PostWebTestEventArgs e)
        { base.PostWebTest(sender, e); }

        public override void PreRequestDataBinding(object sender, PreRequestDataBindingEventArgs e)
        { base.PreRequestDataBinding(sender, e); }
    }
}
```

The next part of the code is for defining the request, extraction rules, validation rules, and the Form Post or the Query String Parameters. These parameter values are set with values retrieved from the parameters bonded with the data source fields. A part of the code looks like this:

```
WebTestRequest request4 = new
            WebTestRequest((this.Context["WebServerName"].
                  ToString() + "/Employee/Insert.aspx"));
request4.ThinkTime = 219;
request4.Method = "POST";
request4.ExpectedResponseUrl =
  (this.Context["WebServerName"].ToString() + "/Employee/List.
   aspx");
```

```
FormPostHttpBody request4Body = new FormPostHttpBody();
request4Body.FormPostParameters.Add("__EVENTTARGET",
        "ctl00$ContentPlaceHolder1$FormView1$ctl02");
request4Body.FormPostParameters.Add("__EVENTARGUMENT",
        this.Context["$HIDDEN1.__EVENTARGUMENT"].ToString());
request4Body.FormPostParameters.Add("__VIEWSTATE",
        this.Context["$HIDDEN1.__VIEWSTATE"].ToString());
request4Body.FormPostParameters.Add("__EVENTVALIDATION",
        this.Context["$HIDDEN1.__EVENTVALIDATION"].ToString());
request4Body.FormPostParameters.Add("ctl00$ContentPlaceHo
lder1$FormView1$ctl04$ctl00$__First_Name$TextBox1", this.
Context["EmployeeDataSource.EmpData#csv.First_Name"].ToString());
request4Body.FormPostParameters.Add("ctl00$ContentPlaceHo
lder1$FormView1$ctl04$ctl01$__Last_Name$TextBox1", this.
Context["EmployeeDataSource.EmpData#csv.Last_Name"].ToString());
```

The first line in the preceding code defines the request and the rest of the code is assigning the values to the Form Post Parameters.

The coded Web Performance Test provides all the properties of the Web Performance Test and requests in the Web Performance Test, which can be used to customize and add more functionality to the test.

Transactions in coded test

In Web Performance Test recording, we have seen inserting transactions to the set of requests for tracking the time taken by all requests within the transactions. The same thing can be done using the code by using the transaction method in the web test. Transaction is the logical grouping of multiple requests in a Web Performance Test. This is like a timer, which collects the start and end time of the group requests under the transaction. Given here is the code, which begins the transaction, requests for two web pages, and then ends the transaction:

```
this.BeginTransaction("FirstTransaction");
WebTestRequest request2 = new
            WebTestRequest((this.Context["WebServerName"].ToString()
                    + "/Employee/List.aspx"));
request2.ThinkTime = 4;
yield return request2;
request2 = null;
WebTestRequest request3 = new
        WebTestRequest((this.Context["WebServerName"].ToString() +
                "/Employee/Insert.aspx"));
```

```
request3.ThinkTime = 35;
ExtractHiddenFields extractionRule1 = new ExtractHiddenFields();
extractionRule1.Required = true;
extractionRule1.HtmlDecode = true;
extractionRule1.ContextParameterName = "1";
request3.ExtractValues += new
            EventHandler<ExtractionEventArgs>(extractionRule1.Extract);
yield return request3;
request3 = null;
this.EndTransaction("FirstTransaction");
```

Custom code

The main advantage of coded Web Performance Test is customizing the code that is generated or creating a new deriving class from the `WebTest` base class and adding additional functionality. For example, the following code checks if the value of the context parameter `AddTestRequest` is yes, and adds a new Web Performance Test request with think time and request method to the Web Performance Test.

```
if (this.Context["AddAbsenceforEmployee"].ToString() == "Yes")
{
  WebTestRequest request6 = new
              WebTestRequest((this.Context["WebServerName"].ToString()
                      + "/Absence/Insert.aspx"));
request6.ThinkTime = 4;
yield return request6;
request6 = null;
}
```

Adding comment

This class is used for adding comments to the Web Performance Test. The code given here is an example which adds a comment to the test result from the Web Performance Test code:

```
this.AddCommentToResult("Test custom comment added to the Web Test
through code");
```

Running the Coded Web Performance Test

We have created the simple code for the Web Performance Test. Running or executing the code is very simple. This is not the same as running the other projects. We need to open the **Test View** or **Test List Editor** window using the **Test** and **Windows** option in the main menu. **Test View** lists all the tests in the current project including the coded Web Performance Test.

From the list of tests, select the coded test and, right-click and choose the **Run Selection** option which starts running the coded Web Performance Test.

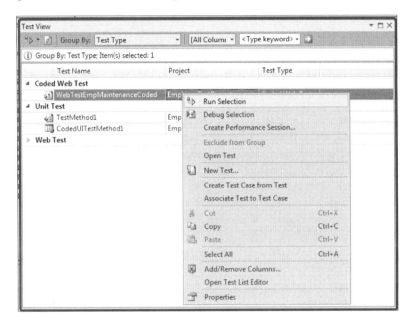

The result of the Web Performance Test is shown in the **Test Results** window, similar to that shown by the recorded Web Performance Test. It shows the status of the test, whether it has successfully passed or failed, or has some errors.

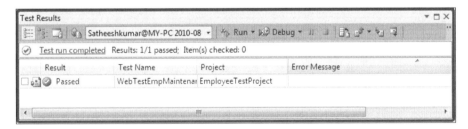

To see the details of the test result, select the result from the **Test Result** window, right-click and choose **View Test Result Details**, which opens a window depicting the details about the web code test. This is the same result details window that we saw for the recorded test.

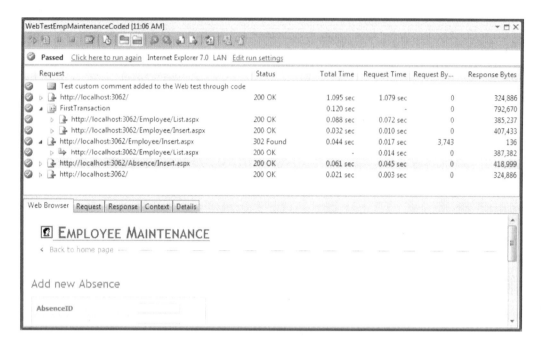

The result details window shows the result of each request in the Web Performance Test. It also shows the information about the request, response, context parameters, and the rule execution details for each request. You can see that the selected request in the result window is the last request added to the Web Performance Test through the additional code mentioned previously. You can also see the additional comment added to the web test through the code. The comment is shown at the top of the test results.

As the code is the normal C# code and the entire Web Performance Test is a class file, we can debug the code as we would for the normal assemblies created in Visual Studio. This is very helpful in getting the runtime information of the Web Performance Test, requests, and the context information from the Web Performance Test.

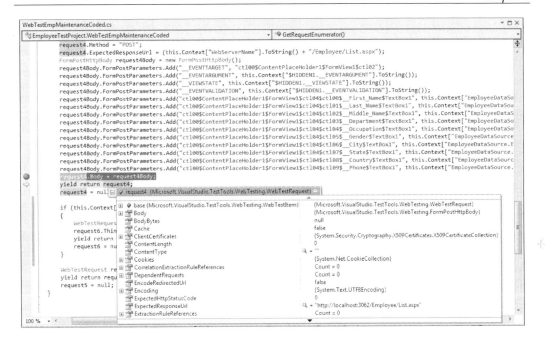

Debugging the Coded Web Performance Test

Web Performance Testing is an integrated tool in Visual Studio, and the Web Performance Test can be coded using the .NET languages and we can debug the code while running the application during the application development. The creation of a Web Performance Test is similar to developing another application, and we may have to debug sometimes when we want to find out the runtime behavior so that we can fix the issue easily. To do this, Visual Studio provides a debugging facility for the code.

Select the Web Performance Test from the **Test View** or **Test List Editor** and double-click to open the Web Performance Test code. Scroll to the method and the line to include a break point for the Web Performance Test execution. Right-click on the line and select the option in the context menu to insert a new breakpoint. Continue doing this at all the places where breakpoints are required.

For example, the following screenshot shows the Web Performance Test with a couple of breakpoints at different locations. Select **Test** from the **Test View** or **Test List Editor** and right-click to choose the option to debug the selection. This option actually runs the Web Performance Test but breaks at the point where we have breakpoints.

```
WebTestRequest request2 = new WebTestRequest((this.Context["WebServerName"].ToString() + "/Employee/List.aspx"));
request2.ThinkTime = 4;
yield return request2;
request2 = null;
     [+] ✓ request2 (Microsoft.VisualStudio.TestTools.WebTesting.WebTestRequest)
WebTestRequest request3 = new WebTestRequest((this.Context["WebServerName"].ToString() + "/Employee/Insert.aspx"));
request3.ThinkTime = 35;
ExtractHiddenFields extractionRule1 = new ExtractHiddenFields();
extractionRule1.Required = true;
extractionRule1.HtmlDecode = true;
extractionRule1.ContextParameterName = "1";
request3.ExtractValues += new EventHandler<ExtractionEventArgs>(extractionRule1.Extract);
yield return request3;
request3 = null;
```

We can step through the code and find out the values for the context variables and the object properties. Different options are provided under the **Debug** menu option.

Now let us step through the code and see some of the object properties and attributes while debugging the code. The following screenshot depicts the debug information for the context variables set at the end of the constructor code. It shows the values of the context variables added to the context and the other properties set for the context.

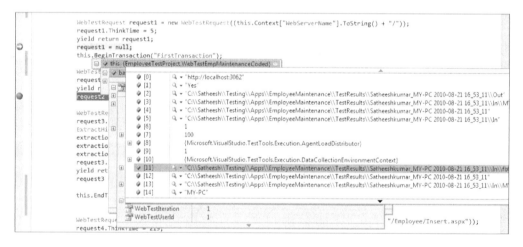

Similarly, we can step through the code line-by-line and find out if the current values depict the status of the objects and the properties. The following is another example of the **PostWebTest** event that refers to the methods in the plug-in `ClassLibrary1forPlugIn`.

```
public class WebTestEmpMaintenanceCoded : WebTest
{

    private Class1 testPlugin0 = new Class1();

    public WebTestEmpMaintenanceCoded()
    {
        this.Context.Add("WebServerName", "http://localhost:3062");
        this.Context.Add("AddAbsenceforEmployee", "Yes");

        this.PreAuthenticate = true;
        this.PreWebTest += new EventHandler<PreWebTestEventArgs>(this.testPlugin0.PreWebTest);
        this.PostWebTest += new EventHandler<PostWebTestEventArgs>(this.testPlugin0.PostWebTest);
        this.Pre  ✓ this.PostWebTest {Method = {Void PostWebTest(System.Object, Microsoft.VisualStudio.TestTools.WebTesting.PostWebTestEventArgs)}}
        this.Post ✓ base {System.MulticastDelegate} {Method = {Void PostWebTest(System.Object, Microsoft.VisualStudio.TestTools.WebTesting.PostWebTestEventArgs)}}
        this.PrePage ✓ base {System.Delegate} {Method = {Void PostWebTest(System.Object, Microsoft.VisualStudio.TestTools.WebTesting.PostWebTestEventArgs)}}
        this.PostPage ⊞ 🔧 Method        {Void PostWebTest(System.Object, Microsoft.VisualStudio.TestTools.WebTesting.PostWebTestEventArgs)}
    }                  ⊞ 🔧 Target        {ClassLibrary1forPlugin.Class1}
                       ⊞ 🔧 Non-Public members
    public override IEnumerable<WebTestRequest> GetRequestEnumerator()
    {
        // Initialize validation rules that apply to all requests in the WebTest
        if ((this.Context.ValidationLevel >= Microsoft.VisualStudio.TestTools.WebTesting.ValidationLevel.Low))
        {
```

Custom rules

When we generate the code for the recorded Web Performance Test, Visual Studio creates the code for the rules that we added for the recorded test. However if we need more custom rules to be added to the Web Performance Test, we can use the `Microsoft.VisualStudio.TestTools.WebTesting` namespace and create a new rule class which derives from the base class. This new class can be part of the managed class library which can be a plug-in. This can be an extraction rule or a validation rule.

Extraction rule

The extraction rules are used for extracting data from the responses received for the web requests. Data can be extracted from text fields, headers, form fields, attributes, or hidden fields. The new custom extraction rule is a new class file derived from the base class `ExtractionRule`, which is in the namespace `Microsoft.VisualStudio.TestTools.WebTesting`. Add a reference to the library, `Microsoft.VisualStudio.QualityTools.WebTestFramework`, which contains the base classes. In the new class, implement the **RuleName**, **RuleDescripton**, and **Extract** methods and build the custom rule as per requirements.

For example, the following screenshot shows a **CustomExtractionRule** for extracting the **Query String Parameter** value from the request:

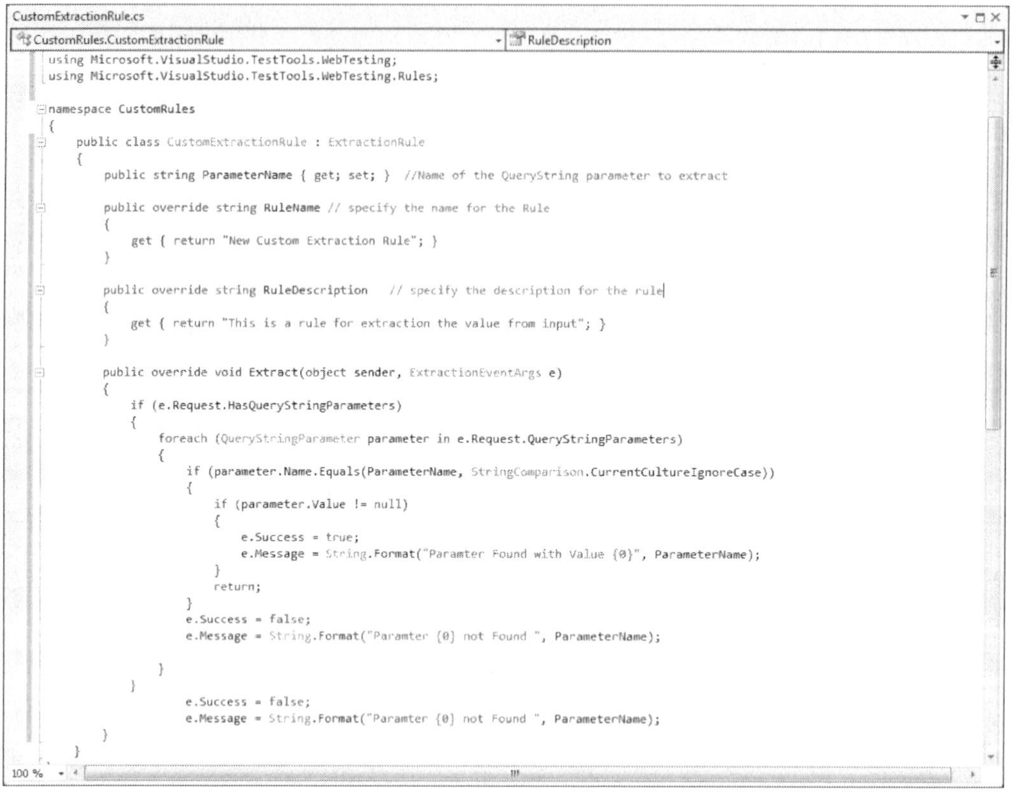

```
CustomExtractionRule.cs
CustomRules.CustomExtractionRule                                      RuleDescription

  using Microsoft.VisualStudio.TestTools.WebTesting;
  using Microsoft.VisualStudio.TestTools.WebTesting.Rules;

  namespace CustomRules
  {
      public class CustomExtractionRule : ExtractionRule
      {
          public string ParameterName { get; set; }  //Name of the QueryString parameter to extract

          public override string RuleName // specify the name for the Rule
          {
              get { return "New Custom Extraction Rule"; }
          }

          public override string RuleDescription   // specify the description for the rule
          {
              get { return "This is a rule for extraction the value from input"; }
          }

          public override void Extract(object sender, ExtractionEventArgs e)
          {
              if (e.Request.HasQueryStringParameters)
              {
                  foreach (QueryStringParameter parameter in e.Request.QueryStringParameters)
                  {
                      if (parameter.Name.Equals(ParameterName, StringComparison.CurrentCultureIgnoreCase))
                      {
                          if (parameter.Value != null)
                          {
                              e.Success = true;
                              e.Message = String.Format("Paramter Found with Value {0}", ParameterName);
                          }
                          return;
                      }
                      e.Success = false;
                      e.Message = String.Format("Paramter {0} not Found ", ParameterName);

                  }
              }
                  e.Success = false;
                  e.Message = String.Format("Paramter {0} not Found ", ParameterName);
          }
      }
  }
100 %
```

- **ParameterName:** This is to specify the name of the Query String Parameter that we want.

- **RuleName**: This is to specify the name of the new Extraction Rule. The extraction rule dialog will show the input field for specifying the rule name.

  ```
  public override string RuleName // to specify the Rule name for
  this rule {
    get { return "New Custom Extraction Rule"; }
  }
  ```

- **RuleDescription**: This is to specify the rule description for the new rule. The **Extraction Rule** dialog will have input field to specify the description.

  ```
  public override string RuleDescription  // to specify the
  description for this rule {
    get {
  ```

```
        return "This is the custom rule for extracting
                the value of input field at index 1";
    }
}
```

- **Extract**: This is the method to extract the data. This method is applicable only for the Extraction Rule. This method contains two parameters: **object** and **ExtractionEventArgs**. The **ExtractionEventArgs** has the property response, which provides the response generated by the request. The response contains the querystring, attributes, and the HTML documents along with all the other details about the response. Once the test is run, the extraction rule gets executed. In the example shown previously, the extract method will find the specified parameter in the Query String and extract the value if a match is found. The method returns with a success or failure status along with the message. The extracted value can be added as the context variable using the code:

```
e.WebTest.Context.Add(this.ContextParameterName, parameter.Value);
```

The context contains the key value pair, where the key is equal to the ContextParameterName and the value is the parameter value that is extracted.

```
// add the extracted value to the Web test context
e.WebTest.Context.Add(this.ContextParameterName, fieldValue);
e.Success = true;
```

The **ExtractEventArgs** object also contains a return value of either **Success** or **Failure**. We should set this to success or failure based on the extraction of the value. The following code shows the sample of an extraction rule, which extracts the value of an input field with the given name:

```
public override void Extract(object sender, ExtractionEventArgs e)
{
  if (e.Request.HasQueryStringParameters)
  {
    foreach (QueryStringParameter parameter in e.Request.
            QueryStringParameters)
    {
      if (parameter.Name.Equals(Name, StringComparison.
        CurrentCultureIgnoreCase))
      {
        if (parameter.Value != null)
        {
          e.Success = true;
          e.Message = String.Format("Parameter Found with value {0}:
                                    ", Name);
          e.WebTest.Context.Add(this.ContextParameterName,
                                parameter.Value);
        }
```

```
        return;
    }
}
e.Success = false;
e.Message = String.Format("Parameter {0} not Found ",
                          ParameterName);
}
```

After completing the class file with the code for the new extraction rule, compile the class library. Add the class library reference to the Web Performance Test project and include the namespace to the Web Performance Test code to make use of the new custom rule. Now to create a new rule for the request in the Web Performance Test code, create a new instance of the `CustomExtractionRule`, which is the class that we created for the custom rule, and set the properties. The following code contains the sample for an example of adding a new rule to the test. The extracted value will be added to the list of extracted values for the requests:

```
CustomExtractionRule extractionRulenew = new CustomExtractionRule();
extractionRulenew.Name = "Parameter1";
request2.ExtractValues += new EventHandler<ExtractionEventArgs>(extractionRulenew.Extract);
```

The custom rule can also be used in the recoded Web Performance Test. To add the custom rule, open the **WebTest** project and add the reference to the custom rule project.

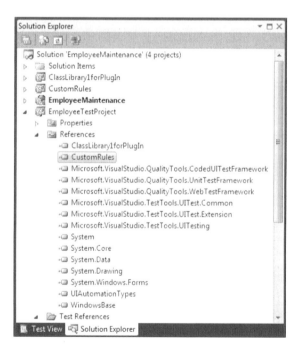

Now open the Web Performance Test project and select the request for which the new extraction rule should be added. Expand the test recording, select the **Extraction Rules** folder for the request and select the **Add Extraction Rule** option which will display all the different types of Extraction rules including the rule we created.

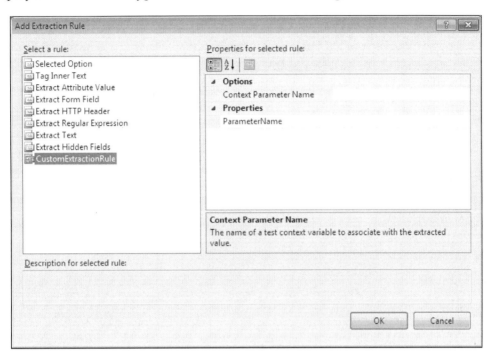

The **CustomExtractionRule** is just like the other rule, but is custom-built for the required functionality.

Validation rules

CustomValidationRule is written similar to extraction rules. It is the custom code written as a class, which is derived from the `ValidationRule` base class. This class is present in the namespace, **Microsoft.VisualStudio.Testtools.WebTesting**. The new class can be a separate class library, which can be added to the Web Performance Test project when required.

Create a new class library project and a add reference to the **Microsoft.VisualSudio. QualityTools.WebTestFramework** assembly.

The validation rule is to check if a particular value is found once or more in the HTML response. The response contains the attributes, parameters, hidden values, and the entire HTML document from which we have to find the value to validate.

The validate rule has similar properties and methods as to **Rule Name**, **Rule Description**, and **Validate.**

The **Validate** method contains two parameters, **object** and **ValidationEventArgs**. The **ValidationEventArgs** object contains the response property that provides the response text for the request through which we can find out the string value and validate the response.

The **Validate** method should set **e.IsValid** to **true** if the validation succeeds, or false if not. The following code is to find a string value in the document. At the same time, **e.Message** should also be set to a message based on the result, which will be shown at the end of test.

```
CustomExtractionRule.cs*                                                    ▼ □ ×
*$ CustomRules.CustomValidationRule                    ▼ | StringValueToFind        ▼

        public class CustomValidationRule : ValidationRule
        {
            public string stringValueToFind;
            public override string RuleName // specify the name for the Rule
            {
                get { return "New Custom Extraction Rule"; }
            }

            public override string RuleDescription   // specify the description for the rule
            {
                get { return "This is a rule for extraction the value from input"; }
            }

            public string StringValueToFind
            {
                get { return stringValueToFind; }
                set { stringValueToFind = value; }
            }

            public override void Validate(object sender, ValidationEventArgs e)
            {
                string htmlDocument = string.Empty;
                if (!String.IsNullOrEmpty(e.Response.BodyString))
                {
                    htmlDocument = e.Response.BodyString;
                    e.IsValid = htmlDocument.Equals(stringValueToFind, StringComparison.CurrentCultureIgnoreCase);
                    e.Message = "The string Found Successfully";
                }

                if (!e.IsValid)
                {
                    e.Message = String.Format("The string {0} is not found", stringValueToFind);
                }
            }
        }
    }

100 %  ▼ ◄                               III                                   ►
```

Now compile the library and add the reference to the project similar to the extraction rule and add **include the namespace**. In the Web Performance Test code, create a new instance of this custom rule and set the properties. Once the test is run, this rule gets executed and the result is added to the requested output.

```
CustomValidationRule validateRule = new CustomValidationRule();
validateRule.StringValuetoFind = "Test";
this.ValidateResponse += new EventHandler<ValidationEventArgs>(validateRule.Validate);
```

The custom rule can also be used in the recorded Web Performance Test. To add the custom rule library created previously, select the recorded Web Performance Test project and add the reference to the library. Open the Web Performance Test and select the validation rules folder, right-click and select the option **Insert Validation Rule**, which opens the dialog, listing out all types of validation rules.

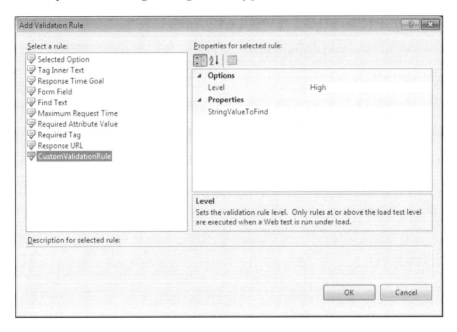

Now set the value of the **StringValuetoFind** parameter to something. Let us say the value is Test. Run the Web Performance Test again and check the results. The following is example of the test which returned failure and the message along with the result:

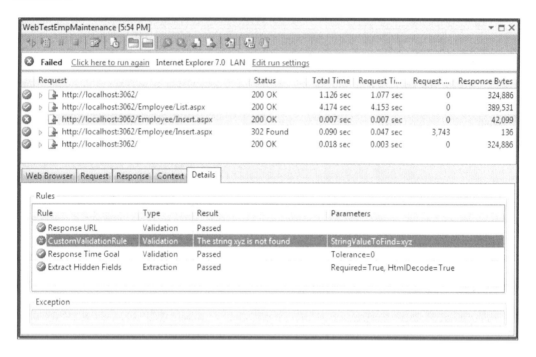

The message says: **String 'xyz' is not found**. We can add as many custom rules like this as we like and validate their responses.

Summary

This chapter explained the advanced features of Web Performance Testing using Visual Studio. All the features covered in this chapter explained the customization of the web testing feature based on our requirements. Writing custom rules are the extension of the in-built Extraction and Validation rules that comes with the Web Performance Testing. And generating code out of the recorded Web Performance Testing gives more control to the tester to customize the testing. We can include looping, calling custom written methods between the requests, adding transactions for requests and adding additional data sources. Furthermore, we can copy and paste the same requests as often as we want and modify them.

7
Load Testing

Load Test for an application helps the development and management team to understand the application performance under various conditions. Load Test can have different parameter values and conditions to test application performance.

Load Test can simulate the number of users, network bandwidths, combination of different web browsers, and different configurations. In the case of web applications it is always necessary to test the application with a different set of users and a different set of browsers to simulate multiple requests at the same time to the server. The following figure shows an example of a real time scenario with multiple users accessing the web site using different networks and different types of browsers from multiple locations.

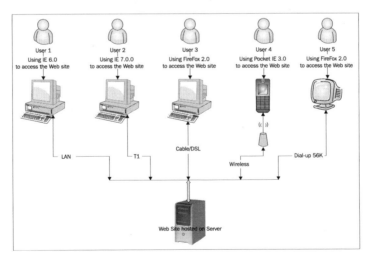

Load Test is not only for testing web application requests and responses but we can also test the unit tests to check the performance of the data access from the server. The Load Test helps to identify application performance in various capacities, application performance under light loads for a short duration, performance with heavy loads, and different duration.

Load Test uses a set of computers, which consist of a **controller** and **agents**. These are called **rig**. The agents are the computers at different locations used for simulating different user requests. The controller is the central computer which controls multiple agent computers. The Visual Studio Test Load agent in the agent computers generate the load for testing. The Visual Studio Test Controller at the central computer controls these agents. This chapter explains the details of creating test scenarios and Load Testing the application. This chapter covers the following topics:

- Creating Load Test
- Editing Load Tests
- Working with Test Result and analyzing Test Results
- Using Test Controller and Test Agents

Creating Load Test

The Load Tests are created using the Visual Studio Load Test Wizard. You first create the test project and then add the new Load Test which opens the wizard and guides us to create the test. We can edit the test parameters and configuration later on, if required.

Before we go on to creating the test project and understanding the parameters, we will consider a couple of web applications. Web applications or web sites are accessed by a large number of users from different locations at the same time. It is necessary to simulate this actual situation and check the application performance. Let's take a couple of web applications that we used in previous chapters. The first is a simple web page, which displays employee details and employee related details. The other application is the coded Web Performance Test that retrieves the employee details and also submits new employee details to the system.

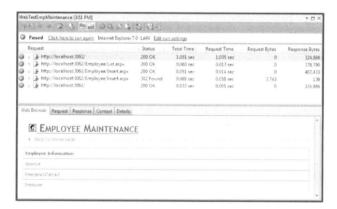

Using the preceding examples, we will see the different features of Load Testing that are provided by Visual Studio. The following sections describe the creation of Load Testing, setting parameters, and testing the application using Load `Test.load`.

Load Test Wizard

The *Load Test Wizard* helps us to create the Load Test for the Web Performance Tests and unit tests. There are different steps to provide the required parameters and configuration information for creating the Load Test. There are different ways of adding Load Test to the test project:

- Select the test project and then select the option, **Add | Load Test...**

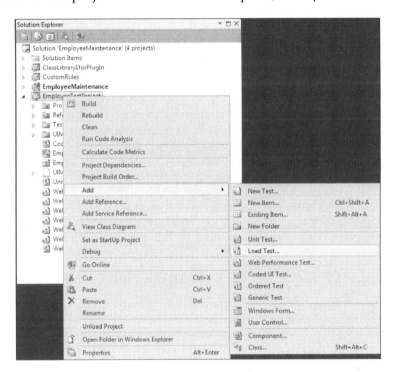

- Select the **Test** menu in Visual Studio 2010 and select **New Test**, which opens the **Add | New Test...** dialog. Select the Load Test type from the list. Provide a test name and select the test project to which the new Load Test should be added.

Both the preceding options open the **New Load Test Wizard** shown as follows:

The wizard contains four different sets with multiple pages, which collect the parameters and configuration information for the Load Test.

The *Welcome Page* explains the different steps involved in creating a Load Test. On selecting a step such as **Scenario**, **Counter Sets**, or **Run Settings**, the wizard displays the section to collect the parameter information for the selected set option. We can click on the option directly or keep clicking next and set the parameters. Once we click on **Finish**, the Load Test is created. To open the Load Test, expand the solution explorer and double-click on the Load Test, **LoadTest1**. We can also open the Load Test by using the **Test View** window in the **Test** menu and double-clicking on the name of the Load Test from the list to open the test editor. The following screenshot is an example of Load Test:

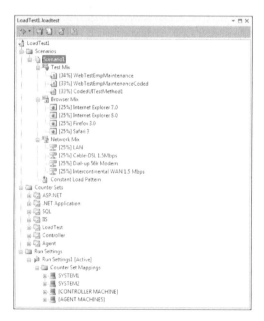

The following sections explain how to set the parameters in each step.

Specifying a scenario

Scenarios are used for simulating actual user tests. For example, in a web application there are different end users. For a public web site the end user could be anywhere and the number of users could be anything. The bandwidth of the connection and the type of browsers used by users also differ. Some users might be using a high speed connection and some a slow dial-up connection. But if the application is an Intranet application, the end users are limited within the LAN network. The speed at which these users connect will also be constant most of the time. The number of users and the browser used are the two main things which differ in this case. The scenarios are created using the combinations which are required for the application under test. Enter the name for the scenario in the wizard page.

We can add any number of scenarios to the test. For example, we may want to test **WebTestEmpMaintenance** with **40 per user per hour** and another test for **WebTestEmpMaintenanceCoded** with **20 per user per hour**.

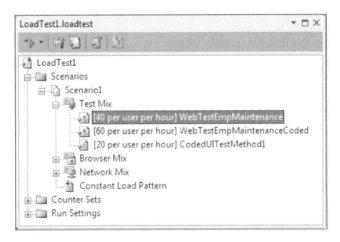

Now let us create a new Load Test and set the parameters for the scenario. From the solution explorer, select the test project and right-click **Add | Load Test** which opens the Load Test Wizard. We will see each step in the wizard and set the parameters.

The first step in this wizard is the *Welcome Page*, which provides the high level information about using the Load Test Wizard. The second step is to set the scenario name and the think time for the test.

Think time

The think time is the time taken by the user to navigate between web pages. These times are useful for the Load Test to simulate the test accurately.

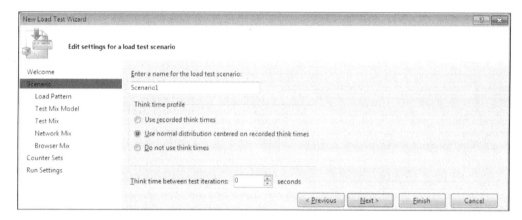

We can set the Load Test to use the actual think time recorded by the Web Performance Test or we can give a specific think time for each test. The other option is to set the normal distribution of the think time between requests. The time slightly varies between requests, but will be realistic to some extent. There is a third option, which configures not to use the think times between requests.

The think times can also be modified for the scenario after creating the Load Test. Select the scenario and right-click and then open **Properties** to set the think time.

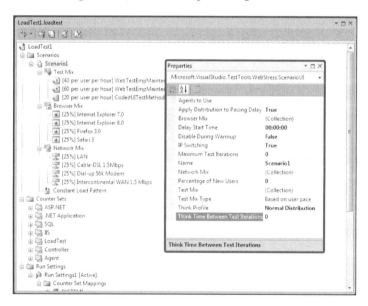

Now once the properties are set for the scenario, click **Next** in the **New Load Test Wizard** to set other parameters for **Load Pattern**.

Load pattern

Load pattern is used for controlling the user loads during the tests. The test pattern varies based on the type of test. If it is a simple Intranet web application test or a unit test, then we might want to have a minimum number of users for a constant period of time. But in case of a public web site, the number of users differ from time to time. In this case, we may have to increase the number of users from a very low number to a maximum number with a time interval. For example, I might have a user load of 10 initially but during testing I may want the user load to be increased by 10 after every 10 seconds of testing until the maximum user count reaches 100. So at 90th second the user count will reach 100 and the increment stops and stays with 100 user load till the test completion.

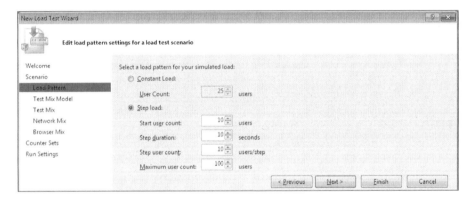

Constant load

The load starts with the specified user count and ends with the same number of user count.

User Count is to specify the number of user counts for simulation.

Step load

The Load Test starts with the specified minimum number of users and the count increases constantly with the time duration specified until the user count reaches to the maximum specified:

- **Start user count**: This specifies the number of users to start with
- **Step duration**: The time between the increases in user count
- **Step user count**: To specify the number of users to add to the current user count

- **Maximum user count**: To specify the maximum number of users count

We have set the parameters for the **Load Pattern**. The next step in the wizard is to set the parameter values for **Test Mix Model** and **Test Mix**.

Test mix model and test mix

The test load model is required to simulate the end users count distribution. Before selecting the test mix, the wizard provides a configuration page to choose the test mix model with four different options based on:

- Total number of tests
- Virtual users
- User pace
- Sequential test order

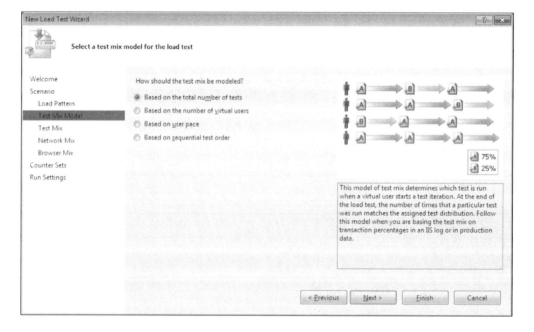

The next page in the wizard provides the option to select the tests and provide the distribution percentage or the option to specify the tests per user per hour for each test for the selected model. The mix of tests is based on the percentages specified or the tests per user specified for each test.

Based on the total number of tests

The next test to run is determined based on the selected number of times, that is, the number of times the test run should match the test distribution. For example, if the test mix model is based on the total number of tests and if three tests are selected, then the distribution of tests is like the one shown in the following screenshot. The percentage shows the distribution for the selected tests:

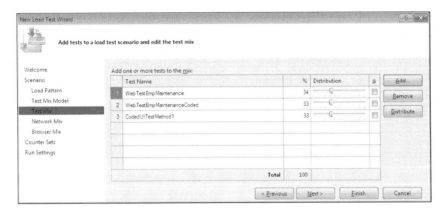

Based on the number of virtual users

This model determines running particular tests based on the percentage of virtual users. Selecting the next test to run, depends on the percentage of virtual users and also on the percentage assigned to the tests. At any point, the number of users running a particular test matches the assigned distribution.

Based on user pace

This option determines running each test for the specified number of times per hour. This model is helpful when we want the virtual users to conduct the test at regular pace.

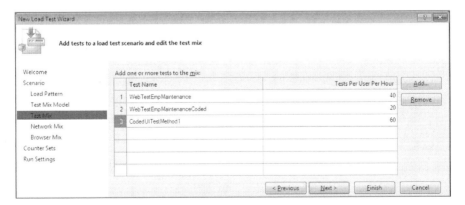

Based on sequential test order

With this option, the test would be conducted in the order the tests are defined. Each virtual user would start performing the test one after the other in cycles in the same order the tests are defined until the Load Test run ends.

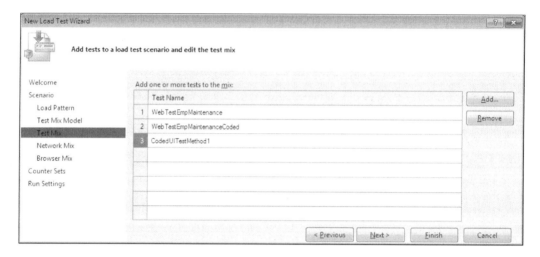

The test mix contains different Web Performance Tests, each with different numbers of tests per user. The number of users is defined using load pattern.

Network mix

Click on **Next** in the wizard to specify the **Network Mix**, to simulate the actual network speed of users. The speed differs based on user location and the type of network they use. It could be LAN network, cable, wireless, or dial-up. This step is useful to simulate the actual user scenario. One thing to note here is that different network types apply only for Web Performance Tests. If we add a unit test to the Load Test then we cannot have multiple network types. When you keep adding network types, the network type is automatically set with an equal distribution. We can change the distribution according to how we want the Load Test to perform. This is the default distribution which shows 25 per cent of the tests will be tested with each type of network selected.

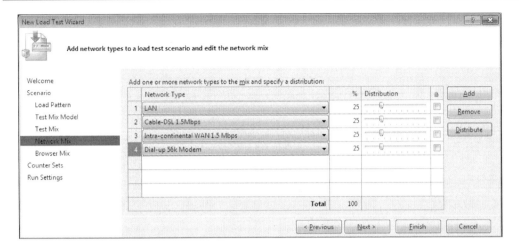

The next step in the wizard is to set the **Counter Sets** parameters, which is explained in the next few sections.

Browser mix

We have set the number of users and number of tests, but there is always a possibility that all users may not use the same browser. To mix different browser types we can go to the next step in the wizard and select the browsers listed and give a distribution percentage for each browser type.

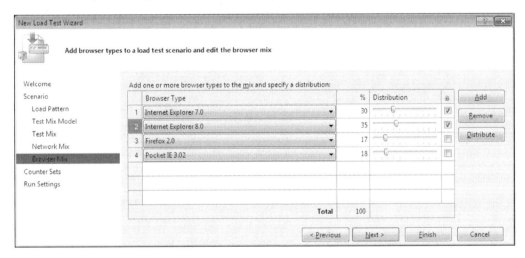

The test does not actually use the specified browser, but it sets the header information in the request to simulate the same request through the specified browser.

Counter sets

Testing the application by Load Test does not contain only the application specific performance but also the environment factors. This is to see the performance of the other services required for running the Load Test or to access the application under test. For example, the web application makes use of the IIS and ASP.NET process and SQL Server. VSTS provides an option to track the performance of these services using counter sets as part of the Load Test. The Load Test itself collects the counter set data during the test and represents it as a graph to display it better. The same data is also saved locally so that we can load it again and analyze the results. The counter set is for all the scenarios in the Load Test.

The counter set data is collected for the controller and agents by default. We can also add the other systems which are part of the Load Testing. These counter set results help us to know how the services are used during the test. Most of the time the application performance is affected by the common services or the system services used.

The *Load Test Creation Wizard* provides the option to add performance counters. The wizard includes the current system by default and the common counter set for the controller and agents. The following screenshot shows an example of adding systems to collect the counter sets during the Load Test:

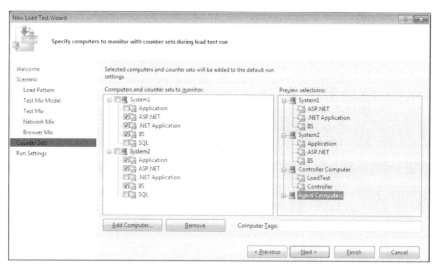

There is a list of counters listed for the system by default. We can select any of these for which we want to collect the details during the Load Test. For example, the preceding image shows that we need the data to be collected for **ASP.NET, .NET Application**, and **IIS** from **System1**. Using the **Add Computer...** option, we can keep adding the computers on which we are running the tests and choose the counter sets for each system.

Once we are done with selecting the counter sets we are ready with all the parameters for the test. But to run the test some parameters are obligatory, which is done in the next step in the wizard.

Run settings

These settings are basically for controlling the Load Test run to specify the maximum duration for the test and the time period for collecting the data about the tests. The following screenshot shows the options and the sample setting.

There are two options for the test run. One is to control it by a maximum time limit and the other is to provide a maximum test iteration number. The test run will stop once it reaches the maximum as per the option selected. For example, the following screenshot shows the option to run the test for five minutes.

The **Details** section is to specify the rate at which the test data should be collected: **Sampling rate**, **Description**, **Save log on Test Failure**, and **Validation level**. **Validation Level** is the option to specify the rules that should be considered during the test. This is based on the level that is set while creating the rules.

Save log on Test Failure is the new option provided in Visual Studio 2010 to capture and save the individual test run details within the Load Test for the failed Web Performance Tests or unit tests. This would help us to identify the problems that occur only while running the test within the Load Test but not outside the context of the Load Test.

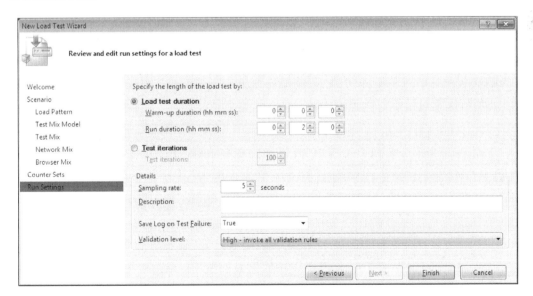

Now we are done with setting all the parameters required for Load Testing. Finish the wizard by clicking the **Finish** button, which actually creates the test with all the parameters from the wizard and shows the Load Test editor. The Load Test editor should look like the following:

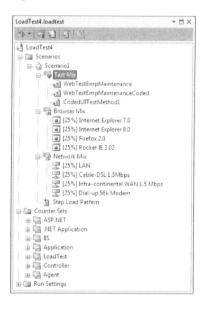

The actual run settings for the Load Test contain the counter sets selected for each system and the common run settings provided in the last wizard section. To know more about what exactly these counter sets contain and what the options are to choose from each counter set, select a counter set from the **Counter Sets** folder under the Load Test, right-click and select the option, **Manage Counter Sets...** to choose more counters or add additional systems. This option displays the same window as the last window in the wizard.

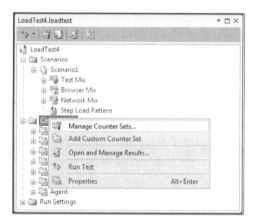

We can also add additional counters to the existing default list.

For example, the screenshot given is the default list of categories under the **.NET Application** counter set, which is shown when you complete the wizard for Load Test creation.

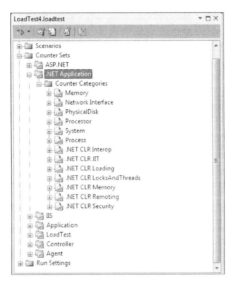

To add additional counter categories we perform the following steps:

1. Right-click on **Counter Categories** and select the option, **Add Counters,** and then choose the category you wish to add from the **Performance category** list. After selecting the category, select the counters from the list for the selected category.

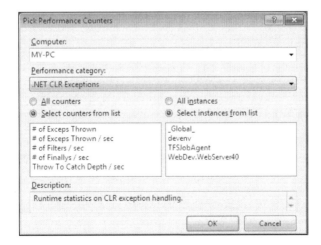

2. The preceding screenshot shows the **.NET CLR Exceptions** category selected with the counters such as the number of exceptions thrown, the number of exceptions thrown per second, the number of filters, and finally filters per second. After selecting the additional counters, click on **OK**, which adds the selected counters to the existing list for the test. The additional counters added are for the specific computer selected. There are many other performance categories which you can choose from the **Performance category** dropdown as shown:

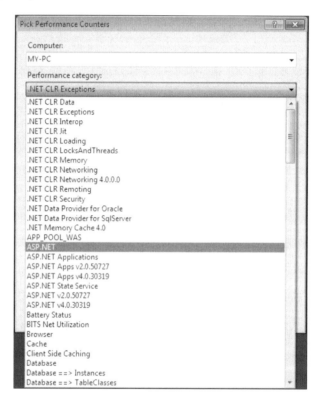

3. What we have seen previously is for the existing counter sets. What if we want to add the custom performance counter and add it to the run settings for the test? We can create a new counter by choosing the option **Add Custom Counter** in the context menu that opens when you right-click on the counters sets folder. The following screenshot shows a new custom performance counter added to the list:

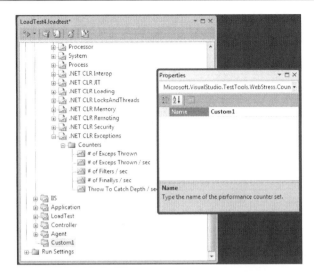

4. Now select the counter, right-click and choose the **Add Counters** option, select the category, and pick the counters required for the custom counter set. For example, we might want to collect the **Network Interface** counters such as the number of bytes sent and received per second and the current bandwidth during the test. Select these counters for the counter set.

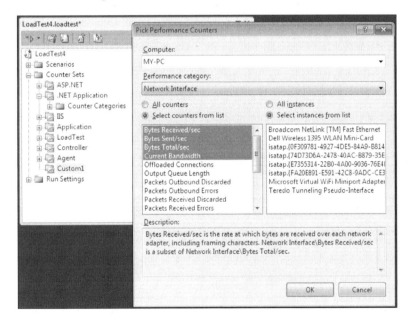

5. Once we are ready with the custom counter set, we need to add this as part of the run settings on all the systems that are part of the test. Select the **Run Settings** folder, right-click and choose the **Manage Counter Sets** option from the context menu and choose the custom performance counter **Custom1** shown under all available systems. The final list of **Run Settings** should look like this:

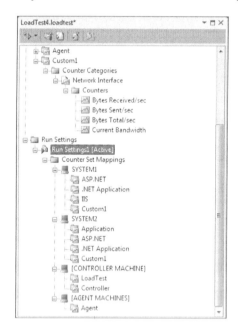

Keep adding all the custom counters and counter sets and select them for the systems used for running the test.

The main use of these counters is to collect data during the test, but at the same time we can use it to track readings. The Load Test has an option to track the counter data and indicate if it crosses the threshold values by adding rules to it, which are explained in the coming section.

Threshold rules

The main use of counters and counter sets are to identify the actual performance of the current application under test and the usage of memory and time taken for the processor. There is another main advantage in collecting these counter data. We can set the threshold limits for each of these data collected during the test. For example, we may want to get an alert warning when the system memory is almost full. Also if any process takes more time than the expected maximum time, we may want the system to notify us so that we can act upon it immediately. These threshold rules can be set for each of the performance counters.

Select a performance counter and choose the option, **Add Threshold Rule**, which opens a dialog for adding the rules.

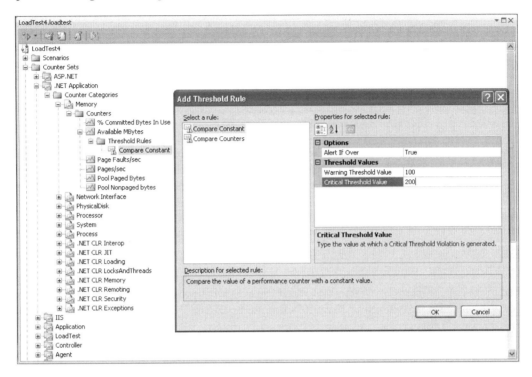

There are two different types of rules that can be added. One is to compare with constant values and the other is to compare the value with the other performance counter value. The following rules explain different ways of setting the threshold values:

- **Compare Constant**: This is to compare the performance counter value with a constant value. For example, we may want a violation, if the Available Mbytes reaches 200 and a critical message if it is less than or equal to 100. The option **Alert If Over** can be set to true or false, where true denotes that the violation will be generated if the counter value is greater than the specified threshold value and false denotes that the violation would be generated if the counter value is less than the specified threshold value.

  In the preceding screenshot, the **Warning Threshold Value** is set to 200 to trigger the warning violation and the **Critical Threshold Value** is set to 100 for the critical violation message.

- **Compare Counters**: This is to compare the performance counter value with another performance counter value. The functionality is the same as in the preceding constants. But here the performance counter values are compared instead of constant.

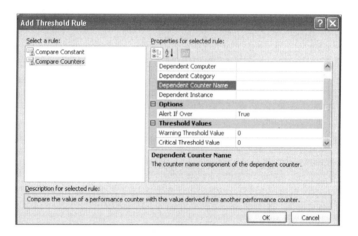

The preceding screenshot shows the options for adding compare counters to the counter set. The warning and critical threshold values are constants, which is multiplied by the dependent counter value and then compared with the current counter value. For example, if the dependent counter value is 50 and if the constant is set to 1.25 for a warning threshold, then the violation would be raised when the current counter value reaches a value of 62.5.

The following screenshot shows the example of the threshold violation whenever the value is above the constant defined in the rule. The test is aborted because the test was stopped before it got completed.

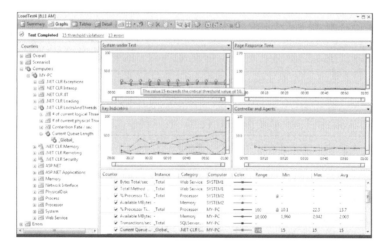

You can see from the graph that there are fifteen different threshold warning messages raised during the Load Test run as shown in the summary information about the test. The graph also indicates when the counter value reached the value above the constant defined in the rule. As the graph shows, the value reached the value **15**, which is over the constant **10** defined in the rule. If the value is above the warning level, it is indicated as yellow, and it is red if it is above the critical threshold value. These rules will not fail the test but provide the alert, if the values are above the thresholds set.

Editing Load Tests

The load can contain one or more scenarios for testing. The scenarios can be edited any time during the design. To edit a scenario, select the scenario you want to edit and right-click to edit the test mix, browser mix, network mix in the existing scenario, or add a new scenario to the Load Test. The context menu has different options for editing as shown:

Add Scenario... opens the same wizard we used before adding the scenario to the Load Test. We can keep adding scenarios as often as we need. The scenario properties window also helps us to modify properties such as think profile, the think time between the test iteration, and the scenario name.

The **Add Tests...** option is used for adding more tests to the test mix from the tests list in the project. We can add as many tests as required to be part of the test mix.

The **Edit Test Mix...** option is used for editing the test mix in the selected scenario. This option will open a dialog with the selected tests and distribution.

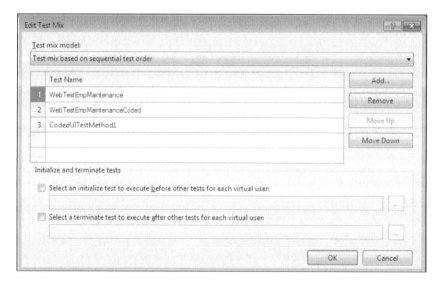

Using this **Edit Test Mix** window we can:

- Change the test mix model listed in the dropdown.

- Add new tests to the list and modify the distribution percentage.

- Select an initial test which executes before other tests for each virtual server. The browse option next to it opens a dialog showing all the tests from the project from which we can select the initial test.

- In the same way as the initial test, we can choose a test which is the final test to run during the test execution. The option is used here to select the test from the list of available tests.

The **Edit Browser Mix...** option opens the **Edit Browser Mix** dialog from which you can select a new browser to be included to the browser mix and delete or change the existing browsers selected in the mix.

The **Edit Network Mix...** option opens the **Edit Network Mix** dialog from which you can add new browsers to the list and modify the distribution percentages. We can change or delete the existing network mix.

To change the existing load pattern, select the load pattern under **Scenarios** and open the properties window which shows the current patterns properties. You can change or choose any pattern from the available patterns in the list as shown in the following images. There are three different patterns available: **Step**, **Constant**, and **Global based.**

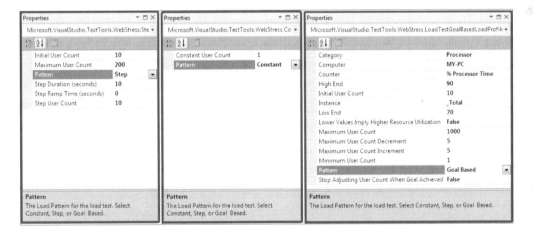

Step load Pattern has the initial user count and the maximum user count with a step duration and step user count. In the preceding image, every 10 seconds the user count would be increased by 10 until the maximum user count reaches 200.

Constant Load Pattern has only one constant user count value. The user count will always be the same throughout the test.

Goal based Pattern has a lot of parameters to target a particular machine and particular counter category and counter. We can also configure the initial user count, minimum user count, maximum user count, user count decrement, user count increment, and adjusting the user count.

Run Settings can be multiple for the Load Tests, but at any time only one can be active. To make the run settings active, select **Run Settings**, right-click and select **Set as Active**. The properties of the run settings can be modified directly using the properties window. The properties that can be modified include results storage, SQL tracing, test iterations, timings, and the Web Performance Test connections.

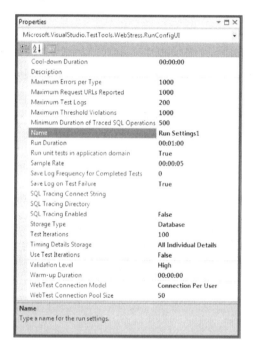

Adding context parameters

We have seen the details of context parameters in the Web Performance Test chapter. The web tests can have context parameters added to the test. The context parameter is used in place of the common values of multiple requests in the Web Performance Test. For example, every request has the same web server name which can be replaced by the context parameters. Whenever the web server changes, we can just change the context parameter value, which will replace all the requests with the new server name.

We know that the Load Test can have Web Performance Tests and unit tests in the list. If there is a change in the web server for the Load Test other than what we used for Web Performance Tests then we will end up modifying the context parameter values in all the Web Performance Tests used in the Load Tests. Instead of this, we can include another context parameter to the Load Test with the same name used in the Web Performance Tests. The context parameter added to the Load Test will override the same context parameter used in the Web Performance Tests. To add a new context parameter to the Load Test, select **Run Settings** and right-click to choose the **Add Context Parameter** option, which adds a new context parameter. For example, the context parameter used in the Web Performance Test has the web server value as:

```
this.Context.Add("WebServerName", "http://localhost:3062");
```

Now to overwrite this in Load Tests, add a new context parameter with the same name as follows:

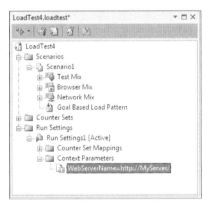

Results store

All information collected during the Load Test run is stored in the central result store. The Load Test results store contains the data collected by the performance counters, violation information, and errors that occurred during the Load Test. The result store is the SQL server database created using the script `loadtestresultsrepository.sql` which contains all the SQL queries to create the objects required for the result store.

If there are no controllers involved in the test and if it is the local test, we can create the results store SQL database using SQL Express. Running the script creates the store using SQL Express. Running this script once on the local machine is enough to create the result store. This is a global central store for all the Load Tests in the local machine. To create the store, open the Visual Studio **Command Prompt** and run the command with the actual drive where you have installed Visual Studio:

```
cd c:\Program Files\Microsoft Visual Studio 10.0\Common7\IDE
```

In the same folder, run the following command, which creates the database store:

```
SQLCMD /S localhost\sqlexpress /i loadtestresultsrepository.sql
```

If you have any other SQL Server, and if you want to use that to create the result store, then you can run the script on that server and use that server in the connection parameters for the Load Test. For example, if you have the SQL Server name as `SQLServer1`, and if the result store has to be created in that store, then run the command as follows:

```
SQLCMD /S SQLServer1 -U <user name> -P <password> -i
loadtestresultsrepository.sql
```

All of these preceding commands create the result store database in the SQL Server. If you look at the tables created in the store, it should be like this:

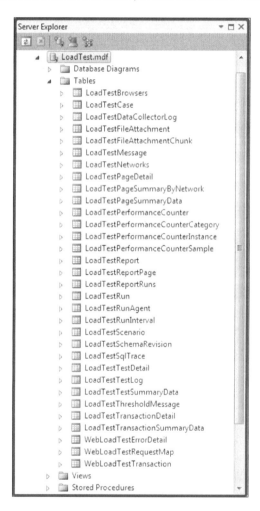

If you are using a controller for the Load Tests, the installation of the controller itself takes care of creating the results store on the controller machine. The controller can be installed using Microsoft Visual Studio Agents 2010.

To connect to the SQL Server result store database, select the **Test** option from the Visual Studio IDE and then select the **Administer Test Controller** window. This option should be available only on the controller machine. If the result store is on a different machine or the controller machine, select the controller from the list or select **<Local-No controller>** if it is in the local machine without any controller. Then select the **Load Test Results** store using the browse button and close the **Administer Test Controller** window.

The controllers are used for administering the agent computers and these controller and agents form the rig. Multiple agents are required to simulate a large number of loads from different locations. All the performance data collected from all these agents are saved at the central result store at the controller or any global store configured at the controller.

Running the Load Test

Load Tests are run like any other test in Visual Studio. Visual Studio also provides multiple options for running the Load Test:

- One is through the **Test View** window where all the tests are listed. We can select the Load Test, right-click and choose the option, **Run Selection,** which starts the Load Tests.

- The second option is to use the **Test List Editor**. Select the Load Test from the test list in the test lists editor and choose the option to run the selected tests from the Test List editor toolbar, which runs the selected tests.

- The third option is the **inbuilt run option** in the Load Test editor toolbar. Select the Load Test from the project and open the Load Test, which opens the Load Test in the Load Test editor. The toolbar for the Load Test editor has the option to run the currently opened Load Test.

- The fourth option is to use the command line command. The **MSTest** command line utility is used for running the test. This utility is installed along with Visual Studio Team System for Test. Open the Visual Studio Command Prompt. From the folder where the Load Test resides, run the following command to start running the Load Test.

```
mstest /testcontainer:LoadTest1.loadtest
```

In all the preceding cases of running the Load Test through UI, the Load Test editor will show the progress during the test run but the command line option does not show the full progress of the test but instead stores the result to the result store repository.

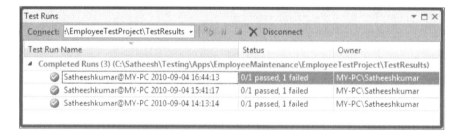

It can be loaded later to see the test result and analyze it. You can follow these steps to open the last run tests:

1. Open the menu option, **Test | Windows | Test Runs**:

    1. From the **Connect** drop-down, select the location for the test results store. On selecting this, you can see the trace files of the last run tests getting loaded in the window.

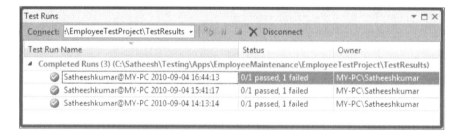

    2. Double-click the test result shown in the Test Run Results window that connects to the store repository and fetches the data for the selected test result and displays in the Load Test window. The end result of the Load Test editor window will look like the following screenshot with all the performance counter values and the violation points:

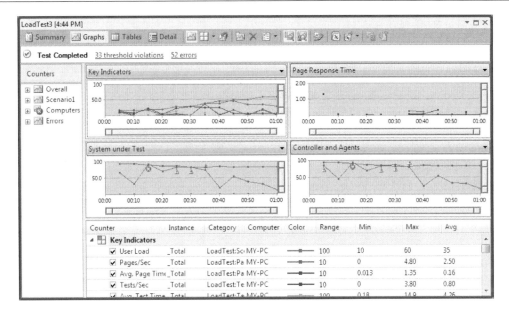

More details about the graph is given in the following section under the *Graphical View* sub section.

Working with the test result and analyzing test results

The result that we get out of the Load Test contains a lot of information about the test. All of these details get stored in the results repository store. The graph and indicators shown during the test run contain only the important cached results but the actual detailed information will get stored to the store. We can load the test result later on from the store and analyze it.

There are different ways to see the test results using the options in the Test editor toolbar. At any time we can switch between views to look at the results. The one given in the following section is the graphical view of the test results. The graphical view window contains different graphs shown for different counters.

Graphical view

The graphical view of the result gives the high level view of the test result, but the complete test result data is stored in the repository. By default, there are four different graphs provided with different readings. We can select the dropdown and choose any other counter reading for the graphical view.

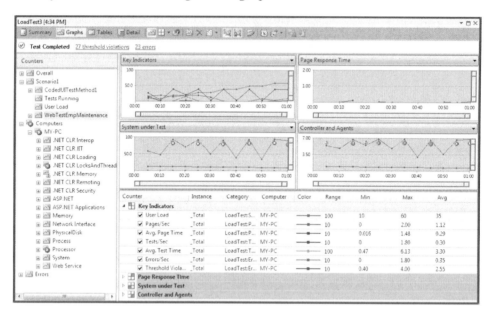

- **Key Indicators**: This graph shows the data collected for average response time, JIT time percentage, threshold violations per second, errors per second, and the user load. The details about the graph are given below the four graphs section, which describe the actual counter data collected during the test with the corresponding color coding with minimum, maximum, and average value for the counter.

- **Page Response Time**: This graph explains how long the response for each request took in different URLs. The details are given below the graphs.

- **System under Test**: This is the graph which presents data about different computers or agents used in the test. The data include readings such as the available memory and the processing time.

- **Controller and Agents**: The last graph presents details about the system or machine involved in the Load Test. The data collected should be the processor time and the available memory.

- **Transaction Response Time**: This is the average time taken by the transactions in Load Testing.

For all the graphs we have more detailed information about each counter in the grid below with color legends. The details show contain information about the counter name, category, range, min, max, and average readings for each counter. The legends grid can be made visible or invisible using the option in the toolbar.

For example, in the preceding image you can see the graph, **Key Indicators,** on the top left of all the graphs. Different types of readings are plotted in different colors in the graphs. The counters from this counter set are also presented in the table below the graphs with all the counters and the corresponding color for the counter used in the graph.

We can add a new graph and add the counters to have the graphical view. Right-click on any graph area and select the option, **Add Graph**, which adds a new graph with the given name. Now expand the counter sets and drag-and-drop the required counters on the new graph so that the readings are shown in the graph as shown in the following sample graph, **Graph1**:

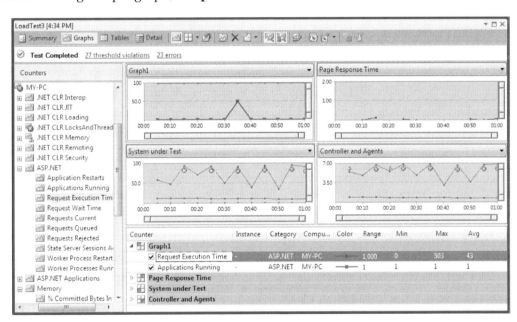

Graph1 is the new graph added to the result with couple counters added to it. The counters and readings are listed in the table below the graphs.

Summary view

The summary view option in the Load Test editor window toolbar gives more information on the overall Load Testing.

The most important information is the top five slowest pages and the top slowest tests. The tests are ordered based on the average test time taken for each test and the time taken for each page request:

- **Test Run Information**: This section provides the overall test run details such as start date and time, end date and time, test duration, the number of agents used for the test, and the settings used for the entire test.

- **Overall Results**: Provides information such as the maximum user load, the number of tests per second, requests and pages per second, and the average response time during the test run.

- **Test Results**: This section shows status information such as the number of tests conducted for each test selected for Load Testing. For example, out of 100 tests run for the Web Performance Test selected for Load Testing, the number of tests passed and the number of tests failed.

- **Page Results**: This section reports information about the different URLs used during the test. This result gives the number of times the page is requested and the average time taken for each page. The detail includes the test name to which the URL belongs.

- **Transaction Results**: The transaction is the set of tasks in the test. This section in the summary view shows information such as the scenario name, test name, the elapsed time for testing each transaction tests, and the number of times this transaction is tested.

- **System under Test Resources & Controller and Agents Resources**: This section reports information about the systems involved in testing and the processor time for the test, and the amount of memory available at the end of test completion.

- **Errors**: This section gives a list of errors that occurred during the test, information such as the error type, sub type, number of times the same error has occurred during the test, and the last message from the error stack.

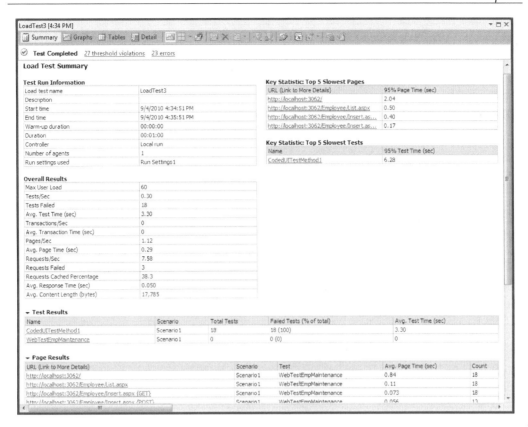

We have seen the Summary view and Graphical view and customizing the Graphical view by adding custom graphs and counter to it. The toolbar provides a third view for the results which is the tabular view.

Table view

In this table view, you can see the summarized result information in table format. By default there are two tables shown on the right pane with the table on top showing the list of tests run and their run details such as the scenario name, total number of tests run, tests passed, number of tests failed, and the time. The second tab shows information about the **Errors** that occurred while testing.

The details shown are the type of exceptions, sub type of the exception, number of exceptions raised, and the detailed error message.

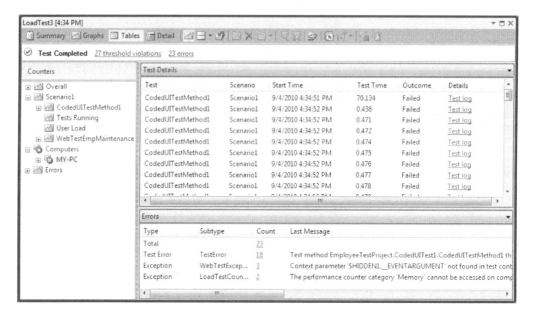

Both of these table headers are dropdowns. If you select the dropdown, you can see different options such as **Tests**, **Errors**, **Pages**, **Requests**, **Thresholds**, and **Transactions**. You can select the option to get the results to be displayed in the table. For example, the following screenshot shows the tabular view of the threshold violations and the web pages during the test. You can see the summary of the threshold violations in the header below the toolbar.

Threshold violation table shows detailed information about each violation that occurred during the test. The counter category, the counter name, the instance type, and the detailed message explain the reason for the violation showing the actual value and the threshold value set for the counter.

The next table below the threshold shows the number of pages visited during the test and the count of total visits per page with other details such as the network used for testing and the average, minimum, and median time taken for the page visits.

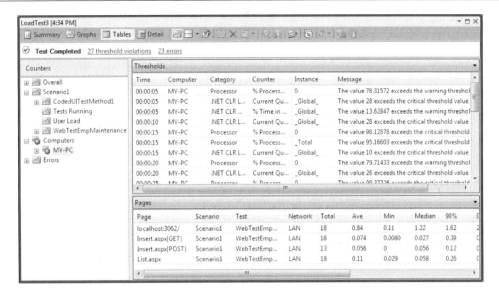

There are many other counter details provided by the tabular view which can be viewed by selecting from the drop-down list.

By selecting **Test details** from the list we can also see that there is a new column, **Details,** which shows as a **Test log** with a URL link for each test that failed. By clicking this test log you can see that a detailed page with all the information about that test opens such as the one shown as follows:

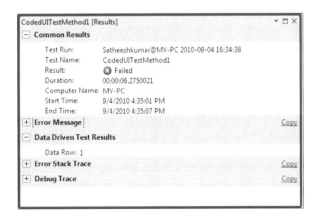

The new page provides information about the failed test such as Test run name, duration, start and end time of the test, details error message about the test, Data driven Test Results, Error Stack Trace, and the Debug Trace about the entire test. The test **fail log** is available only when the option **Save Log on Test Failure** is enabled during the test settings.

Details view

The details view tab shows the virtual user activity chart, which is used for analyzing virtual user activity during the Load Test. The chart also shows the user load, load pattern, and failed or aborted or slow tests during the Load Test. This view contains three sections:

- Select the tests with color code legends
- Filter the results shown in the chart
- Detailed chart

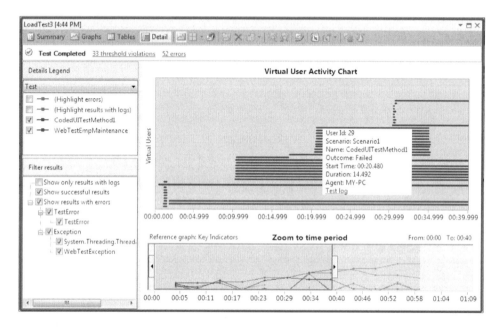

There is also an option to see the time period graph for the entire Load Test. We can scroll to the any time during the Load Test and analyze the activities. On pointing to any of the line in the activity chart, it shows a tool tip message for the selected user with all the activity details such as virtual user ID, scenario, test name, test outcome, start time of the test, duration for the test, and the agent on which the test runs.

Exporting to Excel

We can export the results to Excel using the **Create Excel Report** option in the toolbar of the Load Test result editor:

1. When you choose **Create Excel Report,** Microsoft Excel opens with a wizard to name the report and configure the data required for the report. We do not have to go through the Load Test result to create an Excel report. We can open Microsoft Excel and select the **Load Test Report** option available under the **Load Test Menu** shown as follows. This open directly connects to the Load Test data repository.

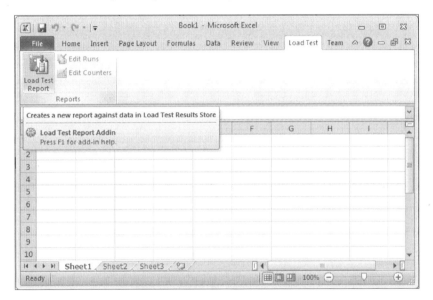

2. The next step is to select the database for the Load Test. Connect to the server and choose the database where all Load Test data are stored.

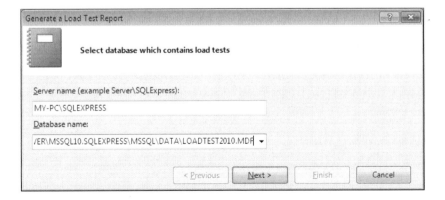

3. The next step in report creation is to select an option either to create a new report, use an existing report as a template, or edit an existing report. Let's choose the first option, which is the default to create a new report.

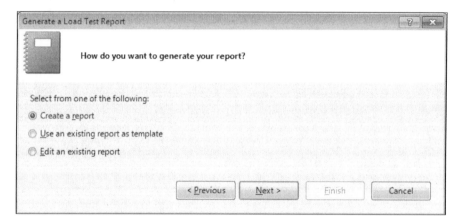

4. The next option is to select the type of report. There are two report types: one to run comparison, and to generate from Trend.

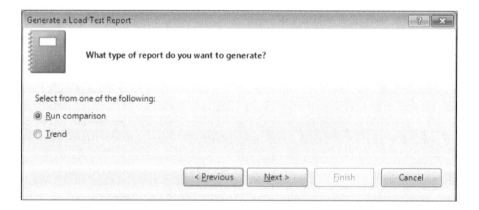

5. Click **Next** in the wizard to go to the next step and provide the report name, select the corresponding Load Test from which we have to generate the report, and provide a detailed description for the new report.

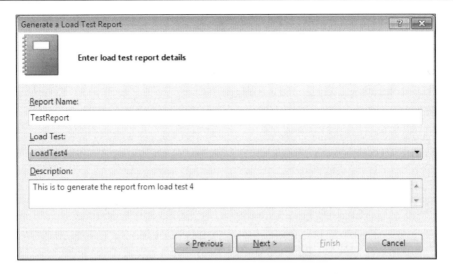

6. On clicking **Next** in the wizard connects to the data repository and pulls the results for the selected Load Test. For each test result the test run time, test duration, user name, and test outcome are shown in the list. We can choose any of the two test results so that a comparison report is generated for the selected test results.

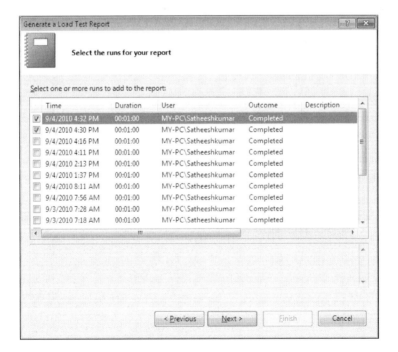

7. The next step is to select the counters from the test results for the report.

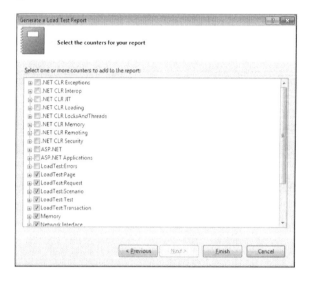

8. After selecting the required counters, click on **Finish** to complete the wizard and start the generation of the actual report.

Now, Microsoft Excel starts gathering the information from the repository and generates five different reports in different worksheets.

There is an initial work sheet which shows the report name, description, and the table of contents for the reports.

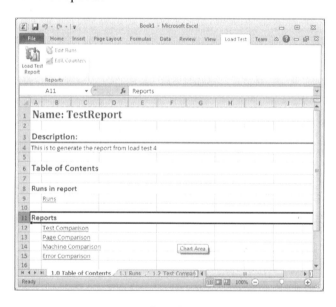

The first report page is Runs, which shows two test results and indicates the type of the results. The first one is considered as the baseline type and the next one is the comparison run.

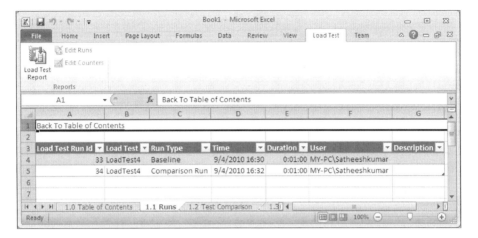

The next four sheets show the comparison between the selected test results. The first one is the Test comparison between the results, the second is the page comparison, the third is the machine comparison and the last sheet shows the error comparison. The following screenshot shows the page comparison between the test results.

The graph shows the average page response time and the performance improvement when compared to the baseline test result:

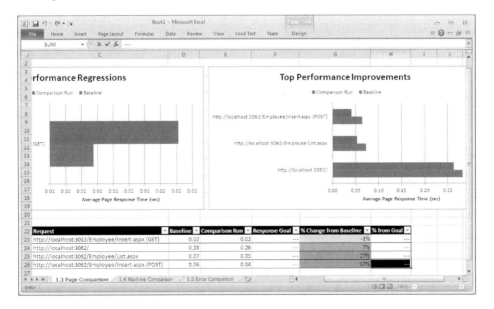

The report also shows the requests by both results and the % change from baseline which shows some significant change in performance. These types of reports are very helpful to compare test results and choose the best test. It should help us to configure the test better for better results.

As we saw the in wizard, there are other options as well: load and edit an existing report, or use an existing report as template. Once the report is generated, we can also customize as per our need as the report is generated directly in Microsoft Excel.

Using the test controller and test agents

The Controller and agents cannot be configured using Visual Studio 2010 as they don't come by default with Visual Studio 2010. To install the controller and agent, you must have Visual Studio Agents 2010 installable and you must be part of the administrators security group.

Test Controller and Agent can be installed on the same machine where you have Visual Studio 2010 Ultimate or you can install on different machines and then configure the settings.

Test controller configuration

The following are the steps for test controller configuration:

1. Install *Visual Studio Test Controller 2010* using Visual Studio 2010 Setup. Provide all the details and then finish the installation. Once the installation is complete, select the **Configure Test Controller now** option to start the configuration for the controller. The **Configure Test Controller** dialog is displayed.

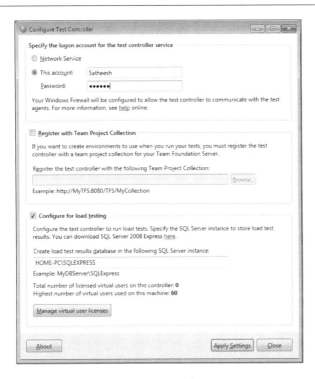

The first section in the configuration is the logon access information. The user account must be a member of the Administrators group to use intelliTrace and the network emulation data. The user should also be part of the test controller's user account to use the controller for testing.

You can also register the controller with the Team Project collection in Team Foundation Server to create environments, provide the Team Project collection URL in the next section.

2. The next step is to provide an SQL server instance name to store the Load Test results. It can be a local SQLExpress or any other SQL instance that you would like to use for storing the Load Test results.

If you have purchased the virtual user licenses then you can also configure the licenses by clicking on **Manage virtual user licenses** which opens a new dialog where you can enter the license.

3. After configuring all the required details, click on **Apply Settings** which opens the **Configuration summary** dialog showing the status of each step that is required to configure the test controller. Close the **Configuration summary** dialog and then close the **Configuration Tool**.

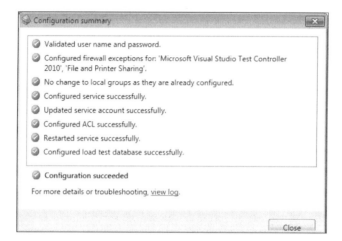

4. After configuring the Test controller, the next step is to install the agents using Visual Studio Agents 2010 setup. The agent can be installed in two ways, one as a service, and the other as an interactive process. If the test interacts with your desktop, such as with coded UI tests, then the agent should be installed to run the tests as an interactive process.

4. Once the installation of Test Agent is complete, the **Configure Test Agent** dialog is displayed. The two options, one as Service, and the other as interactive process, are displayed. Select the required option to configure and click **Next**. Now we need to provide the user details with which the service will run.

In the case of an interactive process, there is an option to select **Log on automatically**. This option encrypts the user credentials, stores them in the registry, and uses the details to run the tests automatically after reboot.

There is another option, **Ensure screen saver is disabled,** for the interactive process to avoid the interference of the screen saver in the case of automated tests that interact with the desktop.

5. The next step is to register the agent with the Test Controller. Select the option, **Register with Test Controller,** and then provide the name of the Controller to register this test agent with the controller to collect the test data. If the test agent is part of a virtual environment created using **Lab Center of Microsoft Test Manager**, we don't have to register the test agent with the test controller. Click on **Apply Settings** to save the configuration. This opens the **Configuration summary** screen which shows the status of each step required to configure the test agent.

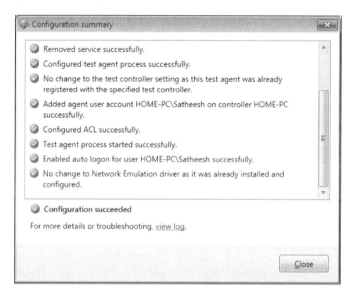

6. Now we can use the test controller and test agent to perform the Load Test. We need to configure the controller and test agent to be used for the Load Test. Open the solution and right-click to add a new item. Select **Test Settings** from the template and then add the new test settings to the solution, which opens the dialog for the test settings. Enter the test setting name, description, and choose the naming scheme in the **General** section, and then click on **Roles**. The roles page is to configure the controller and the agents to collect the data and to run the tests. Select the test execution method as **Remote execution** and then select the Controller name from the Controller dropdown which controls the agents and collects the test data.

7. Click on **Roles** to add different roles to run tests and collect data. The role could be a **Web Server** or **SQL Server**. Each role uses a test agent that is managed by the Controller. You can keep adding roles. To select the role that you want to run the test, click on **Set as role to run tests**. The other roles will not run the test but are used for data collection.

To limit the number of agents used for tests, we can set attributes and filter. Click on **Add** in the attributes section and then enter the attribute name and value for the selected role.

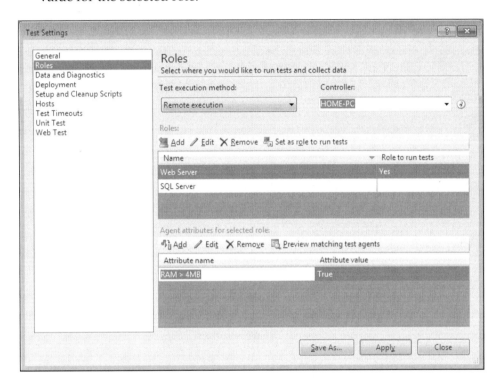

From the Data and Diagnostic page, we can define the diagnostic data adapter that the role will use to collect the data. If there are more data and diagnostics selected for the role and if there are available agents, the controller will make use of the available agents to collect the data. To configure each data and diagnostics, select the diagnostic and click on configure, which opens the dialog where we can configure the selected diagnostic.

Complete the remaining part of the test settings and apply the settings and complete the creation of test setting.

8. Now start creating the Load Test using the new test settings and start running the Load Test. At any time, if we want to load the test result collected by the controller, select the Load Test and right-click to choose the **Open and Manage Results** option, which opens a dialog to select the controller and the corresponding Load Test. After selecting the options you can see the test results collected by the controller. To see the details of each test result, double-click on the result, which opens the Load Test analyzer and shows the details of the test result. The other options available are to import the existing result from the trace file into the controller repository and to export the results to a trace file from the controller repository.

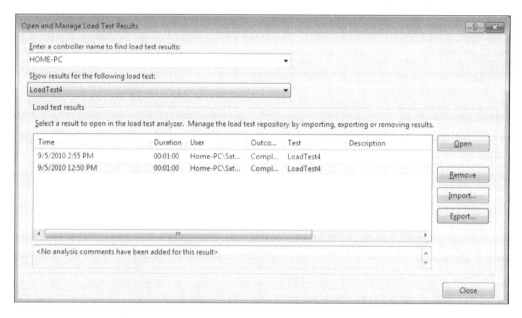

We have now successfully learned the steps for the test controller configuration.

Summary

This chapter explained the steps involved in creating the Load Test using sample web tests. We have seen the details of each step and the parameter values to set in each step in the Load Test creation wizard. There is always a chance to go back and edit the test to change the parameters set or add additional counters and scenarios, which is explained in this chapter. Creating custom performance counters, including the same for Load Testing for different systems and setting the threshold rules for counters and different types of creating the rules are some of the other topics we covered. Once after creating the Load Test we have seen the different methods of running the tests and collecting the test results. And lastly, this chapter explained the multiple ways of looking at the results such as Summary view, Graphical view, Tabular view, and Details View and how useful it is to analyze the test results. Having all these results in test repository may not solve our purpose sometimes. This chapter also explained the configuration of Controller and Agents for the Load Test. Visuals Studio 2010 also provides the creation of Excel report from the test result repository which we have seen in detail in this chapter.

8
Ordered and Generic Tests

This chapter explains the details of creating and using ordered and generic tests. So far, in previous chapters, we have created many tests including Unit Tests, Manual Tests, Web Performance Tests, Coded Web Performance Tests, and Load Tests. Visual Studio 2010 provides a feature called Ordered Test to group all or some of these tests and then execute the tests in the same order. The main advantage of creating the ordered test is to execute multiple tests in an order based on the dependencies. For example, my Web Performance Tests might depend on the results produced by executing the unit tests. So I need to run these tests in an order so that the Unit Test can be executed before starting the Web Performance Tests.

Generic Tests are just like any other tests except that they are used for running the existing third party tool or program, which can also be run using command line.

Let us create sample tests in this chapter and see the usage of both Generic and Ordered Tests. This chapter covers on the following topics:

- Creating, executing, and learning properties of an Ordered test
- Creating, executing, and learning properties of an Generic test

Ordered tests

The following screenshot shows the list of all the tests that we created under the test project in previous chapters. You can see that the tests are independent and there is no link between the tests. We have different types of tests like Unit Test, Web Performance Test, and Load Test under the test project. Let's try to create an ordered test and place some of the dependent tests in an order so that the test execution happens in an order without breaking.

Creating an ordered test

There are different ways of creating ordered tests similar to the other tests:

1. Select the test project from **Solution Explorer**, right-click and select **Add Ordered Test**, and then select ordered test from the list of different types of tests. Save the ordered test by choosing the **File | Save** option.

2. Select the menu option **Test** then select **New Test...**, which opens a dialog with different test types. Select the test type and choose the test project from the **Add to Test Project List** drop-down and click on **OK**.

Now the ordered test is created under the test project and the ordered test window is shown to select the existing tests from the test project and set the order.

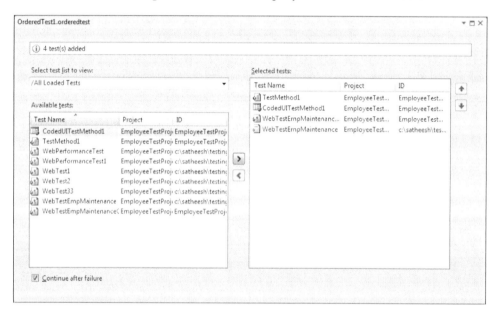

The preceding window shows different options for ordering the tests.

The first line is the status bar, which shows the number of tests selected for the ordered test.

The **Select test list to view** dropdown has the option to choose the display of tests in the available Test Lists. This dropdown has the default **All Loaded Tests**, which displays all available tests under the project. The other options in the dropdown are **Lists of Tests** and **Tests Not in a List**. The List of Tests will display the test lists created using the **Test List Editor**. It is easier to include the number of tests grouped together and order them. The next option, **Tests Not in a List**, displays the available tests, which are not part of any Test Lists.

The **Available tests** list displays all the tests from the test project based on the option chosen in the dropdown.

Selected tests contains the tests that are selected from the available tests list to be placed in order.

The two right and left arrows are used for selecting and unselecting the tests from the **Available tests** list to the **Selected Tests** list. We can also select multiple tests by pressing the *Ctrl* key and selecting the tests.

The up-down arrows on the right of the selected tests list are used for moving up or down the tests and setting the order for the testing in the **Selected tests** list.

The last option, the **Continue after failure** checkbox at the bottom of the window, is to override the default behavior of the ordered tests, aborting the execution after the failure of any test. If the option **Continue after failure** is unchecked, and if any test in the order fails, then all remaining tests will get aborted. In case the tests are not dependent, we can check this option and override the default behavior to allow the application to continue running the remaining tests in order.

Properties of an ordered test

Ordered tests have properties similar to the other test types, in addition to some specific properties. To view the properties, select the ordered test in the **Test View** or **Test List Editor** window, right-click and select the **Properties** option. The **Properties** dialog box displays the available properties for the ordered test.

The preceding screenshot shows that most of the properties are the same as the properties of the other test types. We can associate this test with the TFS work items, iterations, and area.

Executing an ordered test

An ordered test can be run like any other test. Open the **Test View** window or the **Test List Editor** and select the ordered test from the list, then right-click and choose the **Run Selection** option from **Test View** or **Run Checked Tests** from the **Test List Editor**. Once the option is selected, we can see the tests running one after the other in the same order in which they are placed in the ordered test. After the execution of the ordered tests, the **Test Results** window will show the status of the ordered test. If any of the tests in the list fails, then the ordered test status will be **Failed.** The summary of statuses of all the tests in the ordered test is shown in the following screenshot in the toolbar. The sample ordered test application had four tests in the ordered tests, but two of them failed and one had an error.

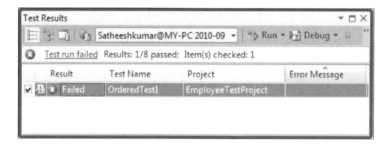

Clicking the **Test run failed** hyperlink in the status bar shows a detailed view of the test run summary:

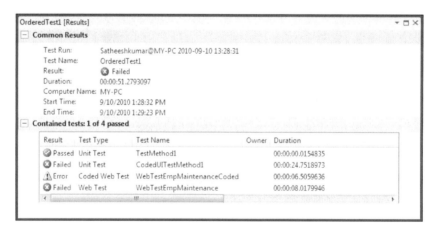

The **Test Results** window also provides detailed information about the tests run so far. To get these details, choose the test from the **Test Results** window and then right-click and choose the option, **View Test Results Details**, which opens the details window and displays the common results information such as **Test Name**, **Result**, **Duration of the test run**, **Start Time**, **End Time**, and so on.

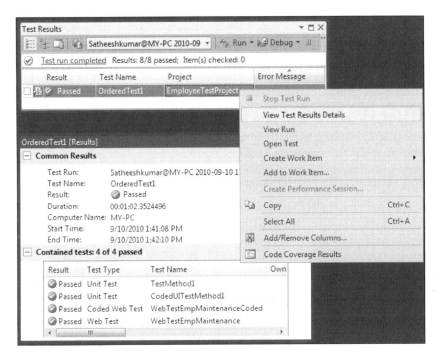

The details window also displays the status of each and every test run within the ordered test. In addition it displays the duration for each test run, name, owner, and type of test in the list. Even though the second test in the list fails, the other tests continue to execute as if the **Continue after failure** option was checked.

Generic tests

Generic tests are ways to integrate third-party tests into Visual Studio. There could be applications which use third party components or services which have to be tested as part of the whole system testing. In this case, we cannot have our own custom test methods or testing created for the third party component as we may not know the logic and the details of how the component is built. In order to test the third party component, Generic Test types in Visual Studio act as wrappers for executing these third-party tests within the boundary of Visual Studio. Once they are wrapped, we can execute these generic tests like any other test through Visual Studio IDE.

The third-party tests should adhere to the following conditions to be categorized under the generic tests in Visual Studio:

- We must be able to execute the third-party tests from the command line.
- The third-party tool must return a Boolean value of either `True` or `False` when executed in the command line.
- It is preferred that the third-party test tool writes an XML file, which contains the list of individual tests. The XML file is the summary results file, which contains the details of all the tests run.

Creating a Generic Test

This is similar to any other test in Visual Studio 2010. Either use the **Test** menu and choose the option of creating a new test or right-click on the test project in **Solution Explorer** and add a generic test or open the **Test View** window and then right-click from there and add a new test. Then provide a name for the generic test. For this example, name it `GenericTestforThirdPartyTest`. A new window opens to set the values or parameters for the generic test.

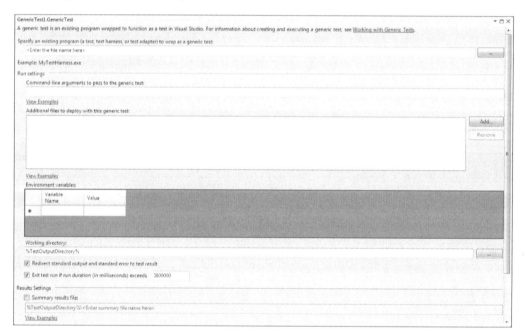

You can see from the form that all the values we have to enter are for executing another test application from the command line by passing parameters. For a command line execution—we may have to set the environment variables, execution parameters, set the working directory, copy or deploy some files, and set the output directory and the file. All these details can be set using the generic test.

The following table explains the different options and their uses:

Parameters for Generic Test	Description
Specify an existing program	This is the name and path of the third-party test application to be executed at the command line; it is the name of the executable application; we can also use the browse button to the right of the text box to find the application and select it.
Command-line arguments to pass to the generic test	This is the place to specify the command line parameters required for the third-party test application; these parameters totally depend on the testing tool's expected value.
Additional files to deploy with this generic test	In some cases, there might be other files required for this test execution; add those files or remove the selected files in the list using the option to the right of the text box.
Environment variables	If the test application uses any environment variables for the execution, we are required to set those environment variables for the execution; using this option we can set the environment variables to be used by the test application.
Working directory	This is to set the current working directory in the command line before we actually run the test application in the command line.
Redirect standard output and standard error to test result	While executing the test application, instead of displaying all the results at the command line, we can redirect those results to the output file, just as we do during the normal command line commands.
Exit test run if run duration (in milliseconds) exceeds how much?	This is to limit the wait time for Visual Studio to move on to the next test in the list, or quit; these numbers denote milliseconds and the default is 60 minutes.
Summary results file	This is helpful if the third-party tests application can write the test results to an XML file; this is the name and path of the XML file in which the output results should be written; if the number of tests in the test application is greater in number, then it will be easy to track the result of these individual tests by having the results in the XML file; not only the result but also detailed information of the test result would be written to this file.

The following is an example of a generic test that executes the `Test.exe` file, which is a third-party test application capable of writing output to the XML file. The command-line parameter for this application is also provided along with the supporting file to be deployed, which is the `Readme.txt` file. You can see `Output.xml`, which stores the output details of the test carried out by `Test.exe`.

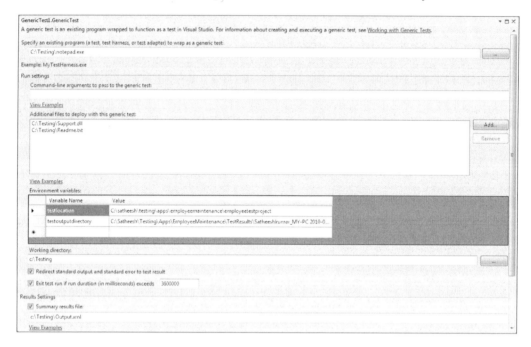

Summary results file

When we execute the above generic test, the third-party `Test.exe` is executed at the command line. The generic test by Visual Studio will get the result back from the third-party `Test.exe` application, which is a single test. But we do not know how many tests are executed internally within the test, and it is not easy to track the results of all the tests of the third-party application using the generic test. But Visual Studio supports the third-party application with a summary results file, which can be used by the application to write the details of the internal test results.

The third-party applications can make use of the class file, which is generated by using the schema file provided by Visual Studio. The schema file is located at the Visual Studio command-line. If Visual Studio is installed in the default `c:` drive, then the path would be: `C:\Program Files\Microsoft Visual Studio 10.0\Xml\Schemas\SummaryResult.xsd`.

The class file can be generated from this schema file using the `xsd.exe` utility on any .NET supported language. The following is an example of generating the default `SummaryResult.cs` class file from an XSD file. The output folder should exist before the command is run. `c:\temp` is the output folder used in the following sample:

`Xsd SummaryResult.xsd /c /l:cs /out:c:\temp`

The class file is the C# file as we have specified C# as the language in the command-line parameter as `/l:cs`. The generated output file would be like this::

```
//----------------------------------------------------------------
-----------
// <auto-generated>
//       This code was generated by a tool.
//       Runtime Version:4.0.30319.1
//
//       Changes to this file may cause incorrect behavior and will be
         lost if
//       the code is regenerated.
// </auto-generated>
//----------------------------------------------------------------
-----------
using System.Xml.Serialization;
//
// This source code was auto-generated by xsd, Version=4.0.30319.1.
//

/// <remarks/>
[System.CodeDom.Compiler.GeneratedCodeAttribute("xsd",
   "4.0.30319.1")]
[System.SerializableAttribute()]
[System.Diagnostics.DebuggerStepThroughAttribute()]
[System.ComponentModel.DesignerCategoryAttribute("code")]
[System.Xml.Serialization.XmlTypeAttribute(AnonymousType=true)]
[System.Xml.Serialization.XmlRootAttribute(Namespace="",
   IsNullable=false)]
public partial class SummaryResult {
```

```csharp
                            private string testNameField;
                            private testResultType testResultField;
                            private string errorMessageField;
                            private string detailedResultsFileField;
                            private SummaryResultInnerTest[] innerTestsField;

        /// <remarks/>
        public string TestName {
          get {
            return this.testNameField;
          }
          set {
            this.testNameField = "SampleTest1";
          }
        }

    /// <remarks/>
      public testResultType TestResult {
        get {
          return this.testResultField;
        }
        set {
          this.testResultField = "Passed";
        }
      }

      /// <remarks/>
      public string ErrorMessage {
        get {
          return this.errorMessageField;
        }
        set {
          this.errorMessageField = "Data not in Expected Format";
        }
      }

      /// <remarks/>
      public string DetailedResultsFile {
        get {
          return this.detailedResultsFileField;
        }
        set {
          this.detailedResultsFileField = @"D:\Testing\Trace.txt";
        }
```

```
    }

    /// <remarks/>
    [System.Xml.Serialization.XmlArrayItemAttribute("InnerTest",
      IsNullable=false)]
    public SummaryResultInnerTest[] InnerTests {
      get {
        return this.innerTestsField;
      }
      set {
        this.innerTestsField = value;
      }
    }
  }
  /// <remarks/>
  [System.CodeDom.Compiler.GeneratedCodeAttribute("xsd",
    "4.0.30319.1")]
  [System.SerializableAttribute()]
  public enum testResultType {

    /// <remarks/>
    Aborted,

    /// <remarks/>
    Error,

    /// <remarks/>
    Inconclusive,

    /// <remarks/>
    Failed,

    /// <remarks/>
    NotRunnable,

    /// <remarks/>
    NotExecuted,

    /// <remarks/>
    Disconnected,

    /// <remarks/>
    Warning,
```

```
    /// <remarks/>
    InProgress,

    /// <remarks/>
    Pending,

    /// <remarks/>
    PassedButRunAborted,

    /// <remarks/>
    Completed,

    /// <remarks/>
    Passed,
}

/// <remarks/>
[System.CodeDom.Compiler.GeneratedCodeAttribute("xsd",
  "4.0.30319.1")]
[System.SerializableAttribute()]
[System.Diagnostics.DebuggerStepThroughAttribute()]
[System.ComponentModel.DesignerCategoryAttribute("code")]
[System.Xml.Serialization.XmlTypeAttribute(AnonymousType=true)]
public partial class SummaryResultInnerTest {

    private string testNameField;
    private testResultType testResultField;
    private string errorMessageField;
    private string detailedResultsFileField;

    /// <remarks/>
    public string TestName {
      get {
        return this.testNameField;
      }
      set {
        this.testNameField = value;
      }
    }

    /// <remarks/>
    public testResultType TestResult {
      get {
        return this.testResultField;
```

```
    }
    set {
      this.testResultField = value;
    }
  }

  /// <remarks/>
  public string ErrorMessage {
    get {
      return this.errorMessageField;
    }
    set {
      this.errorMessageField = value;
    }
  }

  /// <remarks/>
  public string DetailedResultsFile {
    get {
      return this.detailedResultsFileField;
    }
    set {
      this.detailedResultsFileField = value;
    }
  }
}
```

The third-party tool can make use of the preceding class file to write the test result details, or the test application should take care of writing the test result details into the XML file based on the XML schema used. The resultant output XML file should look like this:

```
<?xml version="1.0" encoding="utf-8" ?>
<SummaryResult>
  <TestName>Third party test Application</TestName>
  <TestResult>Failed</TestResult>
  <InnerTests>
    <InnerTest>
      <TestName>Test1</TestName>
      <TestResult>Passed</TestResult>
      <ErrorMessage>Test is Sucessful</ErrorMessage>
      <DetailedResultsFile>
        C:\Testing\Test1Results.txt
      </DetailedResultsFile>
    </InnerTest>
```

```
    </InnerTests>
  </SummaryResult>
```

In the preceding example, we can see that there are two different tests within a single test. One is to export the data to Excel, which is passed, and the other test is to **import** the details from Excel, which is failed. The second test which failed writes detailed information about the test result to the text file. Writing into the log file should be taken care of by the third-party test application in the required format.

Now the **Test Results** window for this generic test would show the result as **Passed** as shown in the following screenshot:

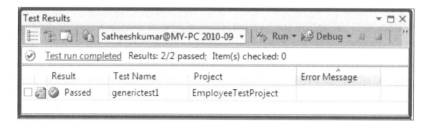

Select the result in the **Test Results** window, right-click and select **View Test Results Details**, which will show all the summary and detailed results based on the XML output as shown here:

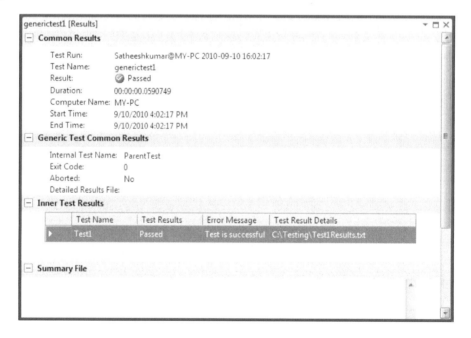

You can see the **Inner Test Results** grid where it shows the results of all the inner tests conducted by the third-party test application. If you look at the **Test Results Details** column, you see the **Test1Results.txt** file which contains the test result details. Now select the row in the **Inner Test Results** grid. On selecting the row, the text file **Test1Results.txt** opens and the details are shown in the **Summary File** area, which is simply the detailed information written by the application about the failed test:

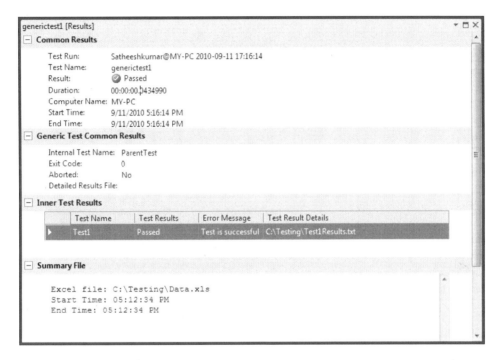

The **Summary File** information is just the content of the text file given in the **DetailedResultsFile**, in the XML output file.

Properties of a generic test

Besides having some properties in common with the other tests, generic tests also have some specific properties. To view the properties, select the generic test in the **Test View** or **Test List Editor** window and right-click to select the **Properties** option. The **Properties** dialog box is then displayed with the available properties for the generic test:

Using the **Properties** window we can associate a test to a work item, iteration, or a project area defined in the TFS. We can also set the input file as arguments, specify deployment items, set the maximum duration for the test run, and many other properties. Most of the properties such as deployment items, description, owner, priority, work item, iteration, and solution are common for all test types, whereas properties such as arguments and target executable are specific to the generic test type.

Summary

This chapter explained the details and usage of different formats of manual testing using Text and Word. Even though both the tests are similar, the Word format gives better formatting features. The section on the ordered test explained how to order the tests and execute them in the same order irrespective of their type. The generic test explained the ways of executing the third-party tests within Visual Studio and showed the tests results collected within the third-party tests.

Each of these different test types has its own properties. Some of them are common, while some are specific to the individual test. There are some common properties to associate the tests to the work items in the TFS. This is very helpful in mapping the test and tracking a set of related work items.

9

Managing and Configuring a Test

So far in all previous chapters, we have created a lot of testing applications, but we have not grouped the tests based on common properties so that we can easily manage them. There are different common properties that we can set for tests using the test run configuration file, which is used by the tests during execution. VSTS provides a utility to edit the common test configuration stored in the `testrunconfig` file. VSTS provides different tools that support easy ways of managing and grouping tests. Using these tools, we can enable and disable tests, select them to run, filter tests from the list of all the tests created for the project, and set properties for an individual test. This chapter covers the following topics:

- Managing tests using Test Lists
- Organizing Test List
- Test View
- Toolbar options
- Configuring Tests
- Editing Test Run Configurations
- Test Properties

Managing tests using Test Lists

The test solution can contain any number of tests. If the number is small we can manage tests easily, but if it is too high it is difficult to identify the tests within the large list of tests. We need to group the tests based on some property to identify and filter them easily. The **Test List Editor** is the main interface provided by Visual Studio for managing all tests under the solution. On opening the **Test List Editor**, using the **Test** menu option in VSTS, you can see all the tests listed in the editor under **All Loaded Tests**, by default. The Test List Editor is divided into two panes. The left pane has the options to choose the list of tests to be displayed on the right side.

By default, the editor displays all tests in the solution irrespective of the type, option to choose the test from the list, the test name, and the project it belongs to.

The **Test List Editor** has a toolbar with options for grouping the tests, filtering the tests, and loading the metadata.

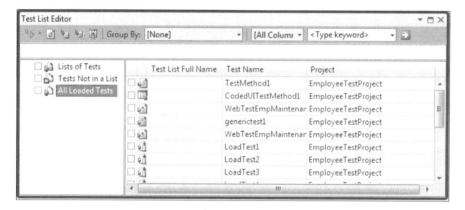

We can select the tests from the list and run them using the **Run Checked Tests** option in the toolbar. We can add or remove the columns to be displayed in the list.

Organizing the Test Lists

The editor window has three different top-level nodes in the left pane to show the test groups based on some property. They are:

- **Lists of Tests**: This is where we have to maintain the tests under the new lists. Initially there won't be any lists created.

Select the **New Test List...** option after selecting and right-clicking the **List of Tests** node. There will be a new screen for entering the Test List **Name** and **Description**. The window will also provide the flexibility to choose the node in the tree to place this new list node. For example, the following image shows the new Test List with the name, **SampleTestList,** added to the root node.

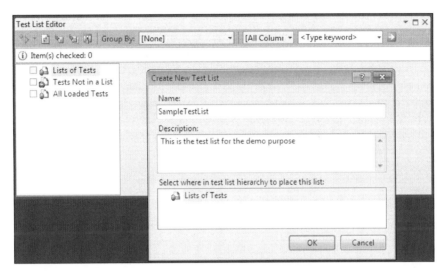

After clicking on **OK**, we can see the new list name added as a new node to the parent node, **Lists of Tests**. This is the same screen used for editing as well. We can edit only the **Name** and the **Description**. We can also delete, remove, and rename the list node from the lists.

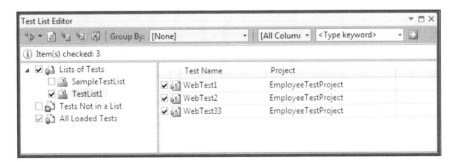

The preceding screenshot shows the **Lists of Tests** added to the solution. If the main node is selected, all the sub-nodes or the lists under the root node will also get selected by default. The new list, **SampleTestList,** is not selected, but grayed out because there are no tests added to the list yet. It's an empty list.

To add the tests to the list, select the tests from the list under **Tests Not in a List,** which are not yet added to any list. After the selection, drag-and-drop the selected tests on the Test List name. We can also use the cut, copy, and paste commands to move the tests under the lists. Now you can see the selected tests added to the list.

Each test can belong to more than one other lists. To copy the tests to the list, without removing it from the original list, press the *Ctrl* key while dragging the test to the new list.

To remove a test from all the Test Lists to which it is added, select it from any Test List, then right-click and choose the option **Remove from All Test Lists**. For example, the following screenshot shows how to remove **WebTest1**, which is then added to the lists, **SampleTestList** and **TestList1**. The other option available is to remove the test from just the selected Test List.

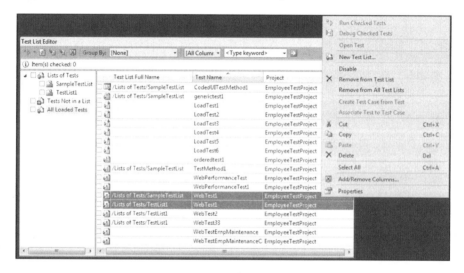

- **Tests Not in a List**: This is to list the tests that are not part of any of the List. Using this list, we can identify the tests that we need to organize and place under a particular Test List.

- **All Loaded Tests**: This option shows all the tests that are available in the solution. Whether it is part of the test or not it will be shown under this option.

Test view

The **Test View** window is similar to the **Test List Editor**, but this one shows all the tests in the solution. We cannot create any lists here, but we can filter the tests based on test properties or names. We can create a new performance session for the **Load Test** and **Web Test** from the Test View to collect the data to study and analyze the application performance. The **Test View** toolbar is similar to the toolbar for **Test List Editor** which provides **Group By**, **Filter**, **Run**, and **Debug** options, as seen in the following screenshot:

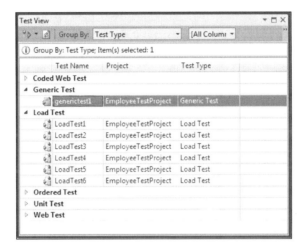

Enabling/Disabling tests

This is the common context menu option available for both **Test List Editor** and the **Test View** window. By default, all the tests listed under a Test List are enabled, which means that the test can be run. If the test is not yet ready to run or if any supporting source data is not available, we can disable the test until it is ready. In the case of ordered tests, we might have more tests. If any of the tests in the order is not ready, or if we are sure that the test will fail, then we can disable the test and run the remaining tests in the order. If the test is ready to run, we can re-enable the test using the context menu option.

Toolbar options

The toolbar options provided by **Test List Editor** and the **Test View** window are almost the same, with features such as filtering and grouping the test based on test properties.

Filtering tests

The Display of tests in the **Test List Editor** and **Test View** window can be controlled using the **Apply Filter** option in the toolbar. Filtering is useful in finding specific types of tests from the huge list of tests available in the solution. Developers might want to list only the unit tests to find out the test for testing the code change for defect fix before delivering that to the test team. On the other hand, the test team might want to list only the Web Performance Test to see if the defect fixed by the developer still exists, or if it is fixed and working as expected.

To filter the tests, use the drop-down provided in the toolbar of the **Test List Editor** or **Test View Window** and select the property on which you want to filter the tests. After selecting the property in the drop-down, enter the string in the **Filter Text** box to find a matching string in the selected property of all the tests. Now click on the **Apply Filter** button which is next to the **Filter Text** box control. Now, the filter is applied, and the editor lists only the test which has matching text in the property selected and the string entered in the **Filter Text** as shown here:

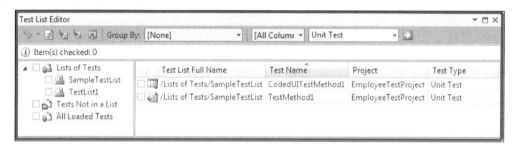

Group by

The **Group By** option is used for displaying the Test List by grouping tests based on a selected property. For example, the following screenshot shows the **Test List Editor** and **Test View** window in which tests are grouped based on properties. The **Test List Editor** groups the tests by the test property that identifies if the test is enabled or disabled. The **Test View Window** groups the tests based on the test type.

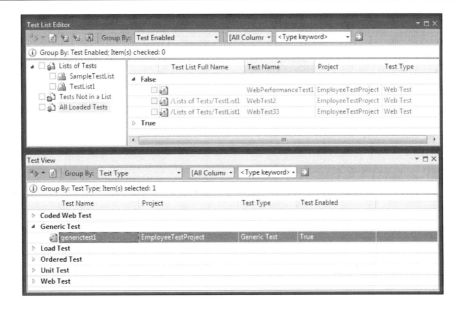

The columns drop-down list in the toolbar is also used for filtering the test. If we do not remember the full test name or type, we can select the column name from the drop-down list and then enter the partial or full text and then apply the filter. This will filter the test that has text matching the text or keyword entered for the filter. This can be a partial or full match. The following sample screenshot shows the filtered result that has returned all the tests which contain the name, **Web,** as part of the **Test Name**:

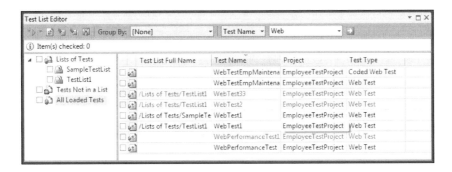

Configuring tests

The Visual Studio solution contains a common configuration file for all the tests under the solution. The common configuration file is used for controlling the test execution. In .NET, all the applications are controlled using the configuration files. The name of configuration file differs with the type of application. Similarly, all the test applications in the solution are controlled by a separate configuration file created by the solution. This file is created under the solution with the extension .testsettings. We can have multiple configuration files, but at any point in time only one configuration file can be active, from which the settings are applied to each test run.

Test settings

To specify or modify the settings in the configuration, we can use the **Test Settings Editor** which opens up on double-clicking the settings file. It has different pages for different sets of configurations.

General

This is the general page for specifying the **Name** of the settings file and the **Description** for the settings. We can also define the naming scheme used for storing the test run results. By default, it takes the current user name and the name of the machine with the run date and time added to the file name. We can also have a user defined custom scheme used for the test result name. We can also specify whether or not to add the current date and time stamp to the name.

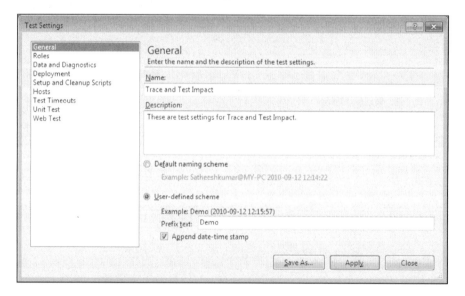

Roles

This is to set whether the test has to be run on the local machine or on a remote machine. By default, it is set to run on the local machine. If the test has to run on a remote machine, we need to provide the controller and the agent names with the roles for the test. The remote machine could be a controller or an agent but a single controller controls and collects data from multiple agents. The roles page is to configure the controller and the agents to collect the data and to run the tests. Select the **Test execution method** as **Remote execution** and then select the Controller name that will control the agents and collect the test data, from the **Controller** drop-down list.

Click on **Roles** to add different roles to run tests and collect data. The role could be a **Web Server** or **SQL Server**. Each role uses a test agent that is managed by the Controller. You can keep adding roles. To select the role that you want to run the test, click on **Set as role to run tests**. The other roles will not run the test but be used for data collection.

To limit the number of agents used for tests, we can set attributes and filter. Click on **Add** in the attributes section and then enter the attribute name and value for the selected role.

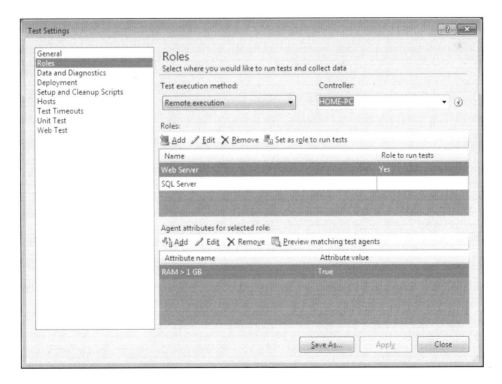

The names and values for the attributes of roles decide which agent should be used for testing.

Data and Diagnostics

From the **Data and Diagnostic** page, we can define the diagnostic data adapter that the role will use to collect data. If there are more data and diagnostics selected for the role and if there are available agents, the controller will make use of available agents to collect data. To configure each data and diagnostics, select the diagnostic and click on **Configure,** which opens the dialog box where we can configure the selected diagnostic.

The roles defined as a part of the **Roles** section are displayed for the diagnostics selection. Select each role from the list and then choose the diagnostics for the selected role. The diagnostics list is displayed only if the controller has any agents with the matching role. For example, the image below shows the Web server role which does not have an agent that matches the selection criteria defined by the attributes.

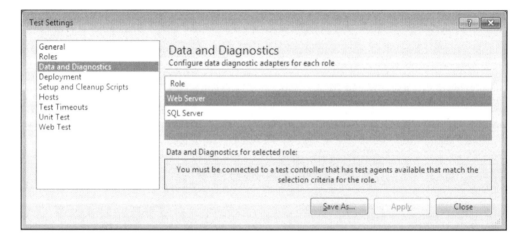

But in case of second role, which is the SQL Server role, the data and diagnostics is enabled, as the controller has a matching agent. We can choose the diagnostic data that we want to collect as part of the test.

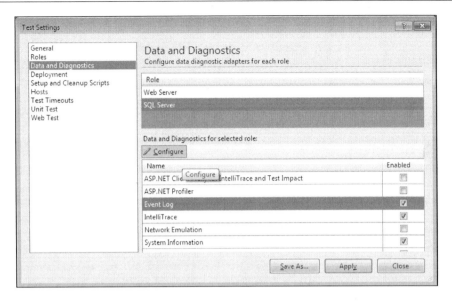

To go into the advanced configuration for the selected diagnostic, choose the **Configure** option from the **Data and Diagnostics for selected role** section, which opens the dialog box to configure the details. The following sample screenshot shows the configuration for the selected Event Log diagnostic. The configuration screen provides the option to choose the event logs to collect, event types, and the maximum entries to log per test. Similarly we can configure the other Diagnostic as well.

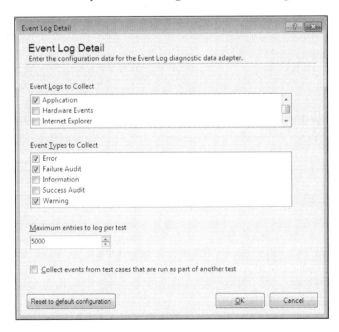

Deployment

Using this page, we can configure the files in the directory to be deployed along with the application. Whatever is specified here determines the additional files copied along with the application files that are going to be deployed. We can also enable or disable the deployment using the checkbox option, **Enable Deployment,** which is, by default, checked.

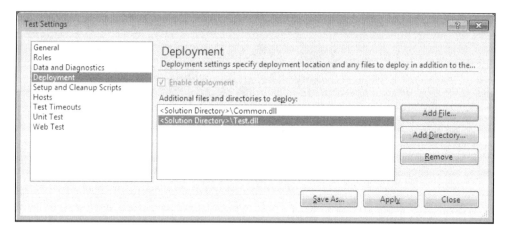

Hosts

There are two options here. One is to select the default host and the other is not to run. This page is for specifying the default host for the tests that cannot be hosted by specified adapters. To run unit tests in the same process as ASP.NET, select **ASP. NET** from the **Host Types** drop-down list. On selecting **ASP.NET**, we can see that the other required detail section is enabled. Provide details like **URL to test**, which point to the application URL. Next, configure if the test has to run with the use of the ASP.NET development server or by using local IIS. If you choose the option to run using the local development server, you need to provide the Website path and the web application root. In case of IIS, we don't have to provide the detail as it is picked from the system itself.

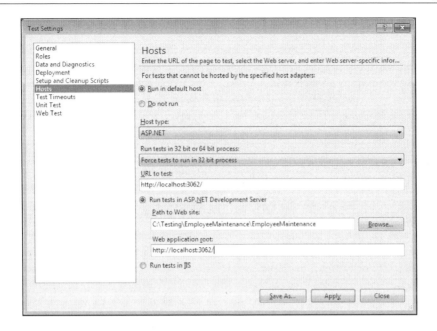

All these details are set as attribute values for test methods while creating the test project and generating the test methods.

Setup and Cleanup scripts

Here in this section, we can specify the script files to be run before and after running the test. This script file is useful in setting the environment for running the test and also in cleaning up the files or other objects used during testing. These are the common scripts for all the tests under the solution. So we should take extra care while writing the script in such a way that it should be common to all types of tests.

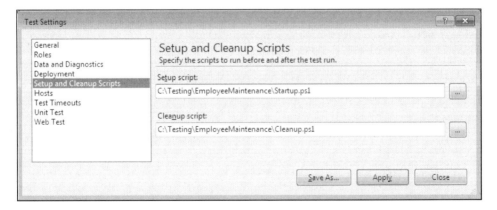

Test Timeouts

These values are specified to set the time limit value during the test run. We cannot wait for long for the test to complete. There are situations where some tests might take a longer time than expected because of many other factors such as environmental issues. In that case, we can set the maximum time limit the test run can take. If it exceeds the limit, the run will be aborted. There are two options for setting the time limit:

- **Abort a test run if its total execution time exceeds**: This is to set the total test runtime limit irrespective of the number of tests and their types. The entire test will abort after exceeding the limit.

- **Mark an individual test as failed if its execution time exceeds**: This is to specify the time limit for an individual test. This applies to all types of tests in the run. On exceeding the time of an individual test, the test will be marked as failed and the subsequent test in the list will continue to run. The timeout property set for the test using test properties will override the default timeout set here.

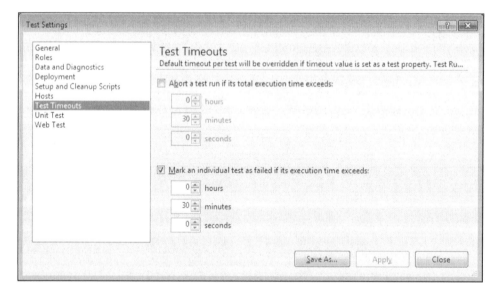

The time limit can be specified in hours, minutes, seconds, or all three. The time limit includes the **Setup** and **Cleanups** Scripts used in the test run. These are the tests with the attribute `AssemblyInitializeAttribute`, `ClassInitializeAttribute`, `AssemblyCleanUpAttribute`, and `ClassCleanUpAttribute` specified for the assembly or a class within the assembly.

Web Performance Test

Web Performance Tests require some specific settings to run. The Web Performance Test can be run in different browsers and with different sets of data. This page has the option to specify the required settings.

Using the first option, we can specify the number of run iterations. It can be a fixed run count where the count is specified, or it can be **One run per data source row**. If the number of run iterations is fixed, the test will run for the specified number of times. If it is mentioned as one row per data, the test will run for each row in the data source attached to the test.

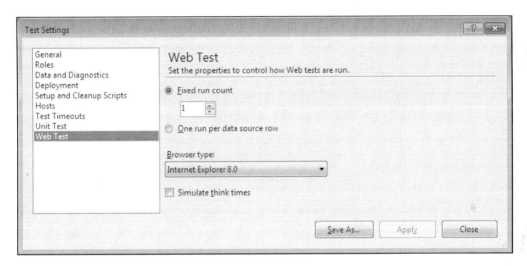

The second option is for selecting the **Browser type** used for testing. The page also has the option to simulate the think times.

Unit Test

There is an advanced option available for configuring unit tests. This is to configure the folders where the assemblies reside for the unit test and the folder to use for the test to run. There is another option to configure additional folders for tests.

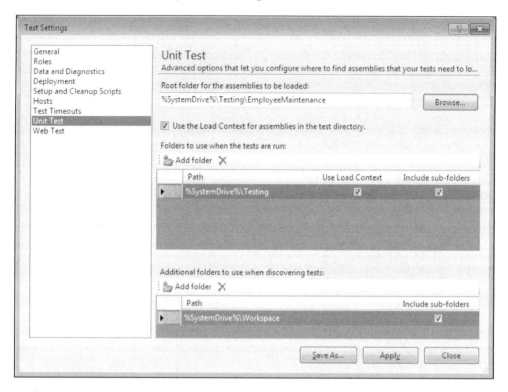

Editing the test run configuration file

The test configuration file contains the same configuration information we saw in the previous section. The editor that we used in the previous section takes care of writing information into the file. But here we are going to see how we can edit the file directly without using the editor. The information edited from both places should be reflected in the same file. It is the normal XML version of the file, which can be opened using any XML editor. As we are not using the test settings editor, we should be careful while updating the file to not break the syntax format.

Let us open the test configuration file using the XML editor and see
what we have and what we can update. Select the test configurations
file from the solution explorer and right-click and select the option
Open with and then choose any xml file editor or notepad from the
list. The XML file contains all the information that was set using
the editor. The following is the sample test settings XML file: <?xml
version="1.0" encoding="UTF-8"?>

```xml
<TestSettings name="TestSettingforLoadTest"
    id="6d1a7bad-a7a9-4c88-920e-fe97c2567242"
    xmlns="http://microsoft.com/schemas/VisualStudio/TeamTest/2010">
  <Description>These are default test settings for a local test run.
  </Description>
  <Deployment>
    <DeploymentItem filename="Common.dll" />
    <DeploymentItem filename="Test.dll" />
  </Deployment>
  <RemoteController name="HOME-PC" />
  <Execution location="Remote">
    <Hosts type="ASP.NET">
      <AspNet name="ASP.NET" executionType="WebDev"
            urlToTest="http://localhost:3062/">
        <DevelopmentServer
            pathToWebSite="C:\Testing\EmployeeMaintenance\
                                        EmployeeMaintenance"
            webApplicationRoot="http://localhost:3062/" />
      </AspNet>
    </Hosts>
    <TestTypeSpecific>
      <UnitTestRunConfig
                testTypeId="13cdc9d9-ddb5-4fa4-a97d-d965ccfc6d4b">
        <AssemblyResolution
            applicationBaseDirectory="%SystemDrive%\Testing\
                                        EmployeeMaintenance">
          <TestDirectory useLoadContext="true" />
          <RuntimeResolution>
            <Directory path="%SystemDrive%\Testing"
                    includeSubDirectories="true" />
          </RuntimeResolution>
          <DiscoveryResolution>
            <Directory path="%SystemDrive%\Workspace"
                    includeSubDirectories="true" />
          </DiscoveryResolution>
        </AssemblyResolution>
      </UnitTestRunConfig>
      <WebTestRunConfiguration
                testTypeId="4e7599fa-5ecb-43e9-a887-cd63cf72d207">
```

```
            <Browser name="Internet Explorer 8.0" MaxConnections="6">
                <Headers>
                    <Header name="User-Agent"
                            value="Mozilla/4.0 (
                                    compatible; MSIE 8.0; Windows NT 5.1)" />
                    <Header name="Accept" value="*/*" />
                    <Header name="Accept-Language"
                            value="{{$IEAcceptLanguage}}" />
                    <Header name="Accept-Encoding" value="GZIP" />
                </Headers>
            </Browser>
        </WebTestRunConfiguration>
    </TestTypeSpecific>
    <AgentRule name="Web Server">
        <SelectionCriteria>
            <AgentProperty name="RAM &gt; 1 GB" value="True" />
        </SelectionCriteria>
    </AgentRule>
</Execution>
<CollectionOnlyAgents>
    <AgentRules>
        <AgentRule name="SQL Server">
            <DataCollectors>
                <DataCollector
                    uri="datacollector://microsoft/SystemInfo/1.0"
                    assemblyQualifiedName=
"Microsoft.VisualStudio.TestTools.DataCollection.SystemInfo.
SystemInfoDataCollector, Microsoft.VisualStudio.TestTools.
DataCollection.SystemInfo, Version=10.0.0.0, Culture=neutral, PublicKe
yToken=b03f5f7f11d50a3a"
                    friendlyName="System Information">
                </DataCollector>
                <DataCollector
                    uri="datacollector://microsoft/HttpProxy/1.0"
                    assemblyQualifiedName=
"Microsoft.VisualStudio.TraceCollector.HttpProxyCollector, Microsoft.
VisualStudio.TraceCollector, Version=10.0.0.0, Culture=neutral, Public
KeyToken=b03f5f7f11d50a3a"
                    friendlyName=
                    "ASP.NET Client Proxy for IntelliTrace and Test Impact">
                </DataCollector>
                <DataCollector
                    uri="datacollector://microsoft/TestImpact/1.0" as
semblyQualifiedName="Microsoft.VisualStudio.TraceCollector.
TestImpactDataCollector, Microsoft.VisualStudio.TraceCollector,
Version=10.0.0.0, Culture=neutral, PublicKeyToken=b03f5f7f11d50a3a"
                    friendlyName="Test Impact">
```

```
        </DataCollector>
        <DataCollector
            uri="datacollector://microsoft/TraceDebugger/1.0"
assemblyQualifiedName="Microsoft.VisualStudio.TraceCollector.
TraceDebuggerDataCollector, Microsoft.VisualStudio.TraceCollector,
Version=10.0.0.0, Culture=neutral, PublicKeyToken=b03f5f7f11d50a3a"
            friendlyName="IntelliTrace">
        </DataCollector>
      </DataCollectors>
    </AgentRule>
  </AgentRules>
  </CollectionOnlyAgents>
</TestSettings>
```

Once the file is opened in the selected XML editor, we can start editing the XML file as we would normally do with any XML file.

Editing the deployment section

For example, the following is the section that identifies the additional files to be deployed along with the application:

```
<Deployment>
  <DeploymentItem filename="Test.dll" />
  <DeploymentItem filename="Common.dll" />
</Deployment>
```

If we have to include more files to be added, we can simply edit it and add the file with the correct attribute. The following code shows the additional files added to the section:

```
<Deployment>
  <DeploymentItem filename="Test.dll" />
  <DeploymentItem filename="Common.dll" />
  <DeploymentItem filename="Readme.txt" />
</Deployment>
```

Test properties

Properties are the configurations meant for the individual tests that are required for running the test. These properties can be set from the **Test List Editor** or the **Test View window**. Some of these properties are directly related to the Team Project Information available in **Team Foundation Server (TFS)**. The projects that are controlled by TFS contain properties such as the iteration, project area, and work items. If the current test project is maintained by the VSTFS integrated version control system, we can specify test properties to maintain the test under a specific work item, specific iteration, and specific project area. The following list explains the properties available for test. You can select the test from the **Test List Editor** or **Test View** and right-click to open the **Properties**. Some properties are specific to the test based on its type.

Property	Is Editable	Description
Arguments	Editable	This property allows us to set the command line argument to be passed to the target program for the test execution.
Associated Work Items	This is editable if connected to Team Foundation Server	We can associate this generic test to the Work item in Team Foundation Server; the work item can be a task, a defect, or a requirement.
Deployment Items	Editable	This refers to the files or folders that need to be deployed along with this test; we have to provide the full path of the files or folders that have to be deployed; there is an option in the property that opens the file open dialog to select the files.
Description	Editable	This property gives us a detailed description of the test.
Environment Variables	Read Only	This property is to set the environment variables for command line execution.
Host Type	Editable	Identify the Host type used for the test. It is either **Default** or the **ASP.NET** host type.
ID	Read only	This property gives us the unique name of the test; it gives the full path of the generic test where it resides.
Iteration	This is Editable if part of Team Foundation Server	This property explains which iteration in the software project life-cycle these tests belongs to; you can set the iterations in TFS.
Maximum Duration	Editable	This property tells how long a generic test can be allowed to execute before terminating the test. The Default Value is **3600000** in milliseconds.
Non-runnable Error	Read only	This property explains the reason why the generic test cannot be executed in this test run; even if a test is included in a test project but for some reason or other this test cannot be executed in this test run; you can enter the reason in this property. This property will be empty if the test is executable for this test run.
Owner	Editable	This property gives the name of the person who has authored the test or is maintaining it.

Property	Is Editable	Description
Priority	Editable	This property is to set the priority of the test; it explains the relative importance of the test and determines which test needs to be executed first; this is also useful for grouping the tests based on priority.
Project	Read Only	This property gives the test the project name to which it belongs.
Project Area	This is Editable if part of Team Foundation Server	This property determines the node in the team project to which this test belongs.
Project Relative Path	Read Only	This property determines the file name of the project where the test resides; the path is relative to the location of the solution.
Redirect Standard Output and Error	Editable	This property allows us to redirect the standard output and the error messages from the target program.
		The value **TRUE** enables the standard output and error message to be redirected.
		The value **FALSE** disables the redirection.
Solution	Read Only	This property identifies the name of the solution that contains the test project to which this test belongs.
Summary XML File	Editable	Identifies the path of the Summary XML Result file.
		This Summary XML result file contains the details of the results from the tests executed within the main test.
Target Executable	Editable	Identifies the path of the third-party command line utility that will be used to execute the tests.
Test Category	Editable	Used to categorize the test and group it under a particular category.
Test Enabled	Editable	This is to enable or disable the test for this run.
		Its default value is **TRUE**.
Test Name	Read Only	This property identifies the name of the test.
Test Storage	Read Only	This gives us the complete path of the file that contains this test; for a generic test, this property is the same as the test 'ID' property.

Property	Is Editable	Description
Test Type	Read Only	This is to identify the type of the test
		In this case the value is 'Generic'; this property is used for Grouping and filtering the tests in the Test view and Test List Editor.
Timeout	Read Only	This property sets the timeout value for the test; how long the test can take to run before it is marked as failed, and abort.
		For a generic test this property has a value of '00:00:00', which we can overwrite by typing the new value.
Use Summary XML File	Editable	By using this property, we can specify whether to use the Summary XML result file, which contains the detailed result of the test execution.
		If **TRUE** then the summary XML result file is used.
		If **FALSE** then the summary XML result file is not used.
Working Directory	Editable	This property determines the working directory of the Target program.

Summary

This chapter explained the different ways of managing the tests in the solution and ways of filtering the tests and grouping the tests in the solution. This chapter also explained about editing the test run configuration using the configuration editor supported by Visual Studio. We have also seen ways of editing the configuration file directly without using the editor.

10
Command Line

We have seen different types of testing and have run tests in Visual Studio 2010 IDE. It is very simple to run the test with the Visual Studio user interface using the *Test List Editor* or *Test View Window* as we have seen in previous chapters. To create or prepare a test project, we need Visual Studio IDE, but once the test is created and ready for execution, we can run the test using Visual Studio IDE or also by using the command line utility.

This chapter explains the command line tool used to run the test with different options and collect the output. This chapter explains the details and usage of the features listed as follows:

- MSTest Command Line utility
- Running a test from the command line
- Publishing test results

MSTest utility

This is the command line utility supported by Visual Studio. Using **MSTest** tool, we can run the tests created in Visual Studio.

To access the **MSTest** tool, add the Visual Studio install directory to the path or access the Visual Studio Command Prompt from the **Tools** section of the Visual Studio group in the start menu.

After opening the command prompt, type MSTest.

The MSTest command expects a parameter to be specified, the name of the test to be run. To see the options of MSTest, just type MSTest /help or MSTest /? at the command prompt.

The help option lists the different parameter options that can be used with MSTest and the description of each parameter and its usage.

Option	Description
/help	Displays this usage message:
	`<Short form: /? or /h>`
/nologo	Does not display the startup banner and the copyright message.
/testcontainer:[file name]	Loads a file that contains tests; you can specify this option more than once to load multiple test files.
	Examples:
	`/tescontainer:mytestproject.dll`
	`/testcontainer:loadtest1.loadtest`
/maxpriority:[priority] /minpriority:[priority]	Execute the tests with priority less than or equal to this value:
	`/minpriority:0   /maxpriority:2`

Option	Description
/category	This filter is used to select tests and run them based on the category of each test. We can use logical operators & and ! to construct the filters or we can use the logical operators | and ! to filter the tests.
	/category:Priority1—any tests with category as Priority1.
	/category:Priority1&MyTests—any tests with multiple categories as Priority1 and MyTests.
	/category:Priority1|Mytests—Multiple tests with category as either Priority1 or MyTests
	/category:Priority1&!MyTests—Priority1 tests that do not have category MyTests
/testmetadata:[file name]	Loads a metadata file.
	Example:
	/testmetadata:testproject1.vsmdi
/testsettings:[file name]	Uses the specified test settings file
	Example:
	/testsettings:mysettings.testsettings
/resultsfile:[file name]	Saves the test run results to the specified file
	Example:
	/resultsfile:c:\temp\myresults.trx
/testlist:[test list path]	The Test List to run as specified in the metadata file; you can specify this option multiple times to run more than one Test List.
	Example:
	/testlist:checkintests/clientteam
/test:[file name]	The name of a test to be run; you can specify this option multiple times to run more than one test.
/unique	Runs a test only if one unique match is found for any given test.
/noisolation	Runs a test within the MSTest.exe process. This choice improves test run speed but increases the risk to the MsTest process.

Option	Description
/noresults	Does not save the test results in a TRX file; the choice improves the test run speed but does not save the test run results.
/detail:[property id]	The name of a property that you want to show values for, in addition to the test outcome; examine a test results file to see the available properties. Example: /detail:errormessage

In addition to the preceding options, there are many other options which can be used with MSTest if *Team Explorer* is used.

Option	Description
/publish:[team project collection url]	Publishes results to the Team Project Collection.
/testconfigname:[config name]	The name of the preexisting test management configuration to associate with the published run.
/testconfigid:[config id]	The ID of the preexisting test management configuration to associate with the published run.
/publishbuild:[build name]	The build identifier to be used to publish test results.
/publishresultsfile:[file name]	The name of the test results file to be published; if none is specified, use the file produced by the current test run
/teamproject:[team project name]	The name of the Team Project to which the build belongs; specify this when publishing test results
/platform:[platform]	The platform of the build against which to publish the test results
/flavour:[flavor]	The flavor of the build against which to publish test results
/buildverification:[yes/no]	The parameter is optional. Identifies the test as a build verification run. The Default value is Yes.

We will run and check some tests using these options using the MSTest command line tool.

Running a test from the command line

Let us see some of the options for MSTest and see the results produced by these options. It is applicable only for the automated tests. Even if we apply the command for the manual test, the tool will remove the non-automated test from the test run.

/testcontainer

The testcontainer option needs the file that contains the information about the tests that must be run. The test container file differs across tests. For example, the unit test information is contained in the Unit Test project assembly file. For the Ordered Test, it would be the <ordertestproject>.orderedtest file, which contains information about the ordered test.

If we have multiple test projects created under the solution, each of these projects has its own container for the tests within the project.

Let us consider an ordered test which contains four different tests such as unittest1.TestMethod1, CodedUITest1.CodedUITestMethod1, WebTestEmpMaintenanceCoded, and webtestempmaintenance.webtest. The name of the ordered test file is OrderedTest1.orderedtest. Now let us try using MSTest to run the tests in the ordered test file. You can see the output of the test as shown in the following image:

First, MSTest loads all the tests within the ordered test and then starts executing them one by one. The result of each test is shown but the details of test run is stored in the test trace file. We can load the trace file in Visual Studio and see the details of the test run.

For Unit Tests and coded Web Performance Tests, the test project file will be an assembly. For example, the following command will load the EmployeeTestProject.dll assembly and run the tests within that assembly:

The preceding image shows the unit test and coded Web Performance Tests within the assembly, which were executed, and the results are stored in the results file.

/testmetadata

The testmetadata option is used for running tests in multiple test projects under a solution. This is based on the metadata file created under the solution. The metadata file contains a list of all the tests added to the **Test List Editor**. Using this Test Editor, we can create a new list of tests from all the available tests under the solution, irrespective of the projects.

The testcontainer option is specific to a test project whereas testmetadata is for multiple test containers with the flexibility of choosing tests from each container.

For example, the following image shows two different Test Lists which contain different tests added to the list from all the available tests in the solution:

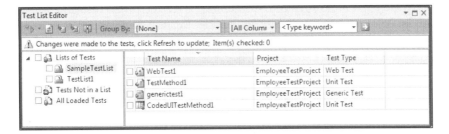

Any change or update made in the Test List editor will be saved in the metadata file. Now, to run only the tests added to the Test Lists in the editor, we use the metadata option. To run a specific Test List, we should use the `/testlist` option along with the `testmetadata` option as shown:

```
mstest /testmetadata:[file name] /testlist:[test list name]
```

The following command runs all the tests added to the list, `SampleTestList`:

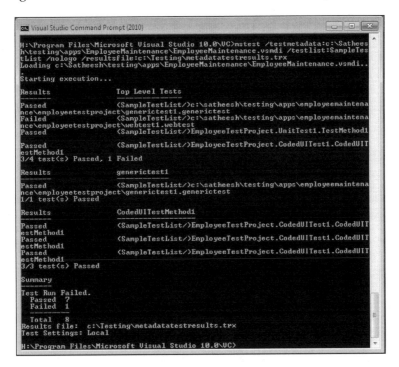

If there are no tests added to the Test List, and if it is an empty list, the `Mstest` command will clearly display a message saying there are no tests to be run in the list.

/test

There are instances when we might have to run a particular test from an available list of tests. In that case, we can use the /test option with the testmetatadata option or the testcontainer option. For example, the following command runs only the generictest1.generictest test from the list:

The /test option can be used along with testmetadata or testcontainer, but not both. There are different usages for the /test option:

- We can specify any number of tests using the /test multiple times against testmetadata or testcontainer option.
- The name used against the /test option is the search keyword for the fully qualified test names. For example, there may be test names with fully qualified names such as:

```
EmployeeTestProject.GenericTest1.generictest
EmployeeTestProject.Service1Test.CodedUITest1
EmployeeTestProject.Service1Test.TestMethod1
```

If the command contains the option /test:EmployeeTestProject then all the preceding three tests will be run, as the name contains the EmployeeTestProject string in it. Even though we specify only the name to the /test option, the result displays the fully qualified name of the tests run in the results window.

/unique

This option will make sure that only one test, which matches the given name, is run. In the preceding examples, we saw three different tests with the string, `EmployeeTestProject`, in its fully qualified name. If we run the following command, all the preceding three tests will be executed:

```
mstest /testmetadata:c:\Satheesh\testing\apps\EmployeeMaintenance\
EmployeeMaintenance.vsmdi /test:EmployeeTestProject
```

But if we specify the `/unique` option along with the preceding command, `MSTest` will return the message saying more than one test was found in the same name. It means that the test will be successful only if the test name is unique.

The following command will execute successfully as there is only one test with the name `Generic`:

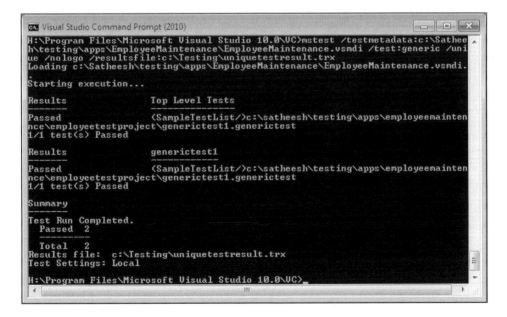

/noisolation

This option runs tests with the `MStest.exe` process. This choice improves test run speed, but increases risk to the `MSTest.exe` process.

Usually, tests are run in a separate process which is allocated separate memory from the system. If we launch `MSTest.exe` with the `/noisolation` option, the tests are run within the MSTest process which avoids having a separate process created for the test.

/testsettings

This is to specify that the test uses a specific test settings file. If the settings file is not specified, `MSTest` uses the default settings file. The following example forces the test to use the `TraceAndTestImpact` settings file:

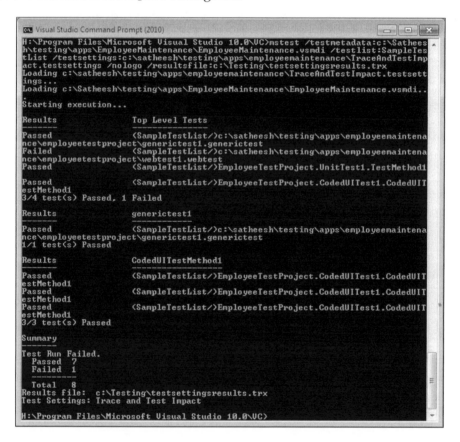

/resultsfile

In all the command executions, MSTest stores the test results in a trace file. By default, the trace file name is assigned by MSTest with the login user ID, the machine name, and the current date and time. We can force the test tool to use a specific file to store the test results. For example, a test result file is created which may be User1_My-PC 2010-06-27 08_00_32_.trx in the default Visual Studio folder. We can use the resultsfile option to change the location and the filename of the results file.

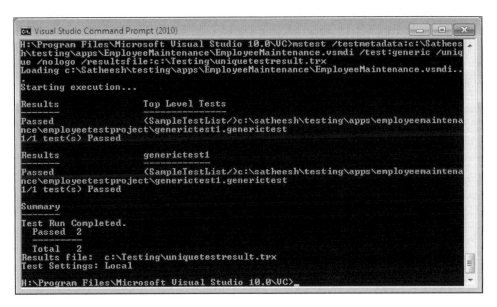

The previous image shows the test results stored at the c:\testing location in the results file, uniquetestresult.trx.

/noresults

This option is to inform the MSTest application not to store the test results in the TRX file. This choice does not store the results but increases the performance of the test execution.

/nologo

This option is to inform the MSTest tool not to display the copyright information, which is shown at the beginning of the test run.

/detail

This is the option used to get the values of the properties of each test run result. Each test result provides information about the test such as error messages, start time, end time, test name, description, test type, and many more properties. Using this option we can get the property values after the test run. For example, the following command shows the start and end time of the test run and also the type of the test run:

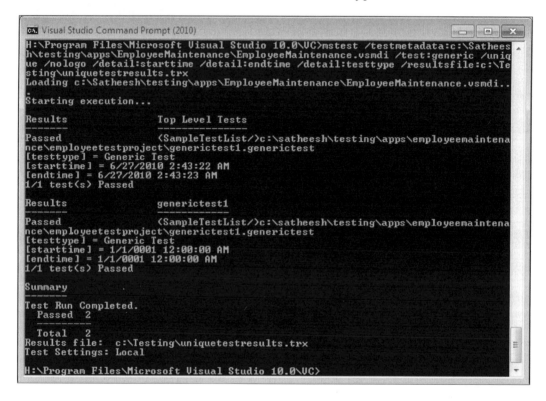

The detailed option can be specified multiple times to get multiple property values after the test run.

Publishing test results

This option is valid only if we have *Team Explorer* installed, and if Visual Studio is connected to **Team Foundation Server** (**TFS**). This publishes the test data and results to the TFS Team Project. Please refer to MSDN for more information on installing and configuring TFS and *Team Explorer*.

Using the command line utility with different options, we can publish the test run results. The publish option with MSTest will first run the test and then set the flavor and platform for the test before publishing the data to TFS. Some of these options are mandatory for publishing the test run details.

We will see examples of different publishing options available for the command line MSTest tool.

/publish

The /publish command should be followed by the URI of TFS, if TFS is not registered in the client. If it is registered, we can use just the name of the server to which the test result has to be published.

`/publish:[server name]`

- Example 1: `/publish:http://MyTFSServer`

  (If the TFS Server is not registered in the client)

- Example 2: `/publish:MyTFSServer`

  (If the TFS Server is registered with the client)

/publishbuild

This option is used for specifying the build name for publishing. This is the unique name that identifies the build from the list of scheduled builds.

/flavor

This is a mandatory option to publish test results to TFS. Flavor is a string value which should be used in combination with the platform name and should match the completed build that can be identified by the /publishbuild option. Before publishing the test run results to TFS, MSTest will run the test and then set the flavor and the platform properties.

`/flavour:[flavour string value]`

- Examples 1: `/flavor:Release`
- Example 2: `/flavour:Debug`

/platform

This is a mandatory string value used in combination with the /flavor option which should match the build option.

`/platform:[string value]`

- Example 1:   `/platform:Mixed Platforms`
- Example 1: `/platform:.NET`
- Example 1: `/platform:Win32`

/publishresultsfile

MSTest stores all test results in default trace files with the extension .trx. Using this /publishresultsfile option we can publish the test results output/trace file to TFS. The name of the file is the input to this option. If the value is not specified, MSTest will publish the current test run trace file to TFS.

`/publishresultfile:[file name string]`

Example 1: `/publishresultfile`

(Current test run trace file will be published)

Trace files

Before publishing the test result we have to store the test results in a trace file. Use the /tracefile option with the MSTest command line to store the test results. The default extension for the trace file is .trx. It is better to use the same extension when we force Visual Studio to use a specific trace file for the test results.

For example:

```
MSTest /testmetadata:TestProject.vsmdi /testfile:TestProject.trx
```

Publishing

To publish the test result, we can use a combination of the different options seen previously, but the only destination is /publishresultsfile.

Let us try creating a trace file and then create a build type for the project. Then we can publish the test result trace file to the build.

Step 1: Create/use existing test project

The following image contains the solution, **EmployeeMaintenance**. The solution contains a Test project, **EmployeeTestProject,** with simple unit test as **CodedUITest1**. The following image shows the test project named **EmployeeTestProject**:

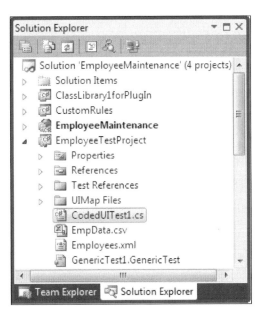

Step 2: Running the test

The test project contains two unit test methods. Run the test and, by default, the test result is stored in the trace files <file name>.trx.

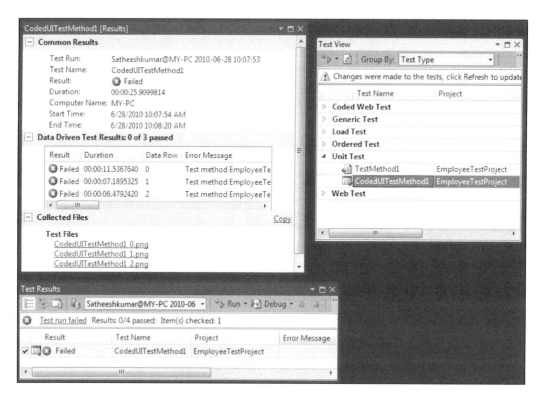

Step 3: Create build

The build service in Team Foundation Server 2010 is a little bit different from the earlier version. The build service has to be configured with controller and agents. Each build controller manages a set of build agents. The steps and the details behind creating the build types are out of the scope for this chapter and book. The following screenshot shows the build service configured with controller and agents:

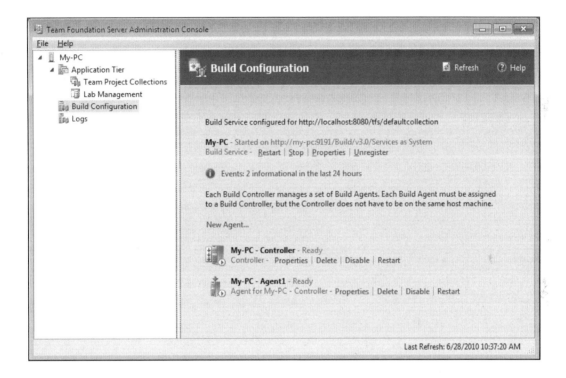

So let us see a quick overview on how to create the build definition using the Team Explorer. Within the Team Explorer select **Build definitions** under the **Builds** option folder, under the Team Project. Right-click and choose a new build definition and configure the options by choosing the projects in TFS and the local folder. In one of the steps, you can see the following screens to select the project and set the configuration information for the build.

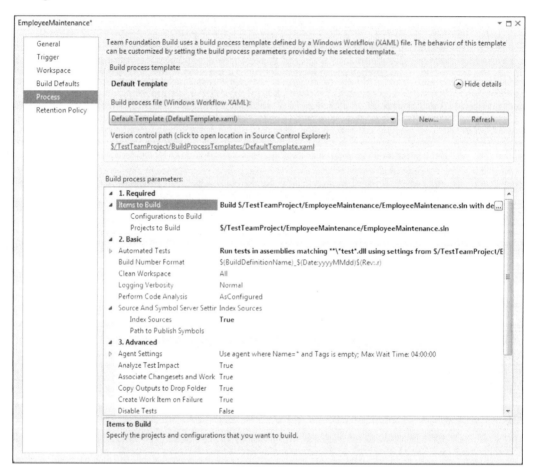

There are different configuration sections where we can select the project to build as part of this build definition. There are settings such as build file formats, Agents settings, work item creation on build failure, among others.

Step 4: Build project

We have created all the projects and set the configurations and properties. We are ready to run the test, build and publish the test results. Select the new build definition and start the build queue process. You can see the build name for the current build. The result details section shows the build summary.

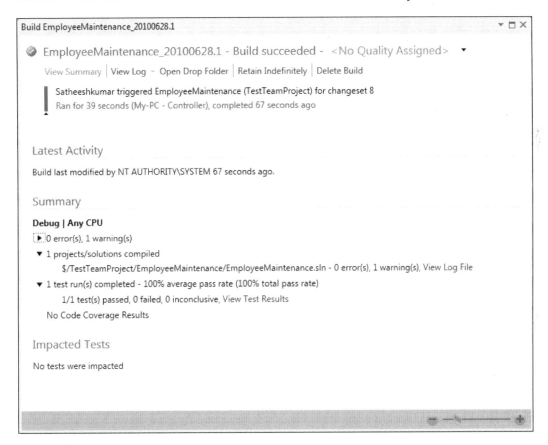

Step 5: Publish result

So far we have run the test and created the test results trace file and also built the project using build definition. The test runs were successful and now we can publish the test results to the build. We have seen the options used for publishing the test results using the MSTest command line tool. The following command publishes the test result to the specified build:

The command line options used in the preceding screenshot show the test result trace file, TFS Team Project, and build against which the test result should be published. The command line also has the platform and the flavor values matching the build configurations.

After publishing the test results, if you open the build, **EmployeeMaintenance_20100628.1**, you can see the test information along with the build summary. The information also contains the link to the trace file.

Summary

This chapter explained the use of the command line utility, MSTest, used for running the test without using the UI. We have seen different command line options for running the test, and their usage. We have not only run the test but also seen how to publish the test results to the corresponding build using the command line options.

11

Working with Test Results

The test result helps us to verify whether the test methods return the expected results but are also useful when analyzing the application quality and verifying the build. We can add the test as part of the *Team Foundation Server* automated build so that we can verify the build and make sure the latest code checked into the source control is working as expected. The build process takes care of compiling the latest checked-in code and creating the project output files and deployment files. If the tests are included as part of the build, the build service runs the tests after building the code and produces test results similar to the tests run using *Test View* or *Test List Explorer*. The test results are stored separately in trace files in the test results folder. The *Test Results Window* helps us to create defects directly into the *Team Foundation Server* as a work item of type defect. The results can also be published directly to *Team Foundation Server* and associated to the code builds available in Team Foundation Server. The following are the main topics that will be covered in this chapter:

- Test as part of Team Foundation Server Build
- Build Report and Test result
- Creating Work Item from Test result
- Publish Test Results

Test Results

All tests run using *Test List Editor, Test View Window,* and the *Solution Explorer* will show the test results in the *Test Result Window*. This window shows the status of the test and the link to the test result details. The test name is the same as the test result .trx file name created by the test run.

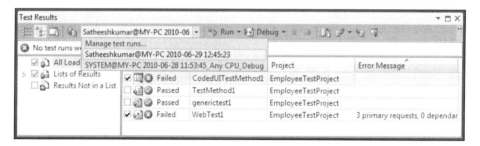

Test as part of Team Foundation Server Build

Team Foundation Server is the place to maintain the code for all projects including the test projects. Let us assume that we have a class library project and the unit test project for the class library and both checked into Team Foundation Server. Whenever there is a change or fix in the code, the test project has to run and verify that the fix is producing the expected result.

Team Foundation Server provides an explicit build service to build the team projects. The build service has to be configured so that the service makes use of the controllers and the agents for the build process.

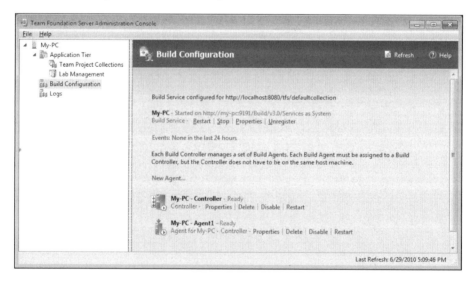

Once the build service is configured and ready for creating the build definitions, we can use Team Explorer to create the build definition for projects. The following screenshot shows the build project which contains the class library project and the test project for the class library:

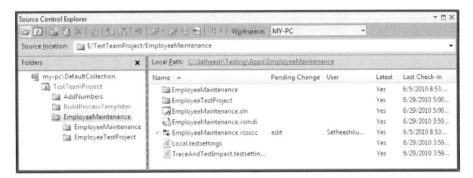

The build project automates the process of taking the latest code from the source control, compiling the project files, and building the project to make sure the code is not breaking. The build process can also run the test project after compiling and building the code to verify the code fix is not breaking anywhere. Creating the build definition involves multiple steps to select the solution files and folders, customize the build process, and set the schedule timing for the builds.

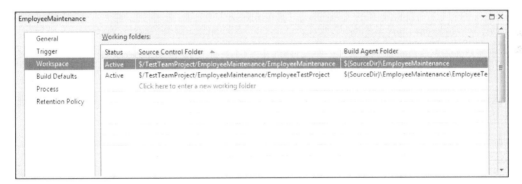

The option shown in the preceding screenshot is one of the steps involved in creating the build definition to select the solution files to build. It can be a multiple or a single solution. During the build process, all the latest code files under this solution folder are compiled and built. You can see that the *Test Project*, which contains all the tests that we have created so far is also included.

The next major configuration section is the **Process** section in which we can configure the projects and tests to be included as part of the build. There are three different parts of configuration: **Required**, **Basic**, and **Advanced**.

- **Required**: This is to include the projects or items to be built as part of the build process.

- **Basic**: The basic section is used for selecting the automated tests and setting the arguments and priority for the testing. We can also select the Test Lists to run as part of the build.

- **Advanced**: This section selects a particular agent for building the projects, sets the option to create work items on test failure, arguments, platform, and drop location to place the output files.

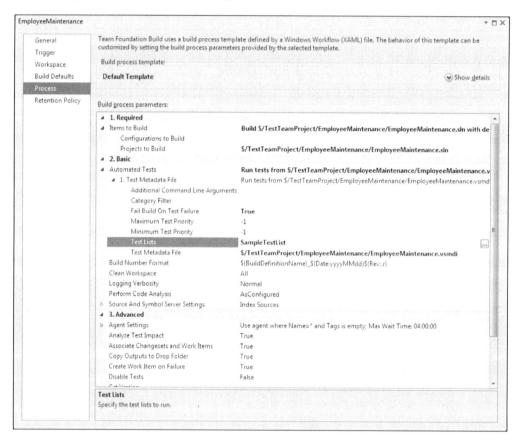

The preceding screenshot shows the *Test Metadata File*, which helps us to select the test metadata file to be used for test selection. We can include the *Command Line Arguments* as the test is executed from the command line during the build process. The **Category Filter** option is used to filter a set of tests from all the available tests. The other filter options available are the minimum priority, maximum priority, to set the option to fail build on any test failure, and choose the Test List. With this section we can select the test settings instead of the test metadata file.

The following screenshot shows the option to select the test setting or the metadata file for the build process. Once the metadata file is selected, we can see the Test Lists listed in the list box to choose the Test List. There is also an option to include all tests in the VSMDI file to run all tests. In this same window there is an option to set the build to fail if any of the selected tests fails during the build process.

The next section is the *Advanced* section, which is used for setting the Maximum **Agent Execution Time**, the **Maximum Agent Reservation Wait Time** and choosing the Agent using *Agent Name* and *Tag*. The other configuration can also be set to analyze the *Test Impact, Associate Changesets* and *Work Items, Copy Outputs* to drop folder, create *Work Item* on failure, get specific version of code, set command line arguments for the MSBuild, and lastly specify the private drop location.

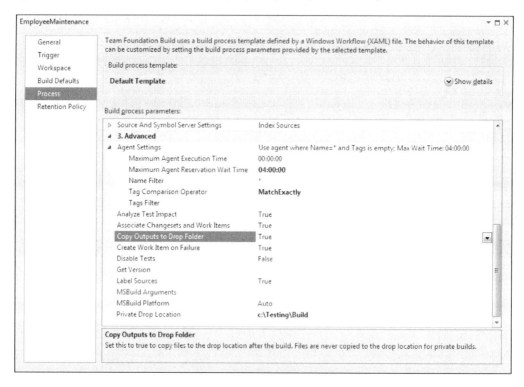

Once we set the process related configuration, the next thing is to set the *Retention Policy* for the test results. There is another section, Trigger, which is used for setting the build schedule to start the build process. It can be set to run Manually so that the check-ins do not trigger the build, Continuous Integration build which happens on every check-in, Rolling builds which accumulates the files until the previous build completes, gated-check in if the files submitted merges and builds successfully, schedule the build to run at a particular time daily, weekly, or every day.

Once we set all these configurations, we are ready with the build definition.

Build Report and Test Result

Select the build definition from *Team Explorer* and Queue new build for the selected build definition. Visual Studio takes the source code from the solution from TFS and builds the projects and reports it immediately. The report is also saved in TFS for future reference. Each and every step is reported in the build report. It consists of getting the source for the project, compiling the projects, compiling the test project, and running the test project if it is set to run after the build. The report also includes the overall build status. The test run status is also reported and the test results are stored in a similar way when the tests are run directly from Visual Studio. The following screenshot is the sample of the build summary report:

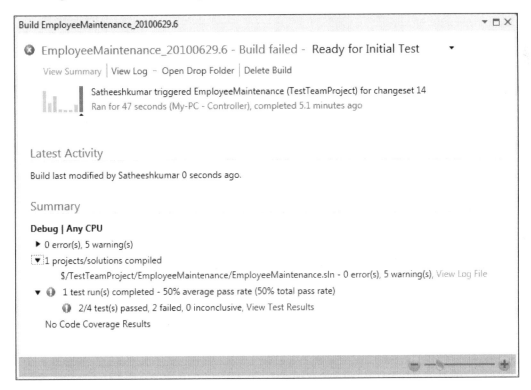

The build shown in the preceding image failed with errors in running the tests. There are five warnings in building the solutions files. Two out of four tests failed and because of that the whole build shows as failed. The **Summary** window has a URL link to View Log, *Drop Folder*, and *Delete Build*. There is another link to the detailed Test results shown as *View Test Results*.

First we shall look at the log for the build that got executed. The following screenshot shows the section of detailed log information which explains the Test execution as part of the build. The log shows that the build used MSTest to run the tests along with command line parameters, flavors, and platform information. The log shows the test results and the *Top Level Test* name. If you scroll further down in the log window you can find the result details for each test. The results also get published to the build.

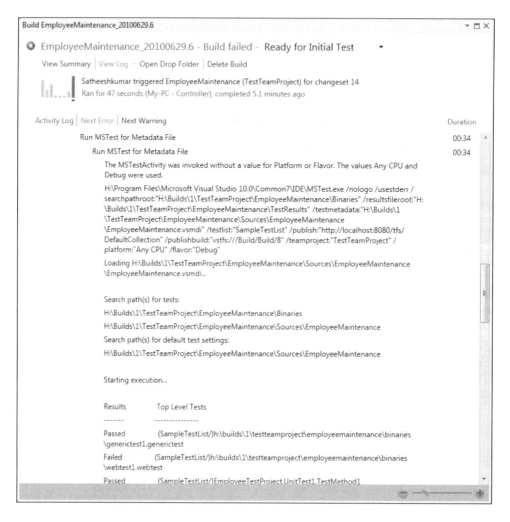

Now let us look at the Test result detail information by clicking on the URL for Test Results, *View Test Results*. This option opens the **Test Results** window and shows the tests executed and the result:

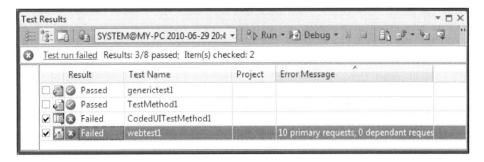

Right-click on the test result and choose **View Test Result Details** to open the detailed test result window which shows the details of the test run. The following screenshot shows the details for **generictest1** which is passed:

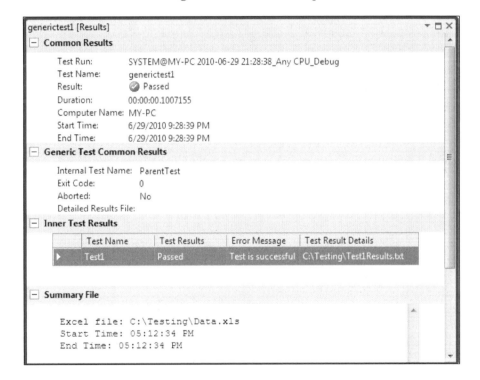

Creating Work Item from the result

Work Item in Team Foundation Server refers to a unit of work with a definite start and end. It could be just an item which is a task or a defect which is a work item of type Bug or it could be an issue or a requirement item. The following screenshot shows the option to add a work item using the **Menu** option in Visual Studio. The option lists the different types of work items.

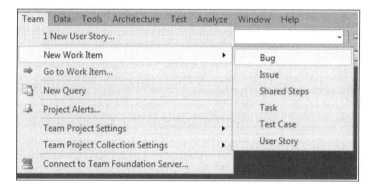

The work item of type **Bug** is used to raise a defect against a failure or error occurred in the application. Now in our preceding example the test result throws an error from the code which needs to be fixed by the developer who wrote the code. Now we can add the corresponding bug work item to TFS using the **Menu** option or we can directly add it from the **Test Results** window.

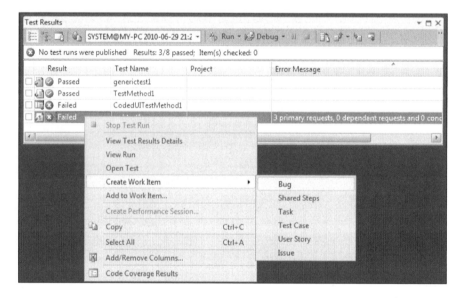

The error is added as a Bug to the Team Foundation work item. It also fills in the details required for the bug. We can overwrite the details as per our requirement if we want. The defect has different sections to it. We can overwrite or fill in additional details to the fields for the Bug.

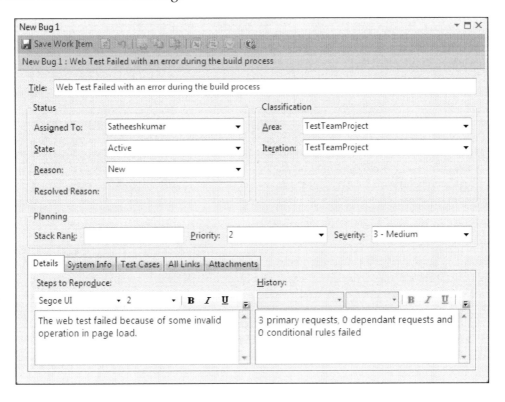

There are other tabs to collect more information related to the defect. Some of them are filled for us raised from the **Test Results** window. The fourth one is the **Links** tab, which contains the link to the corresponding test from which this defect occurred. It is automatically filled by TFS when we create this defect.

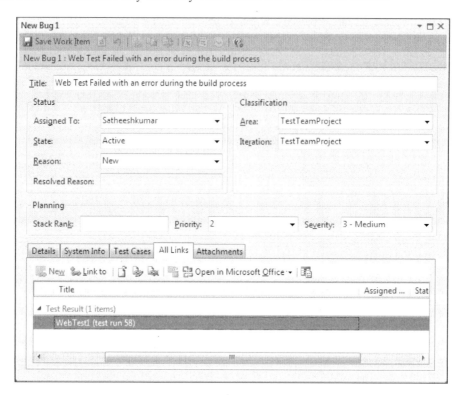

The **Edit** option in the **Links** tab opens the window which contains the link to the test result of the test which is the source of

this defect. We can edit the comment if required. If there are additional links to be added or if the link is moved to a different place, we can add it. The following screenshot shows that the defect is linked to one of the test cases available to create employee details.

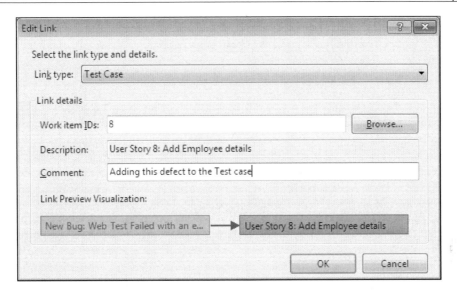

The next tab in the bug work item is the attachment which has the trace file and the test results for the test attached to it. Select the trace file and click on open, which opens the **Test Results** window with the results loaded in the window.

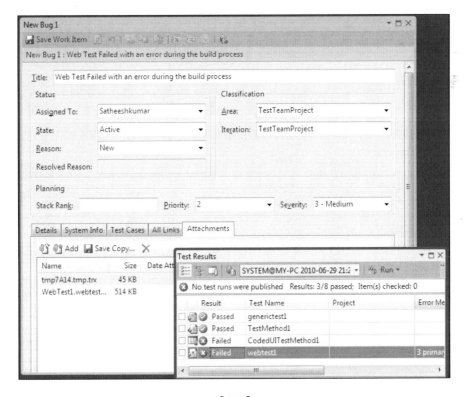

This tab also has different options to add another attachment, save the attachment to a different location, or delete the attachment.

Publish Test Results

So far what we have seen in this chapter, is running the tests, creating the work item for the test result, and setting its properties. If the test is run as part of the build process, then the result will get published automatically based on the build configurations. If the test is run outside of the build process, the test results are stored on the local machine. If the testing is carried out by different testers in different locations, everyone will have the test results on their local machine. To consolidate and keep a history of test results for the latest build of code and let other project teams or the other team members know, *Team Foundation Server* maintains the operational store, which is a central database where all the details are stored for future use.

Visual Studio provides an option to publish the test results to the *Team Foundation Server Operational Store* so that the another team at a different location can easily look at the test results published to a central location.

The **Test Results** window has the option to **Publish Test Results**. Select the check box option against the test results in the window and click on the **Publish** button on the test results toolbar.

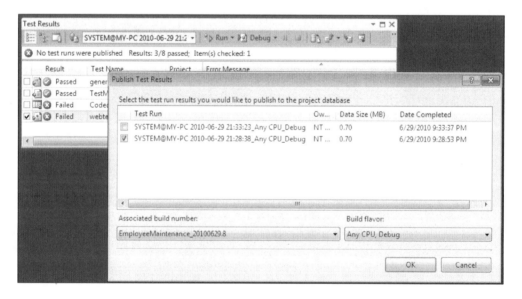

The publish option opens a new window which lists all the test results in the current **Test Results** folder. Select the **Test** to be published and select the associated build number and the flavor to publish the result.

Summary

Whenever a test is run from *Solution Explorer*, the *Test View Window*, or the *Test List Editor*, the results of the tests run are shown in the *Test Results* window. It has different options to filter, import, export, and publish the test to *Team Foundation Server*. The Test Result window also provides a detailed window which shows the error messages for the failed test and the stack trace for the failed unit test result to take us directly to the code where the error occurs. This is very easy for the development team to the cause for the test and the source. The testers also do not have to spend time in logging the defect for the error. The Visual Studio provides the feature to directly log the defect in *Team Foundation Server*. Visual Studio provides better reporting tools, used for grouping the details and presenting the same in graphical and grid formats which we will see in the next chapter.

12
Reporting

We have seen different types of testing methods and run the tests using Visual Studio 2010. Previous chapters explained different ways of running the tests and looking at the test results through the **Test Results** and the **Test Run** window. The **Test View** window, **Test List Editor**, and the **Solution Explorer** window are used for maintaining the tests. The test result summary window displays the selected test result after the test run. But how do we get the collective information about all the tests run based on some specific parameters? Visual Studio 2010 Integrated with Team Foundation server 2010 provides built-in reports to get collective information on all the tests runs. There are several other reports to get information about work items, Team Project builds, and the task level status of the project. These reports are very useful to study and analyze the project quality and status at any point in time.

TFS comes with different process templates that can be used for the team project. Each process template in TFS contains a number of predefined reports. The Team Project is the central place for data to store multiple projects. The data store maintains all the information about projects including source code, build details, and tests. **Team Explorer** is the user interface to get details about work items, test results, and builds.

Team Foundation Server and Visual Studio 2010 integrate with the SQL Server 2008 Reporting/Analysis Services to create and manage reports. SQL Server is the default data store used by TFS 2010 to maintain all information about the projects including the source code, tests, reports, documents, and build information. Whenever a new Team Project is created, a set of predefined reports from the selected process template is created and viewed under the **Reports** folder in Team Explorer. All these reports can be customized based on the requirement. Alternatively, we can also create new reports and share these with the other projects.

Creating reports for Team Projects can be done by using any tool that connects to a Relational database or Analysis database. It could be Microsoft Excel or Visual Studio Report Designer. Excel is easier to use, but provides less functionality when compared to the Report Designer. Some of the important features provided by the Report Designer are:

- Detailed reporting
- Sharing the report using Team Explorer
- Updating the existing reports
- Getting the report faster and managing the reports

All these reports can be exported or printed. The reports can be exported in different formats such as XML, CSV, TIFF, Acrobat (PDF), and Excel. There is a print option that comes along with the report to print the current report result for the selected parameters.

Team Foundation Server reports for testing

TFS has several built-in reports readily available for the selected process template. Some of these reports are specific to defects and some are specific to testing while some others are common to work items. The names and format of reports have been modified in Visual Studio 2010 compared to its older version. The following sections explain a couple of out of the box reports available in TFS

Bug status Report

This report is used to track progress in bug status such as new bugs, resolved bugs, and closed bugs. The report shows the cumulative count of the bugs based on priority, Severity and State of the bugs.

Bugs are the list of defects found during the test run or code compilation or during the build. All these defects can be added as work items of type **Bug** to the team project under TFS. There are different parameters to the work item such as the iteration, area, priority, triage, description, title, and other additional details for the defect. Every time the defect is modified, a history is maintained. The first time the defect is added, the status becomes **active**. Whenever the defect is fixed, the developer can change the status to resolved so that the tester can test the defect in the next deployment of the application and change it to **closed** or **reopened based on the test result**. All these activities are tracked and a history is maintained in the SQL Server by TFS. The details for the defects can be filtered using the start and end dates, iteration and area paths, bug state, and priority and severity.

This report is very useful to see status such as how soon the defects are getting fixed and tested, the priority of defects being fixed and closed, the defects count based on severity and priority, and the module which is getting the most defects which helps us to see the quality of work.

The report provides a detailed graphical view by plotting the number of active, closed and resolved defects against a timeline. At any point in time, the report shows the total count of defects based on the state.

The other pie chart provides the *Active bugs by Priority* or *Severity* with the legends that show the priority/severity values.

Active/Resolved Bugs by Assignment is the horizontal bar chart that provide the total bugs assigned to the team members and the total bugs resolved by the team members.

Status on all iterations

This report is very useful to track the progress in case of projects having multiple iterations. This report provides the graphical view of the number of stories closed, Progress in hours for each iteration, and then the number of Bugs per iteration. To get accurate reports, the project team should plan the Iterations, User stories, Iterations, Area, and defect logging in such a way that everything is tracked on time.

The number of stories denotes the user stories which are closed.

The Progress in hours shows horizontal bars which depicts the Original estimate, completed hours, and then the hours remaining based on the roll up of hours defined for tasks. The tasks are created during the project schedule and the tasks include the duration and start and end date planned for the completion of the tasks. This report is based on the task allocation and the tasks planned for each iterations.

The bug with the numeric value and bar charts denotes the number of active, resolved, and closed defects within each iteration for the project.

These reports help us to see the health of the project at any time. For example, an unhealthy project is one in which the user stories were not closed within the iteration or if there is a wide difference between the estimated and completed hours or number of defects and defect rate is not decreasing after multiple Iterations . But a healthy project would be the one with better progress on all of the iterations and within the estimated schedule.

Other out of box reports

These are the list of reports readily available for getting the project status and the quality:

- *Bug Status Report* — this report provides the total bug count based on the severity, priority, and state, to track the progress of resolving and losing bugs.

- *Bug Trends Report* — this report is used for tracking the bugs which are discovered and resolved over time. This is very useful in the case of bigger teams working towards discovering new bugs and resolving and closing the bugs.

- *Reactivations Report* is used to determine how effectively the team is fixing the bugs. Reactivation refers to reopened bugs, which are resolved or fixed prematurely.

- *Build Quality Indicators* Report is used to collect the test coverage, code churn, and bug counts for a specific build. This is helpful to see the quality of the build before releasing the code.

- *Build Success over Time Report* summarizes the build and test results for a set of build definitions for one or more projects over time. The reports provide day wise information for Build failed, Build Succeeded with No tests, Test Failed, Test passed with Low coverage, and Build Passed.

- *Build Summary Report* provides information about test results, test coverage, code churn, and other details of each build.

- *Burndown and Burn rate Report* — Burndown shows the trend of how much work has been completed and how much remains over a period of time. Burn rate specifies the rate at which the work is completed and the required rate for the remaining work.

- *Remaining Work Report* is useful to track the progress of work and identify if the task completion is on track or if there is any delay.

- *Stories Overview Report* lists all user stories and how much work each story requires. Also provides the completed work status, status of tests for the story, and bugs raised against each story.

- *Stories Progress Report* shows the status and progress of tasks defined to implement the story.

- *Unplanned Work* determines the work that is added at a later point to the iteration after the start of the iteration. This type of work is called unplanned work because the work and tasks are planned before the start of the iteration. The work could be a new requirement, or new test case, or any type of new work item.

- *Test case readiness report* how many test cases are defined and ready to execute.

- *Test plan progress report* is used to determine how much of the testing is complete and how much is remaining. Also provides information on how many tests are passed, failed, and blocking. This report is useful to find out if the testing would complete on time or not.

Creating client report definition using Visual Studio 2010

Visual Studio has the in-built report wizard to create a report definitions file associated with report viewer control. The wizard provides the steps to create report definition by specifying report data and organizing the data in row and column groups in a tablix data region, so select a layout format and choose a style.

Open Visual Studio 2010 and select **file** | **new** | **project** which opens the project templates. Select the **reports application** from the **reporting** templates, which opens the report wizard:

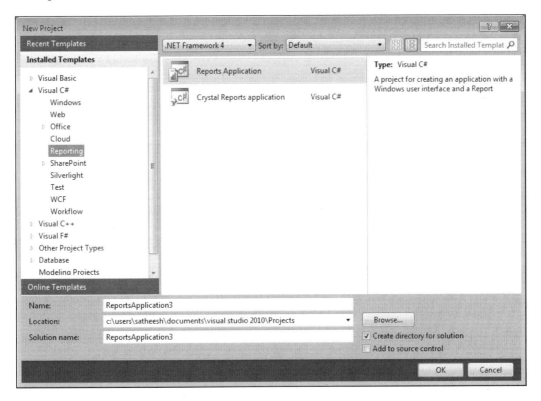

1. The first step is to define the dataset to use from the data source. The wizard provides the list of all data sources such as Database, Service, Object, and SharePoint. Select the required data source and continue. Database is the source for this example.

2. The Next step is to select the database model which could be a Dataset or Entity Data Model. Select Dataset and continue the wizard. Select or create a new connection for the dataset and continue. Select the Database objects from the database after successful connection, such as TestResult table and then provide a name for the dataset.

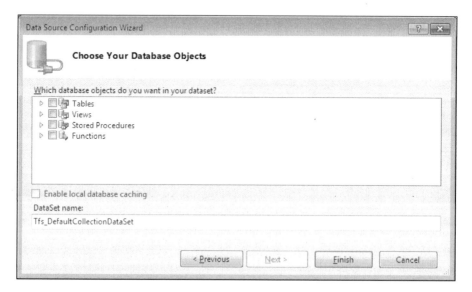

3. The next step in the wizard is **Arrange fields** to arrange fields into row groups, column groups, and detail rows for the tablix data region. Based on the row and column groups, the tablix region displays the data in the grid layout.

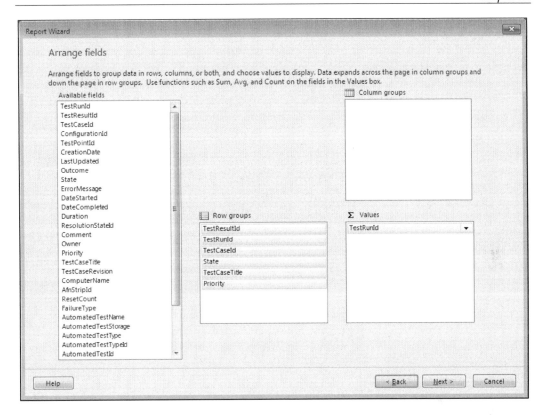

3. The next step in the wizard is choosing the layout for the report. The layout defines the place where the totals, subtotals, and aggregates should be shown in the report.

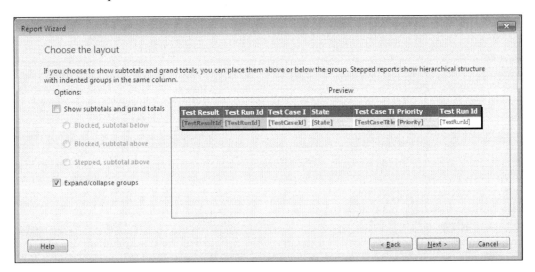

4. The final step is to define the style for the report. Select any specific style from the list of available styles.

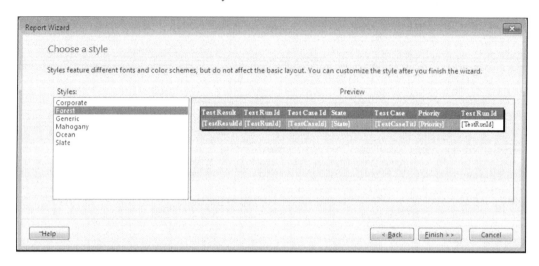

After selecting the style, the report is created and added to the project. Run the project to see the result. The report wizard is flexible to create reports according to requirements.

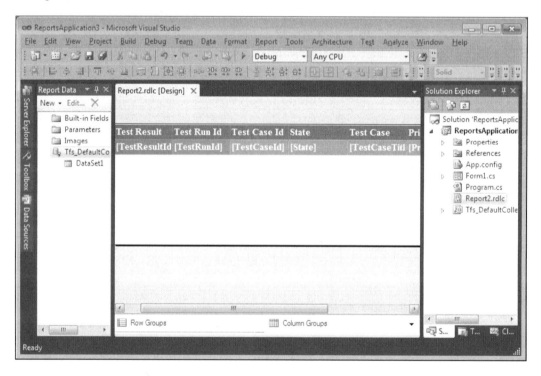

The report can be modified however you want it by dragging and dropping the fields from the Dataset and by defining the layout.

SQL Server Business Intelligence Project

Creating or customizing a new report for the project is always based on the project reporting requirement. In some cases, the existing reports may not be suitable or will not provide enough information required for the project. All information for TFS is stored in MS SQL Server, and it uses the SQL Reporting Service and Analysis Services for reporting purposes. With the existing installation of Visual Studio, we cannot create a new report or customize the existing report. It requires an additional tool called the Business Intelligence Development Studio, which comes along with the SQL Server. There is another option in MS Excel, which uses the option to get external data to get information from the SQL Server databases and present it in a spreadsheet. However, the following are possible if we are planning to use Visual Studio for creating reports:

- Writing your own SQL queries to get the data
- Publishing and sharing the report through Team explorer
- Customizing the report
- High performance report

Creating a new report involves understanding the database structure and designing. Before getting into the actual design of the new report, let's look at the different databases and how the SQL Server databases are structured by TFS for storing the data. It is divided into three different stores, each having its own purpose:

- **OLTP Database**: The Online Transaction Processing store contains multiple databases to maintain all the transactions. It has got database for maintaining the build, version control, work item tracking, and activity logging.

- **Relational Warehouse**: This store is built for queries instead of online transactions. This database is optimized for queries and reporting instead of transactions. Data is transferred into these databases periodically using adapters collecting data from the tools such as work item tracking, build, and other tools.

- **OLAP Cube**: The third one is the Online Analysis Processing Database, which stores the historical data for future reference. It has its own query language. This can be maintained and accessed using the SQL Server Analysis Services.

We will be using the previously mentioned database for building and designing our new report. The warehouse database is broken down into dimensions and facts, which is more important for the reports. The dimensions are the parameters and facts are the actual values. Parameters are used for controlling the data to be fetched from the store while the facts are the actual values such as the count of defects, or build number, or work item ID. You can explore more on these databases and tables using the SQL Server Management Studio.

To get started with reports, we have to make sure we have the required tools. The following are the list of tools required:

- TFS installation
- SQL Server client tools containing the Business Intelligence Development Studio, which is mandatory
- SQL Server Analysis Services
- SQL Server Reporting Services

Analysis Services Project

For the detailed analysis of the progress on development and testing activities, we can create reports from the analysis databases which are created based on the history of records from the transactional data. The SQL Server **Business Intelligence Development Studio (BIDS)** is used to develop and deploy the Analysis Services projects. The databases created from the Analysis Service project are used for reporting purposes and we can create the reports using the Report wizard in Visual Studio. This section provides a high level overview on defining and creating the Analysis Services and Database. Open **BIDS** and select **Analysis Services Project** from the templates list.

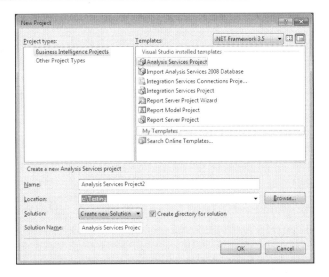

The Analysis Service project is created with empty folders such as Data source, Views, Cubes, Dimensions, and other additional folders. Right-click on each folder and start creating the required data sources, cubes, and dimensions as per the wizard instructions. This chapter does not cover the details of all the steps required for creating the analysis services but the final project should look like the following screenshot with all required configurations and Data sources, Cubes, and Dimensions defined:

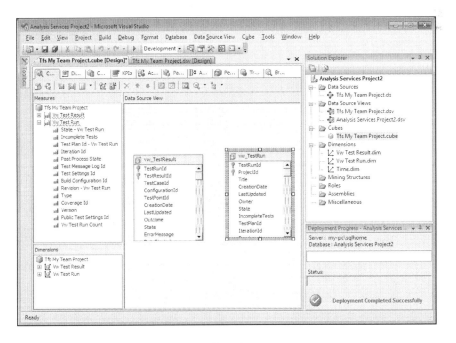

After creating the analysis project, the analysis database has to be created to keep the history of data as per the project definition. The Analysis Services project provides the option of **Generate Relational Schema...** to create the database as per the project definition and the SQL Server connection provided.

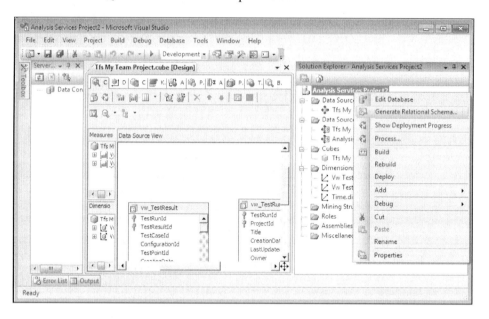

The Schema Generation Wizard does not create the subject area database itself; instead, the wizard creates the relational schema to support the cubes and dimensions in an existing database that you specify. The next step is to deploy the Analysis Service that we created and then process it. Use the **Deploy Analysis Service** option under the menu option **Build** which creates the defined objects in the Analysis Service instance. Processing the objects in the Analysis Service instance copies the data from the data source to the cube objects. Once the objects are created, we need to deploy the project so that the objects are created in the Analysis Service instance.

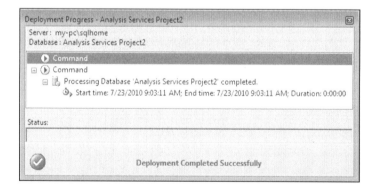

The following screenshot shows the objects and the Analysis Service project created under the Analysis Service instance:

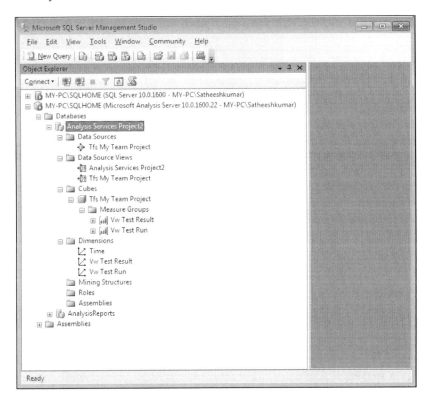

We can modify the Analysis Service if the cube or dimensions or anything has to be modified in the project. After the changes, the project should be redeployed to get the latest changes. Every time the project is redeployed, the database is rewritten with the new changes. Visual Studio provides a warning message before making the changes:

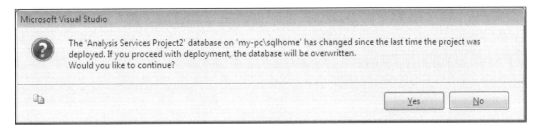

As the Analysis Service project database is ready with the required objects and the data, the report can be designed based on the objects.

Report server project

The Business Intelligence Projects contain the template for creating the Report Server project using the data source. The Analysis Service database is the data source used for designing the new report in this section.

Select **Report Server Project** from the **Templates** of the **Project types** list and provide a name for the project and click on **OK** to create the solution and the project with two folders, **Shared Data Sources** and **Reports.**

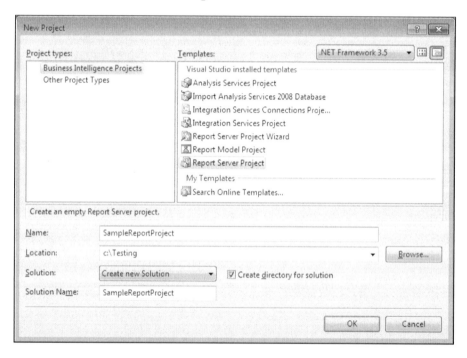

To create the report we need to connect to the Analysis Service database. Create or add the data sources by following these steps:

1. Select the option **Add New Data Source** by right-clicking the **Shared Data Sources**.

2. **Name** the data source as `TfsReportDS`.

3. Select **Microsoft SQL Server Analysis Service** as the **Type** of the data source.

4. Click on the **Edit...** option next to the **Connection String** box and in the new window, select the server name from the list or enter the server name used by Team Foundation Server

5. Select the **Analysis Services Project2** database from the list and click on **OK**. This is the same database created using the Analysis Service project in the preceding section.

The data source required for the Reporting Server project is created and now we can start creating the report using the data source by following the steps defined as follows:

1. Open the Solution Explorer, if not opened and right-click the **Reports** folder and select **Add New Report** which opens the Report Wizard. The first step is to select the data source that we added for the Report Server project, which is **TfsReportDS**.

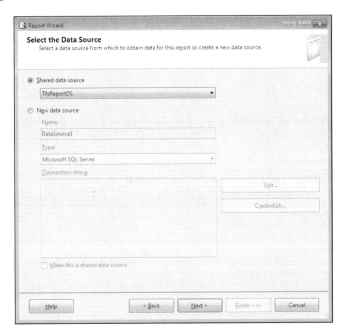

2. The next step is to design the Query using the Query Builder option in the wizard. Click on the **Query Builder** option to start building the new query for the report using the Designer. The designer shows the **Measures** and **Dimensions** from the Analysis Service database from which the required measures can be dragged and dropped on the surface and a dimension rule can be set for the query as shown with a sample query:

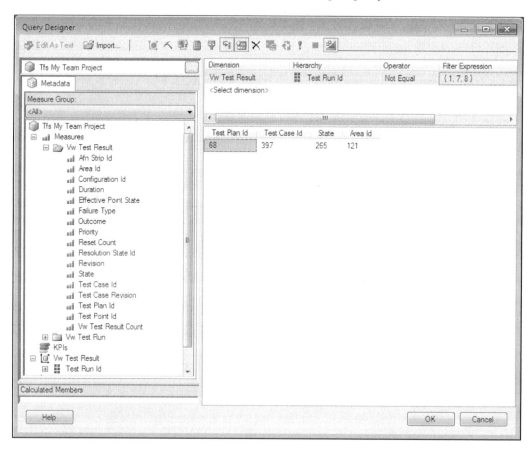

3. The next step in the wizard is the selection of the Report type from two types available, **Tabular** and **Matrix**.

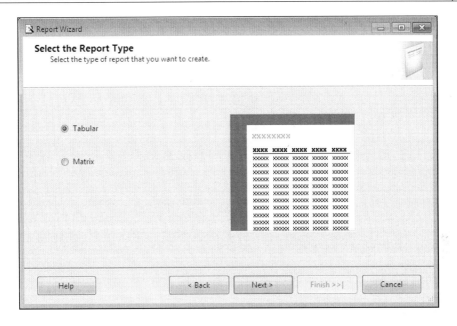

4. The next step is to define the table with the selected fields. This is the table structure that defines the report structure. Select the fields from the available fields into the details section, grouping section, and page section as required for the report.

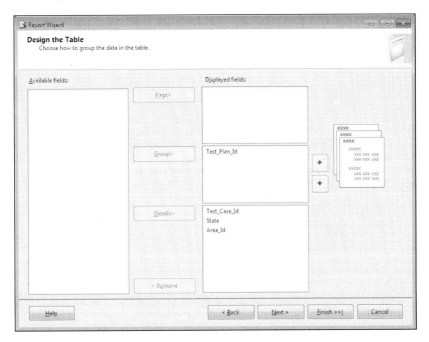

The table is defined but the layout has to be selected as to whether it needs to be a stepped layout or block layout. We can also include the subtotals and enable the drill-down to the report columns from the layout information page.

5. The next step in the wizard is the Table style. This defines the coloring of the texts and the header and detail section styles. Select any style from the available list of styles.

    Selecting the style is the last required information for creating the report. The last step in the wizard is the summary information page which displays all the information that we provided. This is helpful to verify the information before finishing the wizard and creating the report. The report can be further verified using the preview option in the same page.

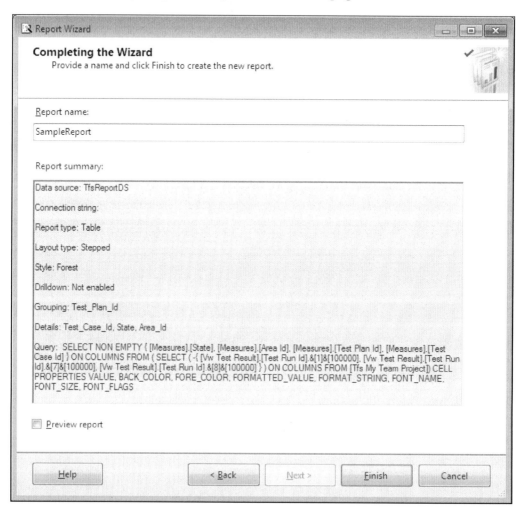

6. Click on **Finish** to create the report definition. The design area of the report shows two tabs, Design and Preview, for the report. The following screenshot shows the final report definition for the *SampleReport* with the tabular layout and the fields selected for the report:

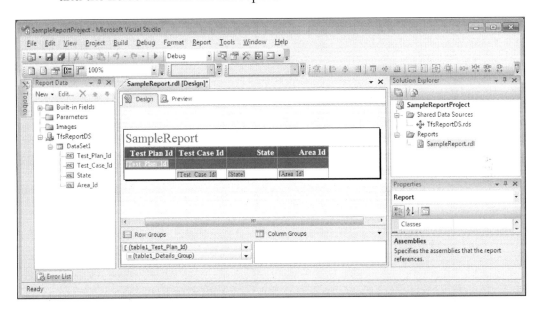

The **Preview** tab executes the report and shows the actual data for the report. Once we are done with the report, we need to deploy the report project to the reporting services so that the report is available at the common repository for reports. This is done using the deploy report menu option under the **Build** menu which connects to the reporting service and deploys the report. After the deployment, the report can be accessed from the reporting service URL.

Create new Report using Microsoft Excel

In the preceding section, we have seen how to create reports using Visual Studio and SQL Server Business Intelligence Studio. Here, we will look at how to create reports using Microsoft Excel. Reporting is not limited to Excel and Visual Studio, but we can use any tool that can create the report and access the SQL Server database. Using Excel we can create a **Pivot Table** and **Pivot Chart** and pull the data from the SQL Analysis Service. Once we create the Pivot Table, we can customize the report based on the columns and the calculations, the table should perform. We can even manipulate the columns and the rows in the Pivot Table that is created.

To get connected to the SQL Server database and the Analysis Service database, the user must have access to read the data from the database to use in the Excel report.

The prerequisites are:

- Microsoft Excel
- Microsoft SQL Server 2008 Analysis Services
- User should have access to the database

Creating the Pivot Table and placing the field is very simple in Excel. The following are the steps to create the report in MS Excel:

1. Open the Excel workbook for creating the report and select the **Data** menu.

2. Select **From Other Sources | From Analysis Services**, which will display the **Data Connection Wizard**. In the **Data Connection Wizard**, Connect to Server and enter the name of the SQL Server Instance for Analysis service.

3. Click **Next** to get the dialog **Select Database and Table**. Select the **Analysis Service Project2** database from the dropdown and select the **Tfs My Team Project** cube from the list. This is the same Analysis Service project and the cube that we created in the earlier sections.

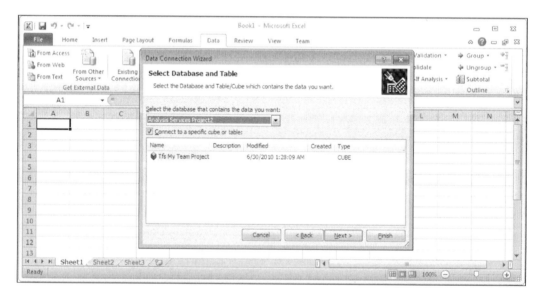

4. Click **Next** and select **Finish** in the dialog window by clicking **Data Connection Wizard | Save Data Connection File and Finish**, which opens the **Import Data** dialog window.

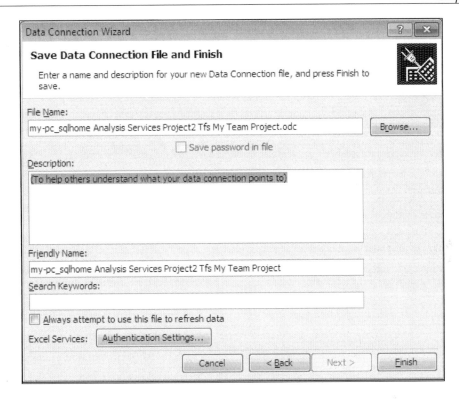

5. Select **PivotChart and PivotTable Report** and click **OK**, which displays the Pivot Table field list and the chart.

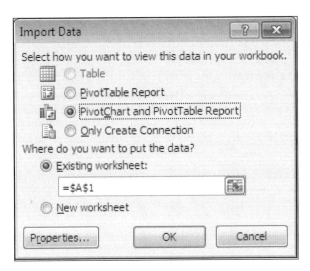

6. From the **Pivot Table** fields list pane, select fields using the checkbox which adds the fields to the report column and the chart. To filter the report, select the fields and drag them to the **Report Filter** box. Repeat this step until all required fields are selected in the corresponding columns and rows.

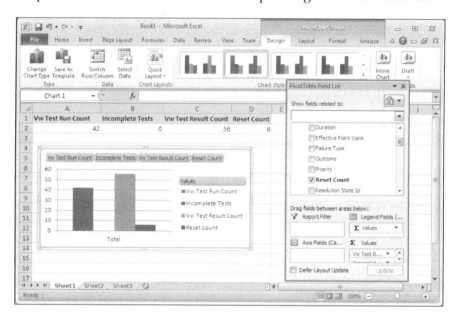

Now the report is ready in Excel. It can be saved in normal XLSX, XML, or in any other supported file format.

Summary

This chapter explained some of the in-built reports and queries to get details from the TFS data store. Using the SQL Server reporting service, Business Intelligence Development Studio, and Visual Studio 2010, it is very easy to create and customize reports. The SQL Server Analysis Service is useful to create the historical data store and based on that, the reports are created easily. Even if the user does not have Visual Studio or reporting services installed on the machine, the report can easily be created using Microsoft Excel and easily customized. New reports can also be deployed to the reporting server, so that the reports are available for the other project team members.

13
Test and Lab Center

Microsoft Visual Studio 2010 contains many new testing features. One of the main features is *Testing Manager*, which is the new tool that works out of Visual Studio 2010 but requires Team Foundation Server. Using this tool, you can plan the testing effort, which includes creating test plans, test suites, test configurations, and test cases with test steps. We can have any number of test plans for a team project. These test plans and test cases can be created and used for both manual and automated tests. The lab center is useful for creating multiple environments and settings to simulate an actual environment and test the application. To create the test plans, test cases, and lab environments, the Test Manager tool has to be connected to the Team Project in Team Foundation Server. The following topics are covered in detail in this chapter:

- Connecting to Team Project
- Testing Center — Plan, Test, Track, and Organize
- Lab Center — Virtual Environments

Connect to Team Project

The *Test Manager* tool requires to be connected to Team Foundation Server to store all *Test Plans, Test Suites, Environments, and Test Results*. The following screenshot shows the step involved in connecting to Team Foundations Server and selecting the *Team Collection* and *Team Project* from TFS. Once we select the team project, all the plans and settings that we create using Test Center will be associated to the team project and saved in the database.

Testing Center

After selecting the Team project, next comes the selection of the existing Test Plan from the Team project or creating a new one. The following screenshot has two test plans already from which we will select the first one to create all Test Plans. The window also has an option to copy the URL to open the Test Plan in the Testing Center. For example, the URL for the first Test Plan in the list would look like `mtm://my-pc:8080/tfs/defaultcollection/p:TestTeamProject/Testing/testplan/connect?id=2,` which would directly open the Test plan when you browse to it.

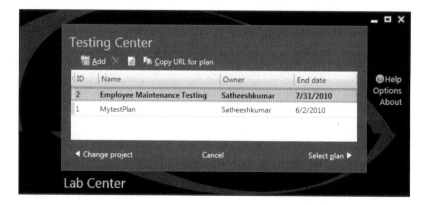

After selecting or creating the *Test Plan*, you can see the **Testing Center** open with existing Test Suites and Test Cases. The Testing Center has multiple tabs like **Plan**, **Test**, **Track**, and **Organize**. The Testing Center contains shortcuts to create new work items such as Bugs, Issue, Shared Steps, Tasks, Test Case, and User Story. Other shortcuts such as choosing another Test Plan or going back to the home page is also available. the following is the list of the descriptions the tabs:

- **Plan**: This tab contains all the features to create Test Suites and test cases. Adding or associating existing requirements to the Test Plan is possible from this tab.

- **Test**: This tab contains features to select a particular test case and then run that test.

- **Track**: Used for building queries to see the status of the Tests. The Testing Center provides multiple queries by default, which we can use or customize to create our own.

- **Organize**: Using this, you can organize or manage *Test Plans*, *Configurations*, *Test Cases*, and *Shared Steps* for Test Cases

Testing Center — Plan

This tab contains two sub-tabs — **Contents** and **Properties**. The **Contents** tab lists all available test suites and test cases associated to the test suite. On the left pane, you can see the list of all test suites and on the right, you can see the corresponding test cases for the selected suite. Each Test plan can have any number of Test suites and each test suite can have any number of Test cases. The right-side pane shows the current configuration selected for the Test Plan and the requirement associated to this test suite.

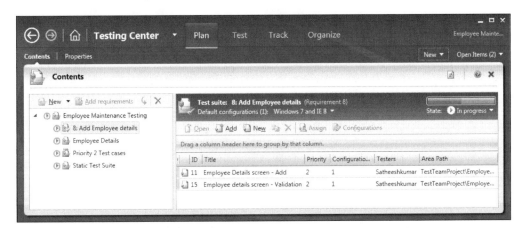

There is also a progress bar that shows the current stage and progress of the test suite. There are different types of test suites that we can create. One is to create a Test Suite and then add test cases to it and the other type is to create a Test suite based on the query to filter the test cases. For example, the previous screenshot contains the test cases that are created or manually added to the suite. At any time we can add or remove test cases from the Test Suite. The following screenshot contains the Test Suite that was created based on a query to select *Priority 2 Test Cases* from all available test cases in the Test plan.

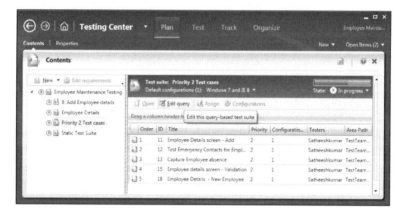

The other option is to add requirements to the Test Plan. Adding or linking the requirements to the Test case helps us to identify those test cases which could get affected in case of any requirement change. Also it is easy to find the related test cases and testing scenarios for the requirement. The following screenshot shows the selection of a requirement from the existing requirements list and adding it to the Test Plan.

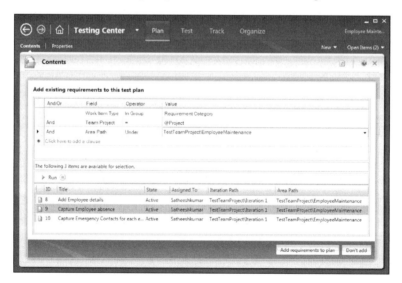

You can set the properties for the **Test Plan** using the **Properties** tab. You can choose the configurations to use for Manual and Automated test runs. The Test Plan can be associated with a build as well. The other common properties such as *Area*, *Iteration*, *Start*, and *End Date* of the task can be set using the properties window. The properties window shows the summary of *Current State of Tests* under the Test Plan.

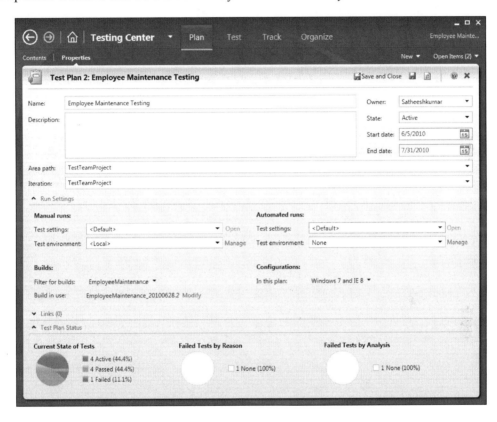

Testing Center — Test

The **Test** tab contains three different sub-tabs: **Run Tests**, **Verify Bugs**, and **Analyze Test Runs**. The first tab, **Run Tests**, is useful to run the test cases and capture the test results. The right pane also lists the test results and the status of each run of the test case. You can select the test case and start running the test with different run options, such as choosing a different build configuration, test settings, and environment. After the test run, we can also view the test result details.

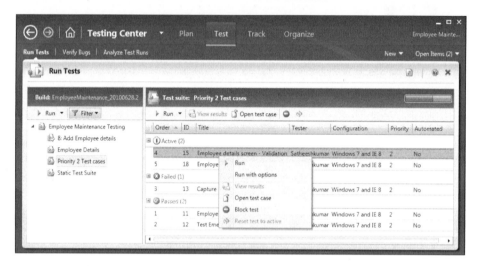

Selecting the test case and running the test opens the window for recording the test actions and the result for each step in the test case. Recording the test actions is optional but is very useful in the case of automating the test. With use of the recording window we can play, pause, and stop the test at any time. Each step shows the actual test step and the expected result for the test step.

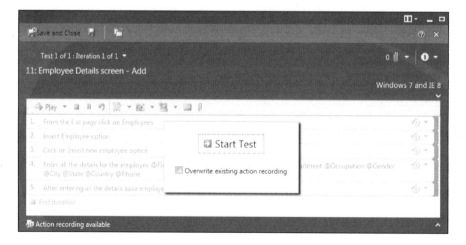

Based on the test result for the particular step, we can set it as pass or fail. After completing all the steps, the test iteration can be set as complete. Clicking on **Save and Close** saves the entire test result and the action recording for further analysis. The toolbar in the window provides other multiple features, such as **Creating a Defect directly from here**, **Taking the Snapshot of the screen**, **Capture the Environment details used at this moment**, and **Adding any other Attachment to this Test Step**.

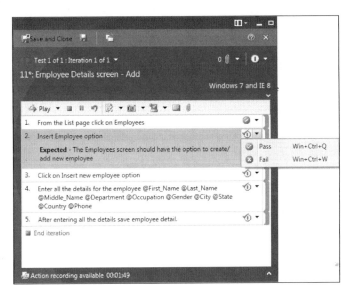

The second tab, **Verify Bugs**, under the **Test** tab is to verify bugs created as a part of the test suite and test runs. We can create a new defect or edit an existing defect from this window. We can also create an entirely new test case based on the defect that arose during the test.

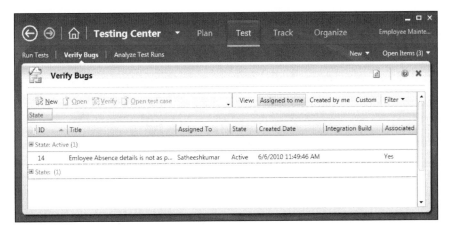

The third tab, **Analyze Test Runs**, is very useful to compare and analyse multiple test runs for the same test. We can change the configuration settings or environments for the test run and have multiple test results collected. We might have to analyse the results of the same test run with different configuration settings later on. The **Analyze Test Runs** window shows the history of test runs and the details of each test run.

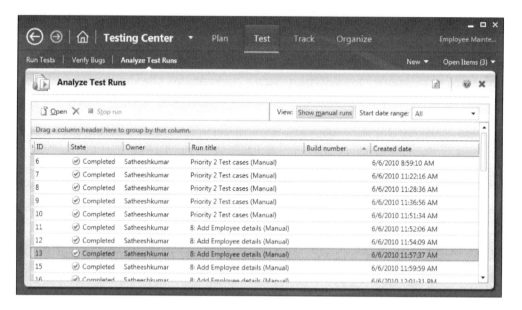

Test Center — Track

The **Track** tab in Testing Center is used for keeping track of the test cases, test runs, and test run results. Assigning builds with work items and getting the test recommendations based on the build change is also provided by this tab.

Using the first sub-tab, **Queries**, we can build queries based on some parameters to get the status of defects and test runs. The Test Manager itself provides a list of built-in queries to track the tasks and defects. For example, the *Active Bugs* is an inbuilt query which fetches the list of all active defects under the team project. We can customize and refine the queries as per our needs. We can build our own brand new queries and save them under the **My Queries** section, which is only meant for the current user who is creating it. We can then can run the query to get the result.

The next tab is the **Assign Build** tab which is used for assigning a new build to the test. This is very useful in situations such as when the development team has fixed some defect that is reflected in the new build, so the testing should happen against the new build and not the old build. To make this change, we can reassign the tests to the new build in which the new defect fixes are available. You can choose the build based on the work items associated to the build.

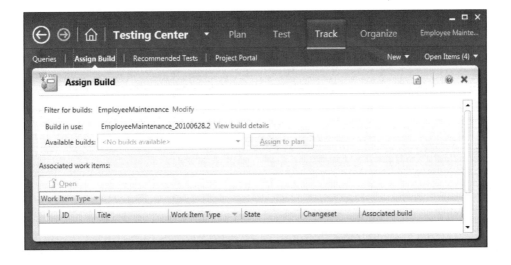

The next tab, **Recommended Tests**, provides an interesting feature that recommends all the tests that need to be re-run based on the changes that are a part of the new build. Because of some requirement change, design change, or code change, some of the tests need to be re-run to make sure the functionality is not broken. We need to choose the builds to compare and identify the differences of work that went into the build. This also helps the tool to identify the changes and the corresponding tests for the change. It then recommends us to re-run the tests. From the resulting list, we can choose the test case and reactivate it or make some necessary changes to the test case to align with the new change in the build.

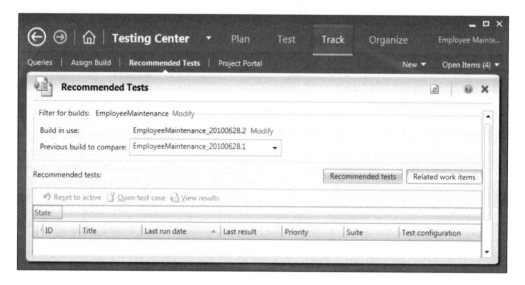

The next tab is the **Project Portal** tab, which opens the website for the team project through which we can get all the information about the team project. This is very useful for all who do not have Visual Studio installed on the local machine but want to access the resources from the Web. For example, if the management wants to know the current status of the project or defects, it is easy to go to the portal and access the corresponding report instead of having Visual Studio installed locally.

Test Center — Organize

The **Organize** tab in Test Center is used for maintaining and managing the Test Plans, Test Configurations, Test Cases, and Shared Steps for test cases. This tab contains four different sub-tabs to manage all of these.

- The first sub tab, **Test Plan Manager,** is used for setting or modifying different properties of the Test Plans.

- The second tab, **Test Configuration Manager**, is for managing and modifying the configurations. We can create multiple configurations based on different parameters such as the Operating system, Browser, version and other system variables.

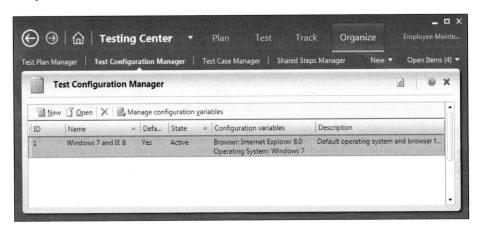

- The next tab is the **Test Case Manager**, where all the test cases in the Test plan are displayed. We can select any of the test cases and modify it or create a new test case or create a copy of existing test case. We can filter the test cases from all existing test cases and then choose the test case to modify.

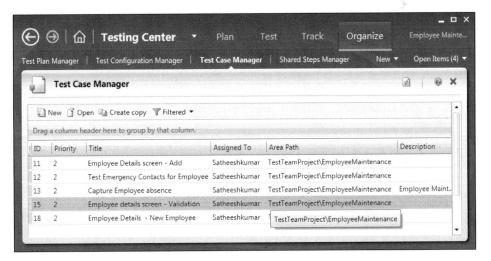

- The next tab is the **Shared Steps Manager** tab, which is for creating and maintaining the test cases that are shared across many test cases. These are called shared steps because they are common steps that are repeated in multiple test case steps. For example, the entering employee details step is the same step used while creating a new employee detail and updating an employee detail.

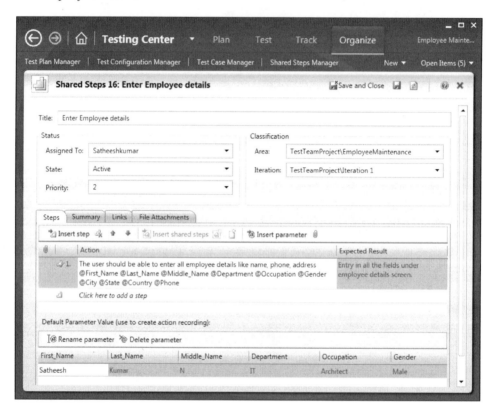

All of these changes are saved to the Team Foundation Server store. As you see in all of these tabs in Testing Center, none of the steps are dependent on Visual Studio. As long as we have the Team Project available in TFS, it is enough to capture the test steps and test cases for the Team project using the Test Center.

Lab Center

Microsoft Test Manager helps us to manage and use virtual machines in testing and developing the applications. The Lab Center in Test Manager is used for managing the Test environments, Test Settings and Controllers used for Testing. The *Lab Management* in Visual Studio 2010 is integrated with *System Center Virtual Machine Manager* (*SCVMM*) to manage multiple physical computers that host virtual machines. To use Visual Studio Lab Management to manage a set of virtual machines as virtual environments, you must first configure Lab Management. Each environment consists of one or many virtual machines for each role required for your application. You can then use Lab Management to deploy your application to these environments and run tests.

Virtual Environments

Creating a collection of *Virtual* machines and managing it with *Lab Management* is called a virtual environment. The integration of Lab Management with System Center Virtual Machine Manager enables us to deploy and test our applications on these virtual environments. We can schedule the Team Foundation Server build to build our application and then deploy and test them on these environments.

The **Lab** tab in the **Lab Center** provides access to the virtual environments deployed on the host groups of a team project. A host group is a collection of physical computers on which virtual environments can be created.

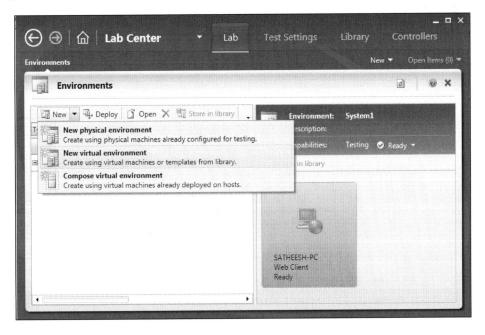

The **Library** tab in the **Lab Center** is used for maintaining and storing the virtual environments and templates that we use to create the virtual environments.

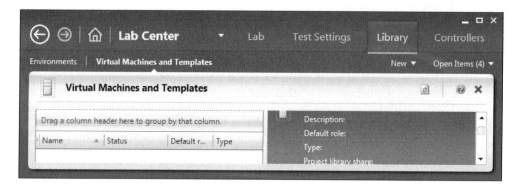

Deployed Environments

A deployed environment is a collection of virtual machines that is located on a team project host group. A deployed environment can be running or stopped.

From the **Lab** tab, you can connect to the individual machines through Environment Viewer, and you can create and store virtual machines and templates in the team project Library

Deployed environments can be created using any of the following sources:

- Using one or more virtual machine templates
- Using stored virtual machines or templates
- Using stored environments
- Using Stored environment from the combination of stored virtual machines or templates
- Using one or more deployed virtual machines

Stored Templates

A template is a virtual machine without any identity. When the template is included in the deployed environment, a new virtual machine is created. The identity is provided when the environment is deployed.

Stored Virtual Machines

The **Library** in **Lab Management** contains the stored Virtual machines. When we include a stored virtual machine from the library to a deployed environment, a copy of the virtual machine is added to the Host in the Lab. It is always a better practice to make sure the virtual machines are workgroup machines instead of domains controlled to avoid duplicate identities.

Environments

The **Environments** sub-tab under the **Lab** tab is used for creating new environments from the virtual machines and templates. The **Environments** sub-tab under the **Library** tab lists the stored environments for the team project. A stored environment contains the configuration information and references to the Virtual machines and templates. New environments can be deployed using the stored environments. There are two different ways an environment can be created.

Creating Environment from stored Virtual machines and Templates

You can create a deployed environment from a stored Virtual machine but you have to make sure each deployed machine has a unique name after deployment. The templates can be configured to provide the unique name automatically.

Creating Environments from stored environments

You can create a stored environment from stored Virtual machines and templates or a deployed environment. When you deploy the environment, you have to customize the names of virtual machines created from stored virtual machines.

Composed Environments

Composed environments are created from *Virtual* machines that are deployed on a Host. The administrator places the virtual machines on the physical machines that are in the team project lab. You can create a new environment by selecting one or more of the machines in a composed environment.

Lab Management environments enable testers to perform the following:

- Store a snapshot of the environment that saves the state of all virtual machines in the environment at any point in time

- Start and stop the Virtual machines

- Run multiple copies of the environments that are stored in Library

The other tabs in **Lab Center** are the **Test Settings** tab and the **Library** configuration tab. The **Test Settings** tab helps us to create multiple test settings. We can define the roles and choose data and diagnostics information for the test.

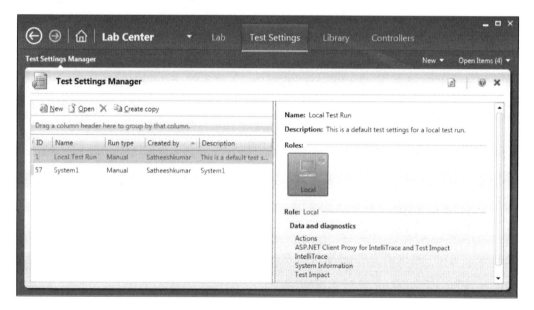

Later on while deploying the virtual machine, the role can be used to choose the corresponding virtual machine to run the tests on.

The **Controller** tab is used to manage the controllers used for the environment. You can select the controller from the list and change the configuration as well. The test controller manages the test agents to run the tests and communicates what each agent should do.

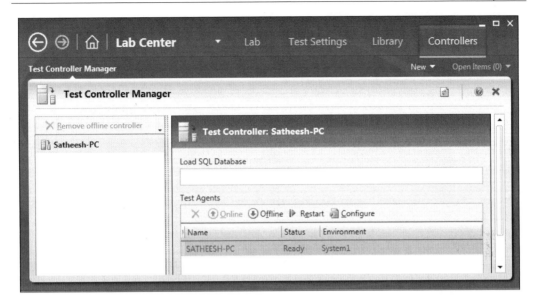

You can configure and monitor the test controller and any registered test agent using the **Test Controller Manager** in the **Lab Center**. To remove any of the test agents from the list, you can simply make it offline so that it won't be available for any of the test activities. Using the **Restart** option, you can restart the selected agents in case the restart is required because of any new deployments or change in settings. You can click on **Configure** and change the configuration information for the selected agent. For example, Load distribution can be changed during the test load.

Summary

The Test Center and Lab Center are the new additions to the Visual Studio 2010 Application Life Cycle product, which helps the testers to manage the test cases and test results using Test Center. The Lab Center is very useful when creating multiple environments using the *Physical* and *Virtual Machines* and deploying the environments for testing purposes. All these tools work without the support of Visual Studio but require to be connected to the *Team Foundation Server*. This helps the testers by having only the Test manager installed and does not require Visual Studio 2010. This tool helps a lot in organizing the Test Plans, Test cases, and configure for the test plans. Tracking the test results and Test plans and running the test cases is also possible from this Testing Center.

Index

Thank you for buying
Software Testing using Visual Studio 2010

About Packt Publishing

Packt, pronounced 'packed', published its first book "Mastering phpMyAdmin for Effective MySQL Management" in April 2004 and subsequently continued to specialize in publishing highly focused books on specific technologies and solutions.

Our books and publications share the experiences of your fellow IT professionals in adapting and customizing today's systems, applications, and frameworks. Our solution based books give you the knowledge and power to customize the software and technologies you're using to get the job done. Packt books are more specific and less general than the IT books you have seen in the past. Our unique business model allows us to bring you more focused information, giving you more of what you need to know, and less of what you don't.

Packt is a modern, yet unique publishing company, which focuses on producing quality, cutting-edge books for communities of developers, administrators, and newbies alike. For more information, please visit our website: www.packtpub.com.

About Packt Enterprise

In 2010, Packt launched two new brands, Packt Enterprise and Packt Open Source, in order to continue its focus on specialization. This book is part of the Packt Enterprise brand, home to books published on enterprise software – software created by major vendors, including (but not limited to) IBM, Microsoft and Oracle, often for use in other corporations. Its titles will offer information relevant to a range of users of this software, including administrators, developers, architects, and end users.

Writing for Packt

We welcome all inquiries from people who are interested in authoring. Book proposals should be sent to author@packtpub.com. If your book idea is still at an early stage and you would like to discuss it first before writing a formal book proposal, contact us; one of our commissioning editors will get in touch with you.

We're not just looking for published authors; if you have strong technical skills but no writing experience, our experienced editors can help you develop a writing career, or simply get some additional reward for your expertise.

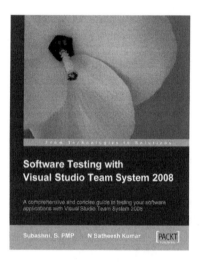

Software Testing with Visual Studio Team System 2008

ISBN: 978-1-847195-58-6   Paperback: 356 pages

A comprehensive and concise guide to testing your software applications with Visual Studio Team System 2008

1. Test your software applications with Visual Studio Team System 2008 and rest assured of its quality

2. Create a structured testing environment for your applications to produce reliable products

3. Comprehensive yet concise guide with a lot of examples and clear explanations

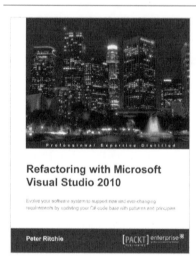

Refactoring with Microsoft Visual Studio 2010

ISBN: 978-1-849680-10-3   Paperback: 372 pages

Evolve your software system to support new and ever-changing requirements by updating your C# code base with patterns and principles

1. Make your code base maintainable with refactoring

2. Support new features more easily by making your system adaptable

3. Enhance your system with an improved object-oriented design and increased encapsulation and componentization

Please check **www.PacktPub.com** for information on our titles

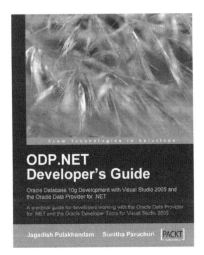

ODP.NET Developer's Guide: Oracle Database 10g Development with Visual Studio 2005 and the Oracle Data Provider for .NET

ISBN: 978-1-847191-96-0   Paperback: 328 pages

A practical guide for developers working with the Oracle Data Provider for .NET and the Oracle Developer Tools for Visual Studio 2005

1. Application development with ODP.NET

2. Dealing with XML DB using ODP.NET

3. Oracle Developer Tools for Visual Studio .NET

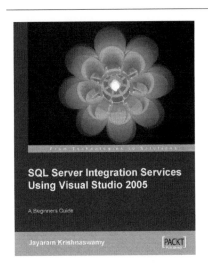

Beginners Guide to SQL Server Integration Services Using Visual Studio 2005

ISBN: 978-1-847193-31-5   Paperback: 320 pages

An ideal book for trainers who may want to teach an introductory course in SQL Server Integration Services or, to those who want to study and learn SSIS in a little over two weeks.

1. Environment set up for Visual Studio 2005 with respect to SSIS and multiple tasking

2. Connect to Microsoft Access, Text Files, Excel Spread Sheets

3. Transform data from a source going to a destination

Please check **www.PacktPub.com** for information on our titles